HOW THE STARS TELL TIME

A Soul Adventure in the Quantum Wilderness

By Astara Raven

How The Stars Tell Time:

A Soul Adventure in the Quantum Wilderness

Cover art "How the Stars Tell Time" by Daria Hlazatova

Astara is available to speak at your live event, workshop, or retreat.
For more information or to book an event visit our website at astararaven.love

ISBN: 979-8-9859800-0-4 (print)
ISBN: 979-8-9859800-1-1 (ebook)

In memory of my parents Lily and Carlyle who gave me my first name and the courage to reach for the stars. Thank you for demonstrating what love looks and feels like in the world.

To my husband Orion, my beloved, best friend, soul mate, fellow alchemist, and space cowboy. Thank you for taking quantum leaps with me in building a new story of intimacy each day.

Contents

Foreword

Over many years I have worked with thousands of people in the field of spiritual development and personal growth as a Master Energy Healer, Coach, Conscious Dance facilitator, and Performance Artist. I've been fortunate to meet many uniquely gifted people in my journey. In the beginning of my career, I was blessed to meet a handful of remarkable people whose influences and friendships would shape my destiny in ways I couldn't foresee at the time. Astara is one of those extraordinarily gifted people. She is a soul family member who continues to inspire me with her capacity as an eternal student and teacher of life's profound yet simple mysteries. Her healing work as a guide elucidating the quantum architecture of the cosmos and human soul continue to serve as reminders that if I stay open, the truths that I hold as foundational to my "inner" standing of reality will be reflected back to me from broader perspectives by allies — time and time again.

Reading about the deep history that made Astara the multitalented soul guide she has become, I have gained greater appreciation for the magic I've been blessed to experience in her company over the past decade.

How The Stars Tell Time is an encapsulation of Astara's important life experiences filled with challenging growth edges and magical time-bending soul retrievals. It's seasoned with humor and ageless wisdom that provides room for readers to grow and evolve as the narrative unfolds. This book can serve as a beacon of truth, a broadening of perspectives, and a permission slip for you to travel safely from your heart into the wide expanse of multidimensional consciousness exploration for your personal growth and happiness.

I first met Astara as a client. She'd been referred to me through a mutual friend in the Ecstatic Dance community. At that time, her name was Lily Marie Livingston. She was living in Oakland working as a sustainable architect in the corporate world. She committed to ongoing energy healing work with me from 2011 to 2012, where I combined reiki healings, spiritual guidance counseling, and channeling. During that time, I was struck by her aptitude to swiftly digest and embody the healing effects of new information that was multidimensional in nature, without the slightest bit of overwhelm — a task not easy to undertake by the uninitiated. During each session it was as if she was spontaneously realizing that she'd forgotten some super profound metaphysical truth and would suddenly remember how it translates from the macrocosm directly into her personal narrative, seamlessly.

I'd witness her connecting dots, thinking out loud, and verbally solving the existential crisis that we were trying to heal — all at once. She'd cry, laugh about it, and find resolution in no time. I quickly realized that I was working with a wise, yet lighthearted, and highly gifted soul. She was a kindred spirit that I was being asked to help in her deep, lifelong self-healing process — one she'd been on far before we met in this life. She was so advanced intuitively, so energetically sensitive, and well versed in all things spiritual — from the new-age to ancient shamanic cosmologies, that I often wondered, *"What does she need my help for? She's already so awake and capable. Am I doing anything for her that she can't do for herself?"*

At that time, I was in my late twenties, working to complete my practice hours required to certify as a reiki master, and I was learning to trust my gifts and their effect on others. Astara's positive feedback and affirmation of my power helped me gain confidence as an intuitive guide and subtle energy worker at a seminal time in my development.

My dedicated ongoing series with Astara — Lily at the time — gave me training ground to experience the difference between working *together* with someone who is actively working on themselves in the realm of personal and spiritual development, in contrast to working *on* a person who's not engaged with their personal responsibility. I was often flabbergasted at how many layers of outdated belief systems, ancestral and cultural programming, as well as karmic soul lessons she was able and ready to resolve in a single session. She promptly became a model client in terms of desired outcomes for growth and development in my soul coaching practice.

In reading *How the Stars Tell Time*, I now recognize that Astara has been doing inner work since she was a child, even if she was unaware of it at the time. In this memoir, she shares several life hacks that took her years to learn. Reading this book can help expedite countless other people's journeys of self-healing and recovery from the traumatic impacts of being a human at this crazy time in history. Her story, albeit deeply personal, is simultaneously universal at its core.

We met at a turning point in her soul's trajectory through life. A part of our soul contract was for me to help her see and embody her multidimensionality unapologetically, and she created space for me to develop my private practice as an energy healer with successful clientele that valued my gifts as an intuitive channel and guide. I am honored to have been there to steward her through the process of her finding her spiritual name Astara. You'll hear more about that in chapters to come. That experience was a significant confirmation of her transformation from my client to my colleague. The transformation of our relationship blossomed naturally, as it does once people complete a dedicated course of internal work, coming out of the chrysalis a new version of themselves, as she certainly did.

The process that Astara has gone through to embody her power, coming out of the spiritual closet while in the corporate world, magnetizing her soul mate after giving up on the prospect of finding him, and emerging into her new life's work as a soul guide, healer, alchemist, spouse, and conscious entrepreneur has been marvelous to watch! Getting to read her story and learning the deep familial and cultural history that inspired her transformation into Astara — the quantum time traveler — has been fascinating.

In her healing work, Astara guides people back home to their true selves through the heart. In this book, Astara shares her love and devotion to the human evolutionary experience, as undertaken through the medium of her own personal development. She shows us how she utilizes the heart, backed by cutting-edge knowledge of quantum mechanics, metaphysics, and shamanic practices, to traverse the matrix of linear time and heal versions of herself across multiple timelines. She then reveals how her time travel inevitably dovetails across dimensions informing her own embodiment of wholeness in the now. A lifetime of inner self-healing work is the mark of a truly capable healer, and it qualifies Astara to serve the empowerment of others with a full cup of inner resources.

How the Stars Tell Time synthesizes a myriad of subjects into a new visionary worldview as it chronicles the history and evolution of western scientific models, systems theory, metaphysics, personal narrative, poetry, and embodied spiritual development. It's sprinkled with enriching quotes, educational tidbits about existential phenomena, and humorous puns. It's a delightful and deeply informative read, and I highly recommend it for all people seeking to broaden their perspective on personal development throughout the lines of time.

Atasiea Kenneth L. Ferguson
Master Energy Healer, Soul Coach, Intuitive Channel
Founder of Angelic Presence Healing with Atasiea
Co-Founder of Ecstatic Dance Los Angeles

Vernal Equinox[1]

By Astara

I am told that you can stand an egg
on its end and it will stay, but only today.

A space of miracles
a small window of opportunity

that is what I am looking for. To stand
perception on its end and watch it stay.

Like the Cereus that only blooms
once a year in the middle of the night.

When no one is looking,
something starts,
shifts,
gains new physics.

Introduction: The Future is Relational

Years before I officially shapeshifted from a sustainable architect into a quantum time traveler and alchemist, I witnessed firsthand a problematic pattern in the building industry around me.

As an architect in a big firm, I was surrounded by visionaries and engineering genius. Yet, the incredible sustainable and regenerative designs we brought forth were often gutted before the decision makers could fund our design. Regardless of the incredible brain power at the design table, as well as beautiful emerging technologies, what blocked the "funding" of our progress was limited human perception.

I knew then that what was next for humanity wasn't big data and technology alone, but rather a shift in *story*.[2] This awareness both deflated and inspired me. I sensed that the long road ahead for humans was the willingness to collectively take an interior journey of healing and evolving — all so that we could shape a better story together.

My heart knew that a more loving view of the cosmos was how we could come together in a healthy way with dynamic Earth-aligned systems. My deep insight was unshakeable; it seeded my eventual exit from sustainable activism and the building industry.

Our human story is broken and rooted in the "win-lose" metrics of an unhealthy ego, which have been around for millennia and are still reflected at every level of our society. Human beings have difficulty feeling together and being together because they're lost inside the paradigm of separation.

Another expression of the "win-lose" tale is the "either-or" narrative, where our reductionism pressures us to choose between two very self-defeating options. It's what I playfully call the "lose-lose" story.

Our rivalrous story generates complicated systems where there's disassociation between the parts; we live in a siloed world where the parts of bigger human-made systems can't see each other or feel each other. Such cultural disassociation inevitably leads to financial meltdowns, environmental destruction, and human violence.

After two decades as an architect passionate to bring positive change, the insight for me was that we do not lack industriousness or inventiveness, we lack intimacy. To get "intimacy ready" as a globe, we first have to face our resistances to intimacy. I believe we have a planetary path of sobriety and recovery ahead. We must face a myriad of human problematic behaviors — our group methods of protecting and self-soothing are destructive and keep our heads in the proverbial sand. As in any recovery process, we must recover the memory of our past to heal the traumatic structures that undermine us.

Our world is poised at a crucial moment in history, where exponential technologies create exponential risk and threaten our future. To shift our trajectory from competitive destruction to mutual generosity in a relational-centered future, we have to remember our future in a new way. Our hope and desire for what is possible is the memory of the future. Our creativity in action stems from our desire — our future — as much as it informs the future.

When we recover our *past*, we can tell a new story and *re-member* our *future* in a new way, helping us be more *present* to each other. This is a quality of intimacy across time which can be experienced individually as well as collectively.

I believe "re-storying" for a healthy relational future starts on the inside and it is a non-linear process. As we reflect in a relational way, we learn about ourselves and each other. Each of us have a "psychological self" waiting to recover the memory of the past to heal. Each of us have a "mystical self" longing to become more aware in the present. Each of us have an "evolutionary self" wanting to vision and co-create a cooperative and fulfilling future. Now, imagine the psychological, mystical, and evolutionary — the past, present, and future — are meant to be integrated inside of us *at the same time.*

It takes a lifetime of practice to cultivate, but such internal coherence is our potential. It is the healthy soil to grow a benevolent and generous human story.

Over the years I have learned that reality is not a fact, it's a story. Reality is a joint venture, and we are writing that story together every day. Your reality and my reality exist side by side, *at the same time.*

When I say "at the same time" I hint at the new human story plot, which escorts the "win-lose" metric of a fractured ego out. The idea of "at the same time," ushers in a "both-and" paradigm of a healthy ego. To me it is a shift to a "win-win" paradigm, where there is room for all of our diversity. This is where we have developed the resilience to hold two or more viewpoints, where your opinion *and* my opinion coexist together. We can visit both past and future, as well as multiple timelines.

We must collaborate to imagine a much better reality — or human story. First, we must summons a vaster and more coherent perspective. To not just live solely inside the vantage point of our current self, but the willingness to see the vantage point of all the other ages inside of us and yet to be. To not just live solely inside the vantage point of the self, but the willingness to see the vantage point of another human. To not just live solely inside the vantage point of humanity, but the willingness to see the vantage point of the entire planet. To not just live solely inside the vantage point of Earth, but the willingness to see the vantage point of another planet or the sun. To not just live solely inside the vantage point of our solar system, but the willingness to imagine the vantage point of another sun, in another star system. And so on.

Only then can a "both-and" or "win-win" universe shimmer into existence.

My current unfolding story has gone farther than the wildest dreams of what my younger self thought possible — it now aligns with what I remember of the future. With the support of a "both-and" story, and the help of my past and future self, I remembered that I have — and we each have — an intrinsic role inside an outrageously wonderful cosmic love story. The cosmic love story is my true story, but it is also your true story. The cosmic love story is also our human story.

A love story doesn't deny the atrocities, war, injustice, and unfairness on the planet. I offer that the shadow of humanity is a challenging, but crucial part of our greater love story. We just have yet to remember it.

When we pull beyond time for a more expansive view, we can see how all our foibles and destructive actions are part of our evolution. With as much compassion and accountability as we can muster, we can do the essential work of recovery, reckoning, and repair. That exquisite difficult work then generates more compassion and accountability. Reparation and compassion feed each other. Life tensions create classrooms for our soul, pressing us inward. When we go inward, that is when the magic of intimacy is available to us. It is also when we meet eternity.

Time travel is a fancy way of saying, "I am standing in eternity." Eternity is not everlasting time; eternity is outside of time. Time travel is powerful because we can commune with the past, present, and future all at once. It is a part of a "both-and" cosmos.

Writing this book reflects my personal journey inwards, which is outside of time. This book harnesses personal stories from years of journal writing since I was a young girl. My diaries tunnel a wormhole across dimensions, sharing soul healing and wisdom with myself. The past dissolves into the present, and the future whispers to the past, while the eternal now is the telephone operator connecting the circuits of time.

With words as my chariot, I begin to integrate my psychological (past), mystical (present), and evolutionary (future) selves. I started writing quite young. While being reunited with my own written history, I reveal my adventure of integration in order to clearly see my own love story. Along the way I've noticed two themes connecting all ages of me — these themes are mine, yet they reflect core principles available to all of us.

The first theme throughout my journals is *wonder*, an unending curiosity that burns bright within my core. I have always suspected there was more to life than I had been taught, and it has been my mission to find out as much as I can. Wonder, or curiosity, is an essential ingredient for us humans to shapeshift our collective story.

Another theme that appears in my writing is *my desire to expand consciousness*. In my early thirties, I wrote:

> *A space of miracles | a small window of opportunity | that is what I am looking for. To stand | perception on its end and watch it stay. | Like the Cereus that only blooms | once a year in the middle of the night. | When no one is looking, | something starts, | shifts, | gains new physics.*[3]

At that age, I had no idea I was describing some of my soul's instructions on this planet. In hindsight, the *new physics* I ached for my whole life can be found at the intersection of wonder and expanding consciousness — it is alchemy.

My two themes synthesized into a common gift: I was learning to become an alchemist. Alchemy is the art of transmuting a story. It took decades to learn alchemy is simply seeing the *space of miracles* already within and around us. An alchemist knows there is nothing that is not God, for God or Source is the energetic infrastructure that informs all creations.[4]

In the last two decades, I began to understand that I am the author, screenwriter, projectionist, director, camera woman, and actor for the life I am living. All my experiences, or scenes, in my movie contribute to learning and evolution. By aligning to my true nature which exists outside of time — what I call my True Self — I began to dissolve my identity as a victim in a "win-lose" drama.

Alchemy is the ability to look at the timeline you are on, and if you don't like it, reframe your story through the lens of Source. This then switches you to a new soul-aligned timeline. The crucial components of switching timelines from competition to cooperation, are creativity and freedom. I decided to get more savvy with creativity and freedom, and this is how I entered into the messy majesty of a "both-and" or "win-win" universe.

Creativity is defined as an act of divine agency, bringing something into being out of nothing.[5] To create more effectively, I gave myself permission to step into *psychic prosperity*,[6] which I translate as an expansion of the physical senses in order to access awareness of other dimensions and create from a wider lens.

The world is larger than our current dimensional construct, the one that we are all in agreement about. You too can give permission to expand your senses, and like the Alice-in-Wonderland-moment in the movie *The Matrix*, you can take the famed red pill instead of the blue one.[7]

Or, in the trial by fire of our complex modern world, you may have learned what it feels like to have one foot in the "win-lose" world (small self) and one foot in the "both-and" world (True Self). When you bravely choose to learn intimacy on Earth, you make space for your small self and True Self and take both pills. You learn to dance between those dimensions until you have the circuitry to jump into one.

Freedom is defined as power or right.[8] I define it as taking responsibility for my life and my reality. This type of responsibility does not place the blame on myself for intense circumstances that are beyond my control. Instead, "response-ability" means just that: my *ability to respond.* Responsibility means I am willing to learn about the soul directive inside any challenge in order to learn and respond.

Such a directive may have been seeded in my soul before I was born, to learn something I didn't quite understand in a previous life. Taking that perspective, I can ask better questions like "What lesson can I learn here?" or "How can I respond with more compassion?" Such a bold step of accountability takes skill building and lots of practice, yet it helps me liberate myself from illusionary fears that bind me. In this way, responsibility is the ultimate freedom.

Practicing creativity and freedom these past two decades allowed me to slowly release the template of *what I should be,* which is formed in fear from the "win-lose" metric, to welcome *what is unfolding from my heart,* which is formed from the "both-and" of the universal laws of holism. I became an alchemist by acknowledging I am a spark of God, and so are you. The fractured ego mistranslates our inherent divine uniqueness as separation. Each day, I still humbly practice creatorship in a "both-and" or "win-win" universe, and each day, I am worse or better at it. That is why it is called a practice.

Jesus was a famous alchemist who understood the foundations of creation. He said, "Behold, I make all things new."[9] Like Jesus, we each have the ability (or creativity) as well as the choice (or freedom) to perceive anew. We can choose to perceive divinity or love inside a moment, rather than deny divinity. When I choose to acknowledge my own divinity, alchemy is the opportunity to live out who I am in truth, what I am in truth, and how I serve in truth.[10]

As you read the pages ahead, I invite you to remember your truth. I invite you to activate your inner alchemist — to no longer deny the divine in you and all things. To practice seeing everything as holy. My truest desire is to expand consciousness on the planet and lift humanity to a higher octave of knowing. My logical mind, or small self, tells me my passion to help humankind re-know themselves as divine is ridiculous and unachievable. My heart, True Self, or Inner Alchemist know it is possible.

I am the action of Spirit.[5] And so are you. Each day, each moment, we can become alchemical masters seeing the world anew.

My heart has understood all along that we live in an interconnected quantum holofractographic[11] multiverse woven from sound and oscillation. That's a mouthful, I know. Let me break it down a little bit.

We are each an integral part of a self-organizing framework. This framework is fractally and holographically present throughout the multiverse. There are similar patterns and geometries found at all scales from our cells to galaxies.[12]

I will expand on such juicy words in Part One of this book.

In simpler terms, I am a small reflection of the whole. As I claim my truth at a higher level, I influence the universe within and around me. As do we all. As I learn, heal, and expand as a soul, so does the world. As the world around me evolves, so then do I.

This book unfolds in two sections:
Part One introduces you to the quantum wilderness for my soul adventure ahead – diving into quantum mechanics, multidimensions,

perception, soul retrieval, the power of the heart, and the universal truth of resonance.

Part Two is a personal narrative of time travel and soul retrieval ignited through words from my own diaries. It is a love story of following my heart and meeting myself intimately, so I can come home to my soul. I reveal how coming home to myself strengthened helped me get "intimacy ready" in my marriage and soul vocation. In time, I build capacity for even another level of intimacy — the ability to hear and translate my Higher Self and soul guides. This channel of love offers me a clear glimpse into the magnificent cosmic love story I am a part of, helping me discover how the stars tell time.

This book is part memoir and part alchemy. It is about time travel fueled by intention. And that intention is love. Love is sharing knowledge between my younger selves and my older selves. Love is embracing my shadow and light. Love is liberating myself and generating new levels of intimacy across time.

As I dive inside my early journals, the unexplainable happens. I encounter time-bending or time-jumping to unwind old stories, gather new insights, and then watch my present world inexplicably, palpably shift.

The stories ahead come from my own direct experience. If you are a skeptic or not, I encourage you to question with discernment as needed. Trust your own knowing.

As you read, I invite you to zoom in on your feelings. It is not your mental experience, but rather your feeling experience, that brings the biggest gifts and energetic unwinding to you. The feeling state helps you embody paradigm-shifting information. Although these are my words and this is my personal story, in many ways, this is your story. I invite you to try your own time travel to your past and future self along the way.

Between the time I put these words to the page and the time this book finds you, what I call "now" may be months or years ahead in my future — your now. Even as I write this, the "win-lose" story is still wreaking havoc on the world. *The time is now*, pun intended, to transform our story.

No matter the time you find yourselves in as you read this book, each word on each page is a vibration encoded with timeless love, creating an energy transmission to lift you to a new octave. This book is a song of re-membering the future. It is a song broadcasting love across time and space, straight from my heart to your heart. Because we are all connected at every level, you have more power than you know to affect active peace in the world. When you step into a new octave of being and remember your divinity, you can remember the future too.

I encourage you to say these words out loud to activate a claim of truth that will support you in going inward as you read this book. I will be saying them with you across time.

> *I am word through my body. I am word through my vibration. I am word through knowing of myself as word. I am the action of Spirit. I know who I am in truth. I know what I am in truth. I know how I serve in truth. I am here. I am here. I am here. I am free. I am free. I am free. I have come. I am in the upper room. I am one with love. Behold, I make all things new.*[13]

We are all soul adventurers in the quantum wilderness, whether we are conscious of it or not. By making the claim out loud, you consciously align in vibration to a higher octave on your adventure, and this becomes your new expression. Like a chord on the piano, you become in *accord* with your own truth at a soul level. From there your vibration radiates love out into the world.

I am forever grateful to all the artists, innovative scientists, and evolutionary thought leaders throughout time who were willing to explore a new story before current science could begin to fathom it. As particles flash into possibility waves and back to particles again, this book unfolds. May it serve as an invitation into your heart. It is the heart that knows how the stars tell time, and the stars know who and what you really are: a shining star inside a cosmic universal love story. But we knew that about you for millions and billions of years already.

The future is relational. To get from here to there, we have a lot of personal and collective intimacy muscle to build. The good news is it has already happened, we only have to remember it.

Happy adventuring.

Wisdom Within[14]

By Astara

As I bow to the light inside my heart
no shadow is cast.
Light flows in all directions
From this source.

When I turn to feel the sun, the moon, the star light outside,
Behind me then trots my shadow,
At times four footed. Wild.
At times my shadow flies,
winged messenger of designs that have yet to form.
It is then I dance with time,
And play in these three dimensions.

As I bow to the light inside my heart
no shadow is cast.
There. Here. More dimensions. Galaxies.
And a wildness that cannot be named.
There is no time. Only now.
Light flows in all directions
From this source. We give it a name.
Love.

PART ONE

Quantum Wilderness

*"There are more things in heaven and earth, Horatio,
than are dreamt of in your philosophy."*

– Shakespeare, Hamlet[15]

More Things

In Act 1 of Shakespeare's play, Hamlet speaks this famous line after the phantom of his newly deceased father appears to him, revealing murder as the dark truth behind how he died. Moments later, Hamlet comes upon his dear friend, a startled Horatio, freshly visited by the ghost of his father as well.

Hamlet's legendary words tumble from his lips expressing both shock and revelation at his father's message from beyond. For me, the phrase *more things* conveys my mission of wonder to dig deeper below the veneer of appearances to reveal hidden truths.

Horatio's name is reminiscent of the Latin word *hora* meaning hour or time, *ratio* meaning reason, and *orator* meaning speaker. In so few words, Hamlet conveys to his intimate friend the veneer of temporal reality and rationality that would keep dark truths hidden in plain sight. And Horatio is the ally who will ultimately carry Hamlet's story forth after he's gone.

In my life, I am Hamlet and Horatio all rolled into one; I am the experiencer and the observer. I am also an amalgam of Hamlet and his father; I am the current evolution of myself as well as my own ghosts from the past who bring messages of truth from my subconscious, my genetics, and other lifetimes. My multiplicity of self helps me explore time, scientific discovery, and befriend my own ghosts so I can love myself to wholeness.

I sought out *more things* early in life. I read voraciously as a young girl and then kept on reading. I loved the science fiction I borrowed from my brother — books exploring wild new worlds, the sentience of other planets and beings, artificial intelligence, time travel, and journeys through ominous black holes. I nourished myself with visions that would take decades for the world to formulate — while some will take centuries more to fathom.

Across the years, I tracked *more things* with the left hemisphere of my brain, prodded on by mathematical curiosity and my talent at seeing patterns. I explored math, physics, biology, engineering, and architecture connecting as many dots as I could.

I was so hungry to comprehend the universal language of math, that halfway through my sophomore year, my college counselor pointed out my linear algebra class surpassed the math requirements for my architecture degree. I was startled I'd sign up for a class I didn't need. Such an instinctive reflex revealed how my passion for *more things* was rooted deeply in the well of my subconscious.

On the hunt for *more things*, I fed my right brain with creative arts. I sang. I played piano as a girl. I danced as early as I could walk, feeling the language of music in my body. I started life drawing as an adolescent. I began making jewelry in high school. I tried glass blowing, ceramics, metalsmithing, sketching, and painting in college. I wrote stories and poems.

Eventually, my reading list broadened into non-fiction. I read topics ranging from creative visualization to feminism, from transpersonal psychology to hypnotherapy. I dove into mystery school studies including past-life research, Akashic records, tarot, sacred geometry, shamanism, and bioenergy. My day job as an architect funded my inner spiritualist. I was learning everything I could about the physics of the soul and consciousness.

As a girl I saw our world was on fire. Now, it is more so than ever. Our fearful and greedy nature has created quite a mess with environmental degradation, extreme climate events, a rise in toxic materials, and failing human systems. We are harming ourselves and our planet in an iterative destructive feedback loop — all because we can't seem to shift from our culture that has normalized fear, scarcity, and separation to a new normal of interconnectivity, responsibility, and love. This new normal is better described as *remembered* because nature in us and around us knows the way.

Since I was a girl, the antidote to the fear-based world waited right outside my window. I felt kindred to nature, where the energy of interconnected systems buzzed around me in a generous dynamic interplay. Nature became my mentor and friend. Connecting to nature uncovered a new world view that was the opposite of what I was taught.

As a girl, I explored outside, befriending the flora and fauna in my yard. Birds, lizards, frogs, bugs, and trees whispered to me that all creatures worked together as part of something bigger. I knew I had my own part to play as well.

Outdoors, I experienced being held and aligned to a benevolent intelligence. Before I had words for it, my heart knew there was no such thing as a closed system in isolation from the rest of the universe. Nature and my heart both invited me to utilize the systems thinking I was born with, helping me innovate inside this strange global playground we find ourselves in.

Nature exposed *more things* as a synergestic effect where the behavior of the whole system is greater than and unpredictable from the sum of its parts. Instead of having to choose between the view of nature as either inherently competitive or benevolent, nature remained neutral. I eventually understood that what seemed dark or destructive in nature was simply an energy exchange of some kind trying for learning and evolution. [16]

The magnetism of nature's intelligence and beauty was, and is, irresistible to me. It was inevitable that nature would become my professional focus inside the art and engineering of architecture. After becoming an architect, I evolved into a sustainable design leader for the built environment.

Left brain. Right brain. Science. Design. Multiple disciplines. Whenever I come across *more things* that ring true, the tingles on my arms, legs, the back of my neck, and the top of my scalp offer me biofeedback. It's a sign I'm onto something. It feels like memory.

The bio-signal of my tingling scalp does not originate from my head brain. In the last two decades, I slowly connected the dots from the HeartMath Institute's research, Dr. Sue Morter's[17] findings, along with many other scientists advancing understanding of human intelligence, to discover we have three brains. That tingling is the intuitive nudge from my heart brain and gut brain. It takes time for the head brain to catch up and make sense of what the two brains at the core of my energy field have known all along.

The heart's the first brain and the most powerful. It has 100 times more electromagnetic activity than my head.[18] It's literally the neutral center of my electromagnetic universe or what I playfully call the *YOU-niverse*. It's the central hub along our channel of energy generating a direct line of communication to the cosmos and our Higher Self.

Many call the gut or enteric nervous system our second brain. I fell in love with the vagus nerve that runs from the gut to the head when I found out it's responsible for 80 to 90 percent of our sensory input to the brain. Our sensory nervous system is one thousand times more abundant in nerve count than our motor nervous system. The gut brain metabolizes and generates responses in our inner realm without having to check in with the brain in our head.[8] This is the nudge from our core when we say, *"I just have this feeling."* Or we say, *"I just know it in my gut."*

We are better off going to the root of energy, which is consistently looking to flow again. Sensing into feelings through our body is a better idea than relying solely on an emotional story through our head brain because our soul sends messages through the core of our being. Listening to the subtle cues of our body is necessary to have a better dialogue with our soul. Working directly from the larger electromagnetic field of the heart and the abundant nerve count of the gut sounds like soul-aligned intelligence to me.

Due to the energetic strength of our core, I call the head brain the third brain. Our head brain works best when all brains communicate coherently along our spine or central channel of energy. The head brain is the radio tower picking up the signal from our core.

All our brains working together creates one *unified mind*, rather than one limited perspective of a singular brain. This state is called *coherence*. Coherence resolves any wobbles in our electromagnetic energy field caused by stress and big emotions. Coherence allows our vital energy to flow unimpeded through the body again so we can capacitate more universal energy. When we get to know the bioenergy of human anatomy better, we may discover even more brains in our miraculous body.

Human society is constructed entirely from agreements we make together that we name culture. And here is the crux, *we see the world as we are* just as *we become what we see.*

Our head brains dominate our field of consciousness, and consciousness is the working state of the soul. If *we see the world as we are*, we are seeing as the protective personality or head brain, and thus our current agreements are born from that protective frame. Most days we experience the head not communicating well with the heart and gut, thus allowing our protective minds to oversee our bodies and our lives.

Even though the highest concentration of energy that we are made of is in our core, many of us still focus on the outside world as the authority over our lives. Ironically, we expand our consciousness when we explore inner space compared to focusing solely on the outer world.

The human body and biofield is made of many energy bandwidths or layers. From the physical body on out we have our etheric body, emotional/feeling body, mental body, and then our spiritual body or pure Source energy. Since we're often stuck in our thoughts and beliefs, head-based anxiety causes us to hover mostly in the mental energy layer, the farthest bandwidth of energy from our body before we connect with pure Source.

Between our mentally focused society, our zeal for the latest technology, and our attention outside ourselves, many of us walk around energetically disembodied like zombies. Most are unaware of the energetic effects of over-thinking and disassociating, yet our collective subconscious reflects this in our surplus of zombie movies.

Although the head knows last, we let it run our personal and planetary show. This is how we agree to the world of limits, separation, and victimization we participate in every day. Such fearful disconnection also determines our scientific outcomes, research, and data.

When we're saturated in stress, we lose access to the center of the brain's visionary hub, as well as the cognitive abilities of the frontal lobe — we lose coherence. The biological instinctive aspect of our mind, our reptilian brain, takes over in fight, flight, freeze, or fawn scenarios. Such a consistent state of stress not only polarizes the brain hemispheres, it holds us in a continual state of emergency.

Since we lead from the head, and the head is often divided and defended, is it not surprising that our world is also? Hence, the left brain, which is science, and the right brain, which is spirituality and creativity, have not been playing well together in our culture for a while.

The world stage reflects this incoherence through perceived scarcity. Our collective protective personality breeds an *us vs. them* mindset. We then out-picture a divisive victim reality. Too often the punitive behaviors of blame and shame become the name of the game. In a world like ours, war seems to be the first answer as a bid for power and drama sells so much better. It is omnipresent in the news, social media, and movies — all the dramatic stories we sell each other and identify with.

Imagine if you were taught in school from a young age how to unite the hemispheres of the head brain to create gut-heart-brain coherence and lived from there. When all our brains communicate beautifully with each other, they form one unified higher mind receiving and sharing wisdom from our center.

Now, imagine a world theater out-pictured from heart coherence on a global scale. Such a reality shift is underway. A shift from the head brain as the dictator to all brains working together with the heart as the leader. It is underway, but still has a long way to go.

My hero's journey thus far taught me the *soul-ution* to every crisis around the globe is to create coherence individually, then collectively. First, we must listen to our heart compass and bravely draw up a new map. Every time I say yes to the fire of curiosity inside me, I become a better cartographer of a soul-aligned map to an authentic life. My heart leads me to *more things* than I ever thought possible, expanding my consciousness each day and sending invitations out to the world. Map by map, we can each make a new atlas together.

"Magic's just science that we don't understand yet."

– *Arthur C. Clarke*

Science is a Verb

Many of us treat science as if it is a noun, or even an adjective, but science is a verb. We like it either fixed or prescriptive, yet it is an ever-evolving process. Discovery after discovery reveal insights that could topple our most treasured realities.

The scientific method is a process of experimentation used to explore observations and answer questions. There are as many versions of the scientific method as there are scientists. Those studying dinosaurs' digestion cannot run medical exams to test hypotheses. Scientists studying a star's longevity cannot fast-forward that star's life. When direct experimentation is not possible, scientists modify the scientific method.[19] They turn to estimation and precedence using intuition and imagination — they theorize.

Scientists aim to explore new ways of conceptualizing the world by asking good questions, carefully gathering the evidence, and examining if all available information can be combined into a logical answer.

We think of the scientific method as a linear process, but we can't help that we mimic the spiraling iterative process of nature. That is because we are nature. New information or new thinking prompts a scientist to back up and repeat steps at any point along the way. No matter how linear we aim to be, all our learning and creating occurs in a circular dance.

Since *we see what we are,* what we measure and call truth can be flat out wrong because when we are biased, we calculate with bias. Quantum mechanics has shown us *we become what we see.* By studying the very small, or quanta, we discover our observations of an experiment can influence the experiment itself. Even the strictest scientific method offering the hard evidence our head craves, is ultimately only proof of what we believe in or are capable of seeing as of yet. What we measure is as accurate as our individual and collective ability to perceive clearly or not. When we see the world from our head-brain solely, our individual and collective vision is distorted.

As we evolve, science evolves. We are in an exciting era where well-loved traditions and institutions are being challenged and re-imagined based on science's influence. To solve many of the issues facing us today, we must reimagine all our systems.

The hunger to comprehend the incomprehensible, the intuitive ability to understand something before it's observed, the poetic capacity to see beyond the visible, and the refusal to accept the present order of things, is historically at the heart of scientific thinking.[20] As the Hungarian biochemist Albert Szent-Györgyi said, "Discovery consists of seeing what everybody has seen and thinking what nobody has thought."

This is why I am drawn to scientists, artists, mystics, and thought leaders orbiting at the edge of culture. I follow those that see past what's visible, honoring the trails of their hunches, fed by study, keen observation, and insight ahead of their time. I have kept my eye on the pulse of quantum mechanics since my college years. My systems-thinking brain kept gluing disciplines of study together, and promising theories excited me.

It can take decades, even centuries, to prove to ourselves and the world what our initial intuitive nudge knows. Listening and then acting on our intuition is brave work. When a scientist is bold enough to share a new theory or discovery that puts mainstream science in question, it is often met with ridicule or outright rejection by the scientific community. The label "pseudoscience" or "misinformation" gets thrown at them or worse.

Cancel culture has been around for a long time and intolerance to scientific innovation is no stranger to us. As George Bernard Shaw famously wrote in his play Annajanska in 1918, "All great truths begin as blasphemies."[21] Invention challenges the status quo, including careers and livelihoods that are built out of the former science. Accepted science ostracizes first and asks questions later. That is why the phrase that *science progresses funeral by funeral* is well-used.

History is filled with those courageous enough to follow their passion, listen to their intuitive knowing before their culture understands, and share the breakthrough. Nicolaus Copernicus, Galileo Galilei, Johannes Kepler, and the list goes on with no end in sight. In the last decade, even the TED conference known for encouraging curiosity and open-mindedness, banned biologist Rupert Sheldrake's talk titled *The Science Delusion*, where he spoke about challenging existing materialist paradigms and the dogmatic resistance received within contemporary scientific society.[22]

Many must agree to a new view before it becomes the norm. To make the necessary pivot to awaken our world and reimagine our systems, we must negotiate through the defense systems of the old guard. What poses a threat to current livelihoods and identity is naturally met with resistance. Dissolution and dissolving of the old will occur and that is not only scary, but also uncomfortable.

Every few centuries — give or take a millennium — humanity stretches in some big way from the old known to a new known, with accompanying conflict and cultural growing pains. Each generation unveils a little more of the truth — even as they are met with stiff opposition.

A famous science paradigm shift began with our star, the sun. In 6th Century BC, the Greek philosopher Pythagoras and his followers initiated the beginnings of a heliocentric[23] revolution and ever so slowly, hospice began for a geocentric[24] paradigm; the risks of his discoveries were so great, he and his allies were all sworn to secrecy and couldn't write anything down.

In 1543, a few thousand years after Pythagoras theorized the Earth was spherical and not the center of our astronomical system, Copernicus published more advanced heliocentric axioms right before his death — demonstrating the sun is at the center of our solar system.

In 1609 and 1618, years after Copernicus was handed a copy of his newly published work on his death bed, Johannes Kepler, one of the few peers to support Galileo Galilei at the time, published his books on planetary motion and the understanding of elliptical orbits — all the while fending off the inquisition from his mother when she was charged with witchcraft. His own culture made it difficult to advance his work, let alone appreciate his genius.

Galileo was the first to craft a telescope to be able to see farther and clearer. His discoveries about the moon, Jupiter's moons, Venus, and sunspots eventually substantiated Copernicus' heliocentric theories. In 1623, he made his work known and with the inquisition's persecution as backdrop, Galileo was charged with heresy and placed under house arrest for the remainder of his life.

Pythagoras, Copernicus, Kepler, and Galileo are just a few of the known science heroes in our time. In their time, their breakthroughs were sacrilege. The idea that the Earth is in rotation around the sun and not the other way around was rejected for over a millennium since it was considered blasphemy in the face of the existing paradigm.

In the 19th century, the German philosopher Arthur Schopenhauer understood that an innovative idea must endure a hostile reception before it is accepted in the scientific community. He said, "First, it is ridiculed. Second, it is violently opposed. Third, it is accepted as being self-evident." It seems that no institution is exempt from this trend because the human condition itself is rife with prejudice, bias, and fright.

In 1687, 60 years after Galileo and Kepler, Newton published *Principia*, a collection of seminal books on the laws of motion and gravity. The culmination of his research would prove the discoveries of Copernicus, Galileo, and Kepler. Many of the frameworks that emerged from Newton are still with us: a materialist, linear, causal, fixed, and deterministic universe. Newton's physics can still successfully plot a course to the moon and engineer a bridge, yet falters when applied to very small objects or objects traveling at or near the speed of light.

Our understanding of light changed in the 1860s thanks to the Scottish physicist James Maxwell, in a watershed moment unifying the fields of electricity, magnetism, and optics. The theory of electromagnetism was born.

Half a century later Einstein stepped in and laid the foundation for a new physics. Einstein was as passionate about light as Maxwell was. He refined Newton's physics with his description of gravity as a curvature of the universe fusing the three dimensions of space and one dimension of time into a fourth dimension known as spacetime.

Newton saw gravity as a push; Einstein saw gravity as a pull. Einstein published his Theory of Relativity in 1905 and its final form in 1916. In the latter part of his life, Einstein attempted a unified field theory to reconcile relativity with electromagnetism; he died trying.[25]

In 1927, Werner Heisenberg's uncertainty principle taught us that our efforts to measure with precision creates more uncertainty. In the same decade, Niels Bohr, Pascual Jordan, and other luminaries took part in a series of physics experiments demonstrating that the act of observing something influences the outcome.

And so, within my grandparents' and parents' lifetime, quantum mechanics reveals how our universe is more strangely connected than we could previously imagine. If everything is made of very small objects and the vacuum of space in between, the old agreements of Newton's and even Einstein's gave way to the ordered chaos and connected beauty of our universe.

Quantum scientists today continue to dive down an Alice-in-Wonderland-type rabbit hole. Physics is now making a world view shift from disconnection to connection, revealing we live in a universe where energy and vibration form matter. Where reductionism and certainty are replaced by complementarity and context. Where relativity hints at an interconnected quantum[26] reality comprised of relations rather than objects.

Decades after Einstein's failed attempt, the unification of physics is still pursued with gusto. After the 1960s, string theory tried for unification and revealed hidden dimensions. Chaos theory led us to the butterfly affect, strange attractors, fractals[27] as patterns of scale, and self-organization[28] affirming my sense of interconnectivity as well as the intelligence inherent in all things.

In 2005, the physicist Nassim Haramein proposes a unification theory called the Haramein-Rauscher Metric. He reveals the fundamental geometry of space that connects us all, describing fractals in a holographic[29] universe from the quantum and molecular to the cosmological scale: a holofractographic universe.[30] In 2013, the physicist Eric Weinstein proposed Geometric Unity — a mathematical theory of everything and released his draft paper in 2021.[31]

I imagine truth to be like a sphere. Much of our science aims at truth as if there is one single answer, yet if quantum exploration shows us anything, it shows that we swim in a sea of paradox. Each scientific theory offers a unique truth, and each theory is true *at the same time*. Imagine each scientific theory as a better question which slowly — one by one — adds another facet to the sphere. The surface area is our aim, not the radius, diameter, or a single point. My point is that we need a large number of theories before we encircle the sphere of truth.

One of humanity's top lessons is to learn how to value the process rather than prioritizing the outcome. Therefore, a well-crafted question can be more valuable than any answer. In general, our attraction to solve a unification theory reflects a shift in consciousness underway from separation and dissonance towards connection and coherence. Overall, I am grateful for the quantum physicists who gave me words to express what my heart has whispered inside me since my youth: *all of life is made of vibration and frequency.*

There are more things in heaven and earth than ever dreamt of before, and we are finding them. Recently, brain scientists have ascertained *more things* through their discovery that novel experiences cultivate synaptic connections and even grow new neurons in the brain. *Neurogenesis* is possible.

This century, geneticists unveiled *more things* through a new field of *epigenetics*, demonstrating genes are not fixed as we assumed.

They discovered trauma leaves a chemical mark on a person's genes, which gets passed down to future generations. Now instead of simply focusing on genetic mutation, science is studying the mechanism by which the gene is expressed.[32]

Regardless of the genetic mark, beliefs, behaviors, and the environment we inherit, it turns out that we have a say in what genes we express. Consciously or unconsciously, we're epigenetic engineers of our DNA based on thoughts, beliefs, and the environments we surround ourselves in.

In my search for *more things*, I observed how truth waits patiently to be seen. The writer David Foster Wallace offers a parable of two fish that aptly describes how we swim in mystery every day, yet we do not realize it.

> *There are these two young fish swimming along, and they happen to meet an older fish swimming the other way, who nods at them and says, "Morning, boys, how's the water?" And the two young fish swim on for a bit, and then eventually one of them looks over at the other and goes, "What the hell is water?"*[33]

Water taught me *more things* about life and memory. Water covers about 71 percent of the Earth's surface, pervades the sky as vapor, and your cells are two-thirds water by volume. Yet, many don't know that the water molecule is so small that 99% of the molecules in your body are water.

In 1969, scientists stumbled onto polywater, laying the groundwork to discover a fourth phase of water. Due to discreditation by the scientific community, research froze — pun intended — for decades until the late 1990s when Gerald Pollack, a bioengineering professor and researcher, began to study a new phase of water. This new phase was named liquid crystalline or structured water and is still controversial today. The four phases of water are solid, *liquid crystalline* (H_3O_2), liquid (H_2O), and vapor.[34]

Liquid crystalline is water that is said to be alive and holds memory. Crystal is a material where molecules are arranged in an orderly formation or *in-formation*. All water stores information, yet tap water holds additional toxins collected from the pipes and the environment — toxins we don't want to drink.

Water is structured by the spiraling torque and spin found in nature — the spiral of your DNA, the way water spirals down a drain, the spiral of a hurricane, and ocean waves. Harmonious resonance through sound or light is also said to structure water. Structured water is a key to our universe. It's in our body, fruits and vegetables, and the water in a running stream or spring.

The discovery of liquid crystalline explains water mysteries such as why your joints work without squeaking, rising water in very tall trees, how ice floats, and the ability of tsunami waves to circle the globe. Reimagining our human-made plumbing and water treatment systems through biomimcry[35] would help us re-create healthy structured water at all scales, with the potential to resolve hidden health issues around the globe.

As a few brave scientists explore the provocative new phase of water, physicists theorize that the quantum vacuum of space, as well as our air, is a superfluid — a very slippery fluid without viscosity. We may soon discover we mimic Wallace's parable of the young fish where truth is hidden in plain sight — we don't realize we are swimming in a fluid universe.

Just like the flatness of the Earth or the revolution of the sun, *more things* recently revealed a universe where time behaves differently than we thought. Theoretical physicist Carlo Rovelli spent his life in the passionate pursuit of understanding time and in doing so, came to know a world without time.

Rovelli discovered time exists as an agreement framed from our human point of view; we demonstrate that with our established time zones. Time is entirely in our minds as memory and anticipation. Time is relational and relative. There is a vast multitude of times, one for every point in space. Time passes slower at sea level than it does in the mountains. Time depends on entropy and heat; without low entropy, the world would go into a state of thermal equilibrium, and past and future, as we understand it, would cease to exist.[36]

The study of the very small revealed that measurement and matter aren't as solid as we think. So many experiment results defy current reality and math inside quantum mechanics that they came up with the phrase *quantum weirdness.*

Quantum weirdness to a scientist is to me the wild backwoods of a universe not yet chartered or understood by our limited awareness. It is the edgy, dark, and wild unknown out of which all possibilities await. I refer to it as the *quantum wilderness.* The quantum wilderness is the interconnected quantum holofractographic multiverse woven from sound and oscillation that Nassim Haramein discovered.

Each hero's journey unfolds to help them wake up to the gift of paradox within the multiple dimensions of the quantum wilderness, either this life or another. Many of us know what it feels like to want to hit the snooze button some mornings. It takes courage to wake up.

It is brave to see the mystery of the quantum wilderness we have been swimming in all along. The heart is the gate into the quantum wilderness and wonder is one of the golden keys. The amazing news is that in a holofractalgraphic universe, your personal healing informs collective healing.

In the 20th century, with quantum goggles more firmly in place, our Western culture gained access to wisdom traditions that are thousands of years old. The *more things* that ancient healing modalities and wisdom traditions around the globe have been practicing for thousands of years are receiving scientific attention. In the 21st century, academics, anthropologists, archaeologists, psychologists, and doctors are still translating core tenets of such teachings in a way that is accessible to the Western mind.

From shamanism to yoga, the Westernization of these wisdom traditions has ushered a renaissance of science and spirituality going on a blind date. There's a dark side though that we'll be sorting through for a while — including colonialization, misuse, and cultural misappropriation. It is easy for spiritual teachings to get taken out of context and much is lost in translation.

Evolution is a given, and progress is inevitable even amid misunderstandings and misuse. The hunger for remembering what is sacred and the pull to vision a new connected paradigm is slowly emerging across the globe. Being visionary is the willingness to turn inward and know thyself. The work to heal and emotionally mature as humans from the inside out is essential; only then can we see deeper layers of truth and possibility regardless of our current comforts, convenience, and fear. Emotional intelligence builds resilience for the path forward and allows us to imagine better institutions.

What lies before us is a new level of accountability to our translations, so that we can build better world systems to positively influence reconciliation, redemption, and restoration planet wide.

I am grateful that the quantum revolution is underway. I bow to the scientists and thinkers before me who violated the agreements of their culture to get to the truth. I am thankful that my soul chose this current culture; so that as a woman and a thinker, I can write my ideas down.

Even now, with all our theories and discoveries, many of the assumptions we have about science and reality are wrong. A musician friend, Mike Tamburo, says it well, "You can fill a universe with what I don't know."[37]

In order to understand something immense, like how the stars tell time, we must be willing to not know and eat a little humble pie every day. We must be more passionate about our questions than our answers. Everything good starts with such unpretentious inquiry. Seeking better questions with an open heart is the path.

Right now, in the "every-when," on our home planet Earth, we are in a post-information age. We are flooded with new global environmental, socio-political, and health factors generating incredibly disruptive times. Disruption gifts us with accelerated change to make room for the possibilities we couldn't see before.

Our established deterministic reality has been on its way-out for years. What used to take generations to evolve an entire cultural paradigm now takes less than a generation. This means you have the power inside you to help mature our view of reality as well as any broken systems within that reality, *in your lifetime.*

Once upon a time we thought the Earth was flat or that the sun moves around the Earth. The Earth moving around the sun is a given now. A new paradigm is rising where energy makes up all things, there is more than one universe, and multiple timelines and dimensions exist at the same time. *Reality itself* can now be examined on purpose, allowing us to come up with better questions, so humanity can begin to participate in the cosmic love story already here.

Although our human experience is relative to the sun we depend on, the rest of the multiverse is not. In looking at the world from the perspective of stars, we embrace a robust reality that allows more dimensions of knowing. Take a moment to imagine a photon's point of view, or our star's vantage point, or the perspective of life elsewhere on other planets.

A less human-centric view can evolve our human experience to become more accountable, conscious, and aware of something bigger than us. We can admit that the universe is filled with what we don't know. We can learn more about the stars we are made of, literally, at the quantum level. This is how we become "humo-luminous." This is how we blaze new trails in the quantum wilderness.

"The words of my heart are also yours. Truth knows truth."

– Astara

Truth's Stretch Marks

Amor fati.

Amor fati in Latin translates as "love of fate" or "love of one's fate." To borrow from my lessons in *alchemy*,[38] which taught me to practice seeing the holy in everything, the poet in me translates Amor Fati as *love everything that happens to you.*

To *love everything*, I must widen my narrow view so I can hold paradox, allowing more than one perspective at a time. Just like scientific theories, when I take in another viewpoint, I begin to encircle the sphere of truth. I learn to hold the trauma and hurt as much as the sweetness and joy. It is no small task. I cringe at pain just like everyone else, but then sooner or later I find myself knee deep in the difficult experience, translating metaphors while gasping at the beauty.

To *love everything that happens to me*, I had to find the toolkit of my heart, open it, and use it liberally. This is the only way to see a bigger truth. The heart is the gateway to the zero point of the quantum field where all connects as one and everything is happening simultaneously. Our hearts can hold the difficult and the beautiful at the same time.

When we are in heart coherence, we become available to our imagination. The imaginal realm is where everything begins. The heart communicates directly with the stars outside of time, and imagination is the secret to creation.

The right brain is where imagination holds court. The left brain gives our imagination structure and form. Our left and right hemispheres continuously emit nerve impulses. Our right brain is in a state of dreaming both when we are awake and when we are asleep. Basically, we are dreaming all the time.[39] If we dream from a state of incoherence and fear, what we form will reflect division and scarcity. When we dream in coherence with the unified field of love, what we form in the world feels truthful and soul-satisfying.

You are dreaming to some extent as you read these words. Dreaming is the aspect of our being that tethers us to the quantum field. We are electromagnetic fields walking around inside of electromagnetic fields, and this electromagnetism we are a part of is more real and influential than what we call solid matter. It is our imagination that moves that field.

In a world driven by the left hemisphere of the brain, we are smitten with evidence, logic, and reason. Right-hemisphere, boundary-less dreaming is undervalued. Our general culture disregards imagination as false fantasy. Yet, dreaming is our most powerful creative act fueled directly by the indefinable source of life; it is pure consciousness animating the clay of our existence.

The ineffable force we are made of holds a very high frequency. Think of the musical metaphor of a chord on the piano. When I say *love everything that happens to you*, I am talking about aligning to a much higher chord than we might be used to. I call it love. I am not speaking to aesthetic or romantic ideals of love we hold as a culture. When we say we are in love with someone, what we are is in the frequency of love with them.

The love I speak of is limitless, like an ocean. Jesus, Buddha, Mohammed, Rumi, Hafiz, and many other great teachers and poets refer to a love like this. The love I am referring to is an expansive resonance that holds space for all of life and not just an expected emotion. We are each a vessel. Any mandates or exclusions we place on love turns the faucet off within us, and we separate ourselves from the good that we are.[40]

Life itself is a great dress rehearsal to practice loving truthfully and loving everything. Every day, I aim to sing a new song of myself — to wake up and marvel at life anew and be available to inquire where love dwells in each life experience.

With love as my guide, years ago I had to give myself a giant permission slip etched in gold that read, *I say yes to my imagination.* I roused myself from cultural agreements that would have me do otherwise. I grew to give merit to all my dreams, both waking and asleep.

If we measure life at the level of consciousness we hold, imagination is subjective. This book paints a world straight out of my heart with my version of life events. If my parents were still alive to tell their version, or if my any of my siblings or friends were to chime in on these pages, the story would be very different. Remember, all stories exist side by side in truth.

As the youngest of four siblings, with piles of family stories as reference, I am no stranger to the convincing nature of my own version of events. Like the game of telephone, truth evolves into fiction with each telling.

From the power of the observer effect, the squirrely nature of the dreaming and creating brain, to the agreements of time, just like perception, memory is a magic trick done with smoke and mirrors. Our individual truth is like a slippery fish in water. The bigger truth is the water itself. What is important is to loosen our grip, leave room for all the slippery magic we each bring, and let the layers of truth flow. We can learn to let our personal truth swim next to another personal truth inside the waters of the higher truth.

In our family, a story could get told so often out of the collective diary, that we could lose sight of whose memory it is or even how it happened. A story becomes so familiar, it could metamorphosize as our own.

Once upon a time, I was visiting my sister Sierra in college. It was exciting to leave my high school world in Los Angeles to visit her college world on the edge of the University of California Berkeley campus.

Sixteen-year-old me arrived in awe as I thought, *I get to hang out with Sierra and her cool sorority sisters!* There I was in her large L-shaped room with big windows overlooking College Avenue. Sierra was across the room on her twin bed at the other end of the L, while I sat on her roommate's bed. We were talking and sharing stories when Sierra sat up to tell me something.

Sierra and I look a lot alike, especially when we were young. In this humorous moment, Sierra had the unique angle to look in the mirror on the closet door and thought she saw me. She looked up and waved at me in the mirror. In short order, the mirror gave her the truth. Sierra laughed out loud as she realized she was waving to herself.

Where things get interesting is that when I tell this story, I feel I was the one on that day who waved at myself in that closet mirror door, not her. Many tellings later, we each insist on our own version of the truth. To this day, I honestly don't know whose memory it is.

How do I *love everything that happens to me,* if I am not sure what is real?

Now, years later, with the help of quantum physics, I believe we were both right. I do know we were both there. To this day, Sierra and I both humorously share our version of the memory. I say yes to the power of imagination and how it dreams our memories and our world into being.

My brother Tim, Sierra, and I still argue over who took a well-remembered photograph of a sunset on a family cross-country road trip in 1975 on our way to see our older sister, Maribel, get married. I would have been days short of five at the time. I was quite young to be taking a photograph, yet my memory has me convinced.

That is the thing about our lives — we were there. And we believe being there instills enough authority that the story happened the way we remembered it. Ultimately, it doesn't matter who owns the story or which version is true. I now understand that truth is not singular but plural. It takes my brother, sister, and myself to reconstruct the beauty of that sunset which would inspire us to hunt for the camera to photograph it.

Truth is a song. In this case, it was sung in a three-part harmony.

If only one person sings, you don't get to enjoy the vocal layers entwining. Truth is not a solo performance; it is a symphony.

What did my sister see in that lowering sun framed by the silhouette of trees? What did my brother see as the tree limbs held the sun's dying glow like a prayer?

Amor Fati. *Love everything that happens to you.* And love what happens to others, for we are all mirrors for one another, helping each other grow.

Loving everything feels like a tall order when it comes to core traumas and violence, and I do not belittle the intensity of anyone's suffering or any crisis around the globe. Life circumstances can engulf our spirit, so it comes down to our willingness to see the divinity within, form a new relationship with our past, learn, heal, chose a new response, and find life again. This is alchemy. It is how we free ourselves and walk around our world with our power restored, able to empower others.

If we are dreaming all the time, we are imagining all the time. Imagination formed from the heart has the power to create, mend, and weave wholeness out of temporal disparate parts. Imagination formed from fear can do the opposite.

Reality is a joint venture; we all imagine our world into being together. Each individual reality exists at the same time. There is room for us all in our differing vantage points and perceptions. Diversity is a given; it's nature's rule. It may take us lifetimes, but we are all here to learn how to meet diversity with compassion and imagine from the heart.

My history reshapes itself in the retelling, and the truth has stretch marks. By entering the timelessness of the heart, I can revisit past impactful events and mend various versions of truth back to love. show. I apply alchemy to the events, which creates uplifting stretch marks way beyond my current earthly existence. The intent is not to change the outcome, it is to change my *story*.

We can learn to love everything that happens to us inside the dream. Let yourself stumble in the pursuit of truth; the stumbling is your best classroom. Then, love it all to a new place.

My version of events are in the pages ahead. I imagine them as a beautiful and distinct movement in a much larger symphony of love that connects me with my family, my ancestors, my soul across life-times, and my soul family. If you are reading this, that includes you.

In the case of that famed photograph of the ebbing sun one summer road trip in 1975, my brother and sister's telling of it informs what happened to me. I can still see that orange disc turning the horizon red against the black outline of trees as we sped past in our Ford station wagon piled high with pillows in the back seats. I remember my brother, sister, and I clamoring for the camera amongst a tangle of blankets. We were desperate to capture that glow, knowing it was a gamble that the photo would ever turn out in the dim light.

"Happiness does not fall from the sky. It's in your hands."

– Eddie Jaku, 101-yr-old holocaust survivor

Ghosts

The law of thermodynamics states that energy does not go away, it just changes shape. I define *ghost* as any expression of lost, stuck, hidden, or unprocessed energy that represents *power loss* through absence or stagnation.

I define *power* as the electromagnetic energy of the universe — the energy we are made of — flowing unimpeded through our body and field. *Power loss* is the depletion of our life force through separation and disconnection. We may give our power away to others or suppress our power in hopes to connect or find worth, but this is not true connection or worth.

Power loss can also be called an *energy leak.* Conscious or subconscious problematic behaviors leak your vital life force energy. Problematic behaviors include negative methods of self-soothing, as well as chronic toxic thoughts and beliefs. An energy leak expresses itself first at the energetic level, and if held long enough, can arrive in the body last as a physical symptom.

Ghosts, or phantoms suffering from power loss, come in many forms.

Like Hamlet's father, when a person dies and their soul still lingers as a ghost, it is because they have unfinished business. Ghosts are a disembodied spirit or discarnate that has decided to hang out in the third dimension after death.

Yet, of all the types of ghosts, **Soul loss**[41] is the primary phantom in most of our lives. The *soul* emanates from Source, what I call

God or the Presence of All That Is. An individual soul emerges and separates from Source through the healthy ego, which mediates between our conscious and subconscious aspects. Think of our *soul* as our essence, our life force, the immaterial or spiritual aspect of being, the part of our vitality that keeps us alive and thriving. The soul is the part of you that is eternal.

Soul loss arises inside larger-than-life occurrences, which can be both uplifting and devastating. Although some big life moments are joyful, like a wedding, promotion, or birth, they can still be impactful enough as to be overwhelming. Some events are shocking and ricochet through our being, like war, cancer, surgery, or deep loss of any kind.

Regardless of the type of experience, from the exuberant to the traumatic, fragments of our soul may step aside for a moment to catch its breath, becoming a ghost. In the shock of a brief high-octane evolutionary moment, a soul part may hit the "pause" button until our body can digest what has occurred. Only then does that part of our soul feel safe to return home. Psychologists call this *disassociation. Shamans*[42] call this soul loss.

We abandon parts of ourselves in the natural course of life. Cultural conditioning, family agreements, and many overwhelming events later, and one day we may look in the mirror and we do not know who we are anymore. Part by part, piece by piece, over the years we slowly and naturally lose track of our inborn wholeness and authenticity. Our identity appears solid, yet deep down, we have become ghost-like.

Soul loss is natural because it is a self-protection mechanism within our human experience. A part of our essence leaves the body so that we don't feel the full impact of what is happening. This is how we survive the pain or even joy that we are unable to endure. A soul fragment may wait an eternity to come home if we don't have the circuitry to capacitate its return. Parts of us can get stuck in time indefinitely.

Accumulated soul loss is prolific in our modern world. Our society does not educate us to know soul loss can occur, let alone train us how to call those parts back. Shamans know that some soul parts do not come back on their own. A shaman dives outside the limits of time into the field of energy to help someone find that missing piece. If we learn to listen to our inner authority, the heart knows the call back, the healing song, and the path home. The heart is capable of magnetism, integration, and alchemy.

When a soul fragment goes missing, we not only experience soul loss, we experience power loss as well. Over time, this can manifest in a myriad of ways affecting physical, emotional, and mental health. When a soul part is returned, it returns the disassociated aspects of one's life and restores intrinsic power.

In addition to ghosts that haunt old castles and ghosts as soul parts stuck in time, ghosts come in a myriad of other expressions as well.

Family legacies haunt us like ghosts. Epigenetic markers of inter-generational trauma hang out as specters in our DNA waiting to be activated. Patterns silently and not-so-silently handed down from grandparents to parents to us. Just as water holds information and memory, our family data also waits in our blood like time-release capsules ready to emerge at just the right moment for healing and release. These echoes of trauma are an effort to heal unresolvedness across generations.

Memory and belief can haunt us as ghosts. Memories of lovers or close friends who left or had important lessons for us that we still haven't learned. Persistent limiting stories about self that create power loss. To maintain our fearful memories and beliefs over the years, we use essential reserves of our life-force, depleting us over the long-haul.

Shadow aspects of ourselves that we have abandoned are hidden ghosts. Shadows are the archetypes or core needs inside us that we suppress or reject outright. It is natural for our inner child to have needs that could not be met when we were young. There may be a grown adult in front of you, but they might be acting out the needs of their inner child through the bad behavior of their outer child. Suppressing our needs ends up suppressing some of our true gifts, and what we are left with are unwanted behaviors and energy leaks.

Past life fears[43] are also ghosts keeping us from our full expression. As energy is eternal and only changes form, when we die, we return to the formlessness of the universe. When we incarnate again, we have soul amnesia and forget our prior life. Yet, the fears from another lifetime can haunt our current incarnation to such a degree that they can shape strange phobias and harmful illusions that govern us until we heal and release them.

In my thirties, I began to remember other lifetimes of experience in a different body, gender, place, and time. Some souls remember even earlier. Some souls do not remember at all.

The hero's journey in movies like Star Wars or The Matrix inspire us to live authentically, but to do so means changing inside and out. We ask ourselves, is the risk worth the reward? In my life, I reached a point where I had to live authentically. When I didn't, I could feel the energy leaks express throughout my system — I hurt physically, mentally, emotionally, and spiritually.

Amor Fati.

To love everything that happened to me, to love all the parts of myself, I had to be like Hamlet and meet my ghosts. I took it further and loved each ghost to a new place. To bring alchemy to the full spectrum of ghosts in my life, I began where success begins, on the inside.

This process revolutionized who was sitting in the driver's seat of my life. All my ghosts held important secrets and keys to my superpowers. With their help, I built more capacity to hold *all of me*, the dark and the light and everything in between. The hidden and the seen. The disliked and the liked. The rejected and the rejoiced. *All of me.*

Time travel turned out to be the willingness to dive into the generous universe and connect with other dimensions inside the quantum wilderness. Because soul loss is a natural part of life, I will be living out this intricate reunion work as long as I am in this body.

Whether it is our own memory or a genetic-hand-me-down, all of us think and live in the past more than any other place. Old traumas and nostalgic memories not felt, faced, and integrated rearrange themselves and take up precious real estate in our subconscious, where our automatic pilot is formed. They also assert themselves in our body and electromagnetic field.

For most humans, somewhere around the age of 35, after many decades of repetition with ghosts and legacies, habits become automatic, and the personality cures into place like concrete. That involuntary aspect of us takes up approximately 95 percent of our functioning brain.[44] This is how our personality creates our personal reality. If our imagination is imprisoned in limiting habits and beliefs, it keeps us narrow and myopic in our vision of what we think is possible for ourselves.

My life turned out to be a training ground in the quantum wilderness to recollect my ghosts and bring them home in order to free my imagination. Now I help my clients learn how to meet their ghosts and love themselves. Soul retrieval is an intimate journey, yet as we empower ourselves, we model for others what wholeness looks like. We become invitations of healthy intimacy from the inside out.

> *"The heart seems to be connected to a type of intuition*
> *that is not bound by the limits of time and space."*
>
> – *Rollin McCraty, Ph.D., director of research, HeartMath*[45]

The Heart of Things

Before I knew a language of consciousness, I was drawn to understand nature, the soul, and the universe. Since I was a child, the first gates to open my awareness were through the art, dance, music, and books I explored. In architecture school, I discovered nature-based design, sacred geometry, and chaos theory. After I graduated at age 25, I studied quantum physics, yoga, massage, Reiki, and more. Left to themselves, no one discipline is complete. The bigger Truth I was searching for came on the heels of many truths woven together. This is why I chose a multidisciplinary path and began earning my living inside the credible field of architecture.

At 31, I discovered the psycho-spiritual tool of tarot as a map of consciousness and a mirror for the soul's evolution. The universal math, patterns, and symbols of the tarot gave me a new framework to delve into the mystery of my nature. I didn't use the tarot for prediction, instead I used it as a self-reflective tool to heal and develop my imagination. The combination of number patterns and visual symbols appealed to my pattern-seeking mind and strengthened my intuition.

At 34, I became a licensed architect in California. Prior to my license, I was able to keep many of my early wounds subterranean. The licensing process forced my anxiety to the surface as physical symptoms so I would begin to face them. I entered therapy to face my childhood traumas, unwind stories, and begin a long road of healing. I discovered conscious dowsing and kinesiology and began to connect with my body and field in a deeper way.

By 36, I learned how to access the Akashic records[46] which accelerated my path as an intuitive. These records hold every experience of every soul across all dimensions and time. The records have been described as a library, the Book of Life, or the tree of life. Some describe it as a matrix or web that mimics a brain, synaptically connecting all information past, present, and future. It's also referred to as the eighth dimension which accesses all dimensions. Using modern technology as a metaphor, imagine the Akashic records as cloud computing or the internet of God where you can download information for insights into personal healing and your relationship to all of creation.[47]

Around age 40, I was guided to meet various wisdom leaders in synchronistic flow. One by one they validated what I sensed my entire life but didn't have words for. My first shamanic training at 41 gifted me hindsight to see I had been dancing between the unseen and the seen all along. Finally, I had a framework for my Inner Shaman, which had been present since I was young.

With a fresh lexicon and new tools at my disposal, I began to journey into the quantum field on-purpose — to translate, co-create, and reflect for others what they couldn't see, as of yet. Although these soulful seeds were in me all along, I discovered each of them in the right timing. One expanding experience led to another, and suddenly, the most interesting information didn't arrive from other teachers, it arose from inside me.

My inner knowing reminded me that love is the energy that makes up everything. I realized that the multiverse is far more interesting and benevolent than our culture knows. I learned that we are each more powerful than we can fathom.

At age 42, all my teachings thus far culminated to reveal the wisdom of the heart. I recognized patterns across disciplines revealing how we are connected to each other and all of life within our heart center. Our entire lives are shaped by the truth that we are either allowing or resisting the heart's knowing. When I discovered that the zero-point of our heart exists free of the constructs of time, things started to get very exciting.

In an epic move from California to Nebraska in 2013, 43-year-old-me activated the last puzzle piece to step fully into my soul instructions. At the surface of my personality, I had no idea such deep magic was unfolding. Initially, it started with my boss at the time calling me at my San Francisco office to ask if I would be willing to transfer to our corporate heart in Omaha. I told him, "Give me a week to say no."

I saw my work transfer to Nebraska simply as a strategic move to climb a ladder of success inside my architecture engineering firm. On reflection, I was at the precipice of stepping off the success ladder built by my culture and redefining success on my terms.

The week went by, and on the morning I had to choose whether to move or not, I laid in my bed in the dark before sunrise. The thought of such immense change weighed on me. I couldn't sleep as thoughts spun through me. *This could be the opportunity of a lifetime. I would have more reach as a sustainable leader by going to the center of the company. But how can I leave everyone I know? How can I leave my family and friends? Will my cat be okay in the snow? Will I meet people I can connect with? How do I leave the beauty of the California coast and the redwoods for a completely new land? How do I live in Omaha, Nebraska?*

Crazy! I decided. *No way.*

As soon as the thought of *no* came, it didn't feel right. I called my dear friend Jessie that had known me for years. I knew she would be up early, and that she would talk straight with me. She gave me perspectives I couldn't see. At the end of our conversation she said, "My mom and I were just saying the other day, why is Astara still in the Bay Area? We both agree it is time for you to go." Her words surprised me, yet they confirmed what my heart knew. After finishing our phone call, I hung up and sat in the dark.

Next, I called my friend James and he said he would be happy to meet me at his office for tea before his first client. I drove to him, and as we sat there sipping our hot drinks, he helped me see all the incredible business success going on in Omaha that I had no idea about. He reminded me that there were spiritual people in Omaha too. I laughed. I thanked him and drove home.

They each gave me words of encouragement and the push I needed. They reminded me to be open and see how this could be right for me.

Back at home again, I mulled over their words. Something inside me chimed in. *Chime* being the operative word. I could hear overtones. A familiar tone rang out inside my brain and body, not my ears. I knew this sound from my Awakening the Illuminated Heart (ATIH) workshop in San Francisco a year before, where I learned how to ignite my heart and activate my *Merkaba* or light body.[48] One of the exercises taught me to listen to the tone of my heart and sing it. Afterwards, helping others illuminate their hearts became my secret mission.

Now, a year later in the early morning hours on the precipice of a big decision, my inner ears rang with that same sound. My inner vision offered me a picture of my heart. I knew it was my Merkaba, with my heart at the center. My heart gave me a clear message, *"Although the surface reason to transfer to the corporate heart of your company is to grow environmental leadership, the actual reason is the heart. You are going into the heart of things."*

A few months prior, I had begun singing songs at the piano with the aim of singing my love to me. I was single and dating was a tiring but consistent reality. At first, I thought my beloved was in the Bay Area, yet here I was contemplating moving 1,500 miles. It hit me that there was a reason I hadn't found him in the Bay Area. And then my heart whispered, *"That's because he isn't here."*

I giggled out loud. The universe had such a sense of humor. I saw the heart theme clearly: the *heart* of my company, the *heartland*, my yearning to illuminate other's *hearts*, and my *heart's* yearning for my beloved. The heart of things indeed!

I called my boss later that day and said *yes*. The move went quickly from there. I was inside my new Omaha home in less than two months. Such flow felt like validation from the universe.

A year after moving, I found out my song not only led me to

him, my song led him to me as well. Only a year after I met my future husband and business partner Ryan, we formed our company Illuminating Hearts[49] and began our adventure into the power of sound. We began to play powerful ancient instruments in sound healing sessions at our home office and in group events out in the world. We started with gongs and singing bowls. Ryan layered in his didgeridoo and flute. I began to sing, finding my voice. Ryan bravely started to sing too. In time, other unique instruments found us and joined in.

Day after day we played just inches away from these incredible instruments. As we healed our clients, we were healing ourselves too. Those powerful resonators were dissolving the noise, or "self-noise," and resistance in our bodies and fields at a rapid rate. Accelerated change was the new normal for both of us.

A year or so into offering Sound Alchemy[50] with Ryan, it was our music that unlocked the gate of time. I had known shamanic journeys were possible through sound. When drumming mimics the rhythm of theta brain waves, it entrains a person's brain and body to a wakeful dream or visionary state. Ryan and I eventually understood that our instruments, singing, speaking, and writing (all vibrations) could initiate a theta brain state, as well as the restorative alpha, delta, and gamma brain waves. When partnered with an awakened heart, this coherent theta state opened the gate of time for us and our clients. The heart of time travel is sound. Pun intended. We began calling our instruments the time machine.

The vibration of written memory inside my journals came alive through our intentional sound. Our music generated resonant attunements that helped me explore inner space. A few years into writing this book, I learned how to set up a permanent conference call with the cosmos, channel my guides, talk to the spirit of deceased loved ones, and connect with my younger and older selves in order to retrieve lost parts of my soul. I was able to heal deeper than therapy could take me a decade prior. I felt the cumulative benefits of a few decades of conscious soul return for I had more capacity inside me to live my intuitive gifts into the world as my full-time vocation.

If you have found this book, my heart magnet found your heart. You likely feel an indefinable yearning to embody the fullness of your being and step into your soul adventure on purpose. The quantum wilderness is participatory, connected, and creative. Infinite possibility exists simultaneously, and you create your reality with your thoughts, feelings, and words. You carry this wisdom in your heart and body. May my adventure ignite a pathway into your core, where a holistic connected reality wants to be remembered and lived consciously.

A Song Singing You into Being[51]

By Astara

There is a song singing the universe into existence right now.
A song that sings you into being again and again.
A song with no beginning and no end,
endlessly singing before time was invented.

The song that is you started
before the wind that moves the trees.
It started before math, microscopes, and telescopes.
It started before words, yet is inside every single one you speak.
Your song started in the quiet of the night sky
that isn't quiet at all.

We can't hear the melodious roar
coursing through the sun's core,
causing the fiery globe to move in and out rhythmically.
Instead, the sun's song thrums towards us as warmth,
growing every garden.

Your lungs, your breath, your lips the flute.
Your heart the drum,
as your pulse stretches through your fingertips.

Your throat finds the note,
a golden key opening everything.
Words swirl in the air around you,
forming galaxies.

As you sing in the shower, the car,
and at the kitchen sink,

notice what you sing into being.
Perhaps a song of separation and lack.
Or even better, a melody with the greater chorus
of the soil beneath you
in multi-part harmony with the sun and moon.

All the while, above you,
raven colors the blue-black backdrop
to the stars with her caw.
Around you, trees continue to chant to the dirt
as their leaves whisper secrets to the sky.
And downstairs, crickets offer their
delicate stringed instruments
to your coats in the front closet.

Meanwhile, panther,
invisible in the dark of a far off jungle,
fur rippling in response to the symphony you just began,
walks the unknown beside you, listening.

PART TWO:

Time Travel

*"When you become your own Guardian Angel, you
discover the dark had to happen, and love was there all
along. Your soul calls for you to remember."*

– Astara

Soul Stars

*In my journey, I am standing in a field below a starry sky. The sky,
and its stars, begins to swirl down and a black panther is running
toward me. The panther's skin ripples with stars reflected across dark
shimmering fur.*

I ask panther, "What do I need to know?"

*Panther is silent. Panther shows me a prairie, a field of grasses. With
a paw, panther paints another swirl of stars across the grass swaying
in the night breeze.*

*Panther's wordless message forms as thoughts. 'This is what you
are. You are the field, the grasses. You are the stars spinning through
the land.'*

*I inhale audibly, mouth wide. As the stars' swirl, they slowly join,
forming a larger brighter star. It is as if they are coming home to each
other. I exhale, mouth wide. Panther speaks, "You are a star. You give
birth to stars."*

I open my eyes.

…

It is Friday night, March 11, 2016. I am 46.

I sit upright looking around the room at the workshop circle I am
a part of. Men and women sit in different chairs, some with their
eyes still closed. Ryan is sitting in the chair to my right with his

eyes are open; he's looking around until his eyes meet mine with a smile. Others are slowly coming back into the room, slowly coming back into this now.

Each attend the shaman workshop for differing reasons — some to learn shamanic techniques, some to practice, and some to feel community connection. We each come to understand ourselves and our relationship to the universe better. I come to enjoy a container for my own journeying; it's refreshing to have someone else do the drumming.

My journey transcends words, yet I rush to write down my experience. It felt like the stars had their own language. My skin shivers and my arm hairs alert to the air. I am alive with energy. Right there, sitting amongst strangers in a plush armchair, my hands busily scribble words to the page. I am rising beyond the known into a realm where star song translates dirt, fire, leaf, water, blood, and bone in a new way. In my journey I'm reminded how allies are everywhere; inside the stars, elementals and nature allies are all communicating with me.

I drive home as thoughts arrive. *Life is the question itself, ever expanding, ever evolving my presence in the place of things. I am learning to live into the life my soul intended. Yet, how do I give birth to stars?*

I park in the driveway and walk to my front door. I walk in, and I go down to the basement. I find the box of my journals that have been calling to me for weeks and start pulling them out of the cardboard storage box. I set them in piles and start to organize them by year; I begin the delicate process of meeting myself across time.

Stars begin to swirl upon this earth.

*"Every beginning | is only a sequel, after all, | and the
book of events | is always open halfway through."*

– Wislawa Szymborska[52]

The Middle

My story begins in the middle. All stories start somewhere in the middle; there is no beginning or end in the book of life.

It is Sunday, October 8, 2017. I am 47. I am at home sitting at my writing desk. I face a pile of journals stacked before me on the dark wood. My journals contain words like busy summer bees; they have been buzzing at me since last spring. When I first unpacked them from their moving box, I meticulously organized them by date and labeled them. The emotion and insights waiting for me, patiently waited some more. All I could do at that time was lift them, hold them, and glance at them enough to arrange them.

I must have room inside me now for I am no longer ignoring their hum. Each journal has its own hive. I fancy that if I open them, sweet honey will ooze out. The Queen bee is me.

My mind hears the smallest journal buzz, *start with me.* A small red hard-bound diary sits on top. Logic and chronology win out; I will start with my youngest self.

Sure, why not, I think, unaware that the linear thread of time is about to unravel.

I pick up the small book and turn it in my hands. The tips of my fingers run across the title *Secrets* written at the top in dark brown bold lower-case letters. A light brown teddy bear caricature sits below. It's stubby cartoon arm lifts a key embossed in shiny silver. I click open the brass latch at the fore edge where the front and back cover boards lock shut.

As I open the cover, I recall the original key was lost when I first got the diary. My secret past is perpetually unlocked, waiting for me.

I scan entry after entry, taking in my adolescent tone. In this first diary, I write for just two months. It is the winter of 1983. At first, I cringe a little at my writing abilities at age 12. I wrote to God — the father-like God I was taught about in church. Each entry ends with a prayer. The pages are riddled with exclamation points.

I read my short report of the winter of 1983 again. Although it is such a brief diary, just one sentence ignites memories in high definition.

At school today I found out I made the softball team!!! Thursday, January 6, 1983.

Although I could pick up choreography easily when I was at dance, I was surprisingly uncoordinated within competitive sports. I tried out for softball to show my father I was good at sports. He loved sports. I loved him. It was a simple equation. Even though I was awful at them, I kept trying to please him.

My heart wasn't in it, which led me to low confidence and slow reflexes. I had two left feet and little arm strength. I could barely catch or throw. I made the softball team by pure mercy. Not surprisingly, I was given the farthest left outfield position.

I was a distant point in the low grass under the glare of the high Southern California sun. I'm daydreaming again with my heart somewhere else entirely. A classmate hits a ball squarely, sailing it into my field. The smack of ball against bat wakes me out of my reverie, but it is too late. He's running the bases. I miss the play, the ball, everything. My cheeks turn pink.

My coach shouts to me, "What's your name?"

With my hands cupped to my mouth I yell, "Lily!"

I was far enough outfield that my coach couldn't hear my name. He shouts back, "Philly?"

Thus, I was temporarily nicknamed Philly Cream Cheese in the seventh grade. It made for great comedy for the whole class.

I went to Egremont, a private school in the San Fernando Valley in Los Angeles County. As a small class, any nickname was a big deal. If something degrading happened, or someone turned on you, or didn't like you, everyone knew. It was enough humiliation to discourage me from continuing with softball.

I tried basketball that same season. I broke my right index finger while dribbling and got blocked. I thought soccer might be the answer; the fancy footwork felt like dance. Then, wham! The soccer ball whizzed with great speed right into my mouth full of braces. A bloody painful mess. Embarrassed and defeated, I kept trying. Next was track. I often dragged in last for each event. My sports insecurity piled higher and higher with each try.

Today was the dance! At the dance, all I danced with practically was Liam. We had fun. I danced with lots of other boys. Then, Liam and I had the last slow dance. He kissed me goodnight! January 7, 1983.

My first kiss at my junior high dance with Liam Brown who was taller than me. The rough texture of his suit jacket rubbed against the skin of my face and neck as we dance. I can still smell the faint scent from the rose pinned to his lapel. Anticipation raises my pulse. I dare to look up at him. He leans down slowly so our lips can briefly meet for the first time.

Today is the day! Rejoice! Rejoice! Liam, Stuart, Dawn, and I all had lunch at my house. We played games and saw a movie at the Galleria. We saw the movie Best Friends. It was good. Liam and I sat together in the waaaay back. We kissed a lot! We also held hands. Liam is really great! I'll never forget today. My first date! Saturday, January 22, 1983.

Weeks after the dance, the dark of the movie theater engulfs us. We sit in the back with no one behind us. Our fingers entwine until our palms sweat. Intermittently, bravely, our lips come together; then we pull back shyly to watch the movie some more.

Memories come in a flash of senses and feelings. In the diary, I talk about how good the movie was, yet I don't remember it now. I search the movie *Best Friends* online and watch the trailer. How synchronistic that the plot of this first date movie starring Goldie Hawn and Burt Reynolds echoes my life.

In my current timeline, Ryan and I are best friends who fall in love and begin to work together just like the best friends in the movie. In the film, the two best friends marry. Ryan and I got engaged four months ago. Subtle patterns offer just enough quantum strangeness across time for me to smile and take note.

I read passages again. What I first dismissed as childish writing, I see with fresh insight. My brief journaling from January 1 to February 9, 1983 is an incredible road map to my life at that age. I flip to the back of the book, and two small items fall out.

A thin bundle of papers even smaller than this red journal lies on the floor. My Egremont School identification card from 1983-1984 lands face up with my 13-year-old self smiling up at me. There I am just months after writing these entries.

I pick up my school card ID and the ripped spiral bound red diary cover with three pages stapled together. On the cover, I scratched out the brand name Mead with black pen. I also wrote my given name "Lily Marie Livingston" at the top and then crossed out my last name in black pen. I laugh. It looks like a redacted top-secret document. In big letters, I wrote "Dear Diary" and drew a small heart.

This small collection covers two days in February 1980 when I was nine. I wrote *date*, *day happened*, and *person talking about*, above the two short excerpts. The earnestness of my miniature self-made journal warms me from head to toe.

Dear diary, on Thursday, January 14, I was asked to be Ricky's girlfriend. He's so nice. He gave me a paper, it said, "Lily love ♡, I am crazy about you sweetheart. Will you be my girlfriend?" I was thrilled. I marked yes. Thursday, February 14, 1980.

In my mind's eye, I can still see the small paper Ricky gave me. It had small square boxes next to the options of "yes" and "no." I checked the box "yes." Excitement and fear swirled together inside me.

Dear diary, after school Ricky came up to me and said, "Lily, my bus driver wants to see you." I said, "Me?" He said, "Yeah." I went to the bus. The bus driver said, "Ricky said he would introduce me to you." I said, "Me?" Friday, February 15, 1980.

Here was a tiny but potent index of my first crush in fourth grade. The chemical zing of anticipation in my body. The hint of new beginnings. I can feel the surge of joy echo across time.

I hold two journals in my hands. Three pages at age nine in my left hand. Thirty-nine pages at age 12 in my right. Yet I don't write in a journal again until age 18. From 18-yrs-old and on, the writing continues for decades. The six-year gap grabs my curiosity. I open my diary from 1983 again. In the very back, there is a short glossary of one term: BBFF.

Memorandum: BBFF means Best Best Friends Forever – refer to February 2.

Glossary, date references, and footnotes. I beam at my young self and how she thinks. I turn to my entry on February 2nd.

Me and Denise are BBFF, all the way! Wednesday, February 2, 1983.

At age 12, Denise Kee was my BBFF. In this now, I haven't talked to Denise or know much about her since I last saw her in high school. We were close in junior high. By the time we graduated, we were no longer in the same friend circles.

I find Denise on Facebook and "friend" her. Looking at her online picture over three decades later, I feel a tug in my core. Even now her gentle kindness radiates off her photo. A soft fog of memory wafts over me like a distant scent or a soft warm breeze. I can't see anything clearly but remember feeling cared for and wanted.

Feeling cared for and wanted is essential to young me. The idea of *Forever* is very attractive to young me too. I had a deep yearning for indomitable love for I was seeking an antidote to my unstable world. I stop dismissing my young words as foolish.

I am the only adult who can be a forever caring presence to that young version of me. As I gain skills to reparent my inner adolescent, I have finally become my own BBFF. The experience, discernment, self-esteem, and compassion that my younger self longs for in a friend or adult is me meeting me.

I stand up and set these small journals atop my own private library spanning decades. It is the second month of my partner Ryan's three-month sabbatical in Joshua Tree, California. Our dog, Brown Dog, is not here. He is wandering the desert with my partner sniffing out coyotes and little pocket mice, helping Ryan care for our mutual friend's land, four goats, one dog, and six fish. I am at home alone. It is just me and our cat Orion, also named after our favorite constellation.

I look across the basement to my orange tabby cat curled in a nap spiral on our gold couch. I can hear the whistle of his light snore as he sleeps.

The wireless is off. The cell phone is powered down. The news, social media, and the drip of online content is turned off. Quiet, blessed, pared down solitude. No electronic alerts beeping. No podcasts on morning walks. No online research for work content. No texts, emails, or voice mail to clients. No streaming music. Only one CD of instrumental handpan music I keep on repeat in the car, or what I play at the piano and sing at home.

Inspired by Ryan's self-care, I create my own at-home-sabbatical and give my left brain a week-long vacation. Ryan, friends, and family know I am off-grid and device-free for a week. Goodbye cues of linear time. Hello me.

"Times are legion: a different one for every point in space."

– Carlo Rovelli[53]

Los Angeles

My throat is dry and tight. My solar plexus is tight. I sip from a glass of water and look back at the little red book. Reading through just a few moments in the life of 9-year-old and 12-year-old me, I recall feeling lost inside a confusing world with few tools.

After healing my inner world with grand determination for decades, I have the internal muscle to read each small passage again. I am feeling my way to my young self.

At age 12, I was unsure of how to reconcile my youthful hope with the strife I experienced in my immediate family. The intimates surrounding me were doing their best with their own fear and trauma, even if that meant projecting their tension on me and mine on them. It wasn't personal for any of us, but I didn't know that then.

I was an empath and intuitive without any training or tools to navigate my sensitivity or theirs. Because of that, their frictions permeated my own small existence to such a degree I thought they were my frictions or my fault. Even with so many beautiful and joyful moments in my loving family, any discord and fighting around me was enough to eclipse my memory of the good.

My mom's moods affected me most. My intelligent, kind, beautiful mom was a paradox, for she expressed emotions recklessly, often overwhelming my senses. I didn't know then that it was her outer child exploding with intensity, rooted in her unactualized inner child hurts. Her spontaneous storms affected my whole family, and we each responded in differing ways. Learning to navigate my mom and the outfall of her emotions became the sun around which I learned to orbit.

Twelve-year-old Lily's words pull me into her orbit.

Today is 1983!!! Well, hello new diary, I hope you like me. I had to type a lot today, because my finger was broken, and I missed four weeks of typing. Also, I looked at pictures of a long time ago. My grandma said Connie's sister died of kissing!! (ha, ha) My grandma makes me so mad. Sometimes I feel sorry for her. Dear Lord, I've been sinning a lot, help me not to. Saturday, January 1, 1983.

My broken finger clues me into my remembered attempt at playing basketball. Out loud in my time zone, I say out loud, "Oh sweetie, sin is not what you think it is."

I close my eyes connecting with young me and my feelings of fear. I hear a familiar high pitch hum. When I open my eyes, I am not at my desk in my Omaha basement. I am in my childhood room in Los Angeles.

The room is painted orange except for the gregarious wallpaper on the accent wall in front of me, a geometric pattern of gold, silver, orange, and pink. A kitten calendar hangs on the wall above my bed next to a wall-mounted bright green Snoopy pen dangling from a plastic spiral cord.

Three years from this now, I get to repaint my room a nice neutral color. Before I do, this orange bedroom with 1950's ornate metallic wallpaper is my backdrop. I will eventually have the pleasure to scrape that wallpaper clean. My arms will be happily sore for days.

My 12-year-old self is on the bed in front of me lying on her belly. Her hair is long and straight and falls below her shoulders. She still has braces. She is propped on one arm writing the diary entry I just read. She doesn't see me. Her face is tight with concentration as she puts words down.

I tentatively put my hand to the edge of the bed to see if I am solid. I'm not sure I can chalk this up to just a dream anymore. My fingers hit the bed.

Young me startles at my movement. She rolls to sit up abruptly and face me, staring. All the while the small red diary and pen fall off the bedspread onto the floor.

She recognizes me and looks startled, but not scared. It must be our same hazel eyes. My long hair is pulled back into a bun from my morning walk. The flecks of grey hair at my temples are revealed; when my brown wavy hair is down, the greys are hidden.

I try to speak to her, but there is a snapping sound, a whoosh in my head, and I am back at my desk in my present house. My hands are vibrating. My heart beats fast.

How is this possible? She saw me!

Shock waves move through me. I quickly grab the red book. All I can think is to keep reading for clues. I underline key passages that stand out to me. Not sure what to expect, I reread the entries; they are the same and do not mention my visit.

What felt like childish writing is transformed. I am staring at a portal. I place stickies marking key pages so that short pink, purple, and turquoise markers begin to stick out like plastic feathers.

I didn't go to church today. Sometimes I'd rather not go to church, the people are mean and stuck up. Sunday, January 2, 1983.

I remember Bel Air Presbyterian Church in the Mulholland hills. People would smile and say loving words, yet I also saw them act small-minded and judgmental. At 12, I didn't understand pretense. I look the word up and read *duplicity, two-facedness, falseness, double standards.*

I want to convey to my younger self how we give words meaning by our beliefs. How we define words defines our lives. But I am not sure how to get back to her timeline.

I grew up reading the Bible in school and church. By age 12, I am versed in the verses. The word sin has different definitions depending on family, culture, upbringing, and language. Sin as a concept was prevalent in all the worlds I circled in as a child: home, church, and school. Growing up, sin meant an immoral act considered to be a transgression against God and divine law. I was taught original sin in Sunday school, which meant we were born sinners. Even though I was meant to follow the authority of parents and teachers, I never agreed with that concept.

I feel young Lily's thoughts as my own. *How do we come into this world with sweet innocence yet already we are a sinner?*

The use of the word sin in my journal told me my young self believed in the definition I was taught. I reread the first entry on the first day of 1983.

Dear Lord, I've been sinning a lot, help me not to.

It's time to talk with 12-year-old me about a better definition of sin.

"Many particles have characteristics that challenge our perception of linear time and orderly space, by manifesting into existence, then disappearing again only to repeat the cycle. We have observed matter vanishing into energy, then winking back in somewhere else as a different type of particle."

– *Dawson Church*[54]

Time Portal

It is Monday, October 9, 2017. It is morning. I am back at my desk holding the small red portal to myself. I flip to a page tabbed with pink plastic and read an underlined section.

There's a fight going on now. It's because of me. I feel so bad! I wish they and I could stop fighting and be happy. Dear Lord, help our family. Wednesday, January 5, 1983.

I want to give young me a hug and let her know it is not about her. A pulse of energy fills my whole body. I feel her insecurity, sadness, and aching. My heart tightens. This single memory catches the thread of a pattern in place for years.

Out loud I say, "It's not about you. It's not about us. It never was."

The vibration of my words fires up the center of my chest. Tingling sensations move along my arms and legs. I close my eyes to feel what is happening. I hear a subtle tone, like a sustained bell sound. But there is no sound in the room.

When I open my eyes, I am standing again in my childhood room in Tarzana, a suburb of the valley. Our house sat on its own small hill below the Santa Monica Mountains within the megalopolis that is Los Angeles. I look at the sheen of my metallic wallpaper again in the light.

Lily is lying face down on her bed, sobbing into her folded arms to muffle her sounds and block out the world. The bed moves as I sit down. Lily feels my presence and lifts her wet face.

"Don't be scared," I quietly offer.

My arrival distracts her from her tears for a moment. Her eyes find mine.

After a tremendous stretch of holding my breath, I announce on the exhale, "I am you from the future." It comes out like a sigh. Out loud my words sound strange. Lily's face is puffy and her eyes are red from crying. I fear she is too tired to handle the impossibility of my arrival. Yet her heart recognizes me.

She looks up, and asks what any human would in this situation, "What?"

"I am sorry to interrupt a good cry," I tell her. "I know how important they are." Her long hair falls to her waist. It is wild to see my own eyes staring back at me.

She wipes her eyes and face, sniffling. She looks from my head to my toes and back.

I continue, "I am future you. I just turned 47 a few months ago. I found our diary, the one you are writing in right now, sitting on this bedspread. Somehow, it is helping me travel in time to meet you. I believe I am here to bring you love and support from the future. After what you just wrote, I sense you could use some good news right now."

She wipes her eyes and says, "I could."

"We, I mean, I go by a different name in the future. I, we, recently changed my name, our name, to Astara." I don't know whether to say I, we, me, or you. I sigh again.

"Astara?" She swallows, rolls over, and sits up. My young self is now quiet, considering. We love the sky and stars and space. At that age, she gobbles up any science fiction literature our older brother

Tim is willing to share. Because she can read my mind but doesn't yet know it, she repeats, "Astara? As in a star?"

"Yes." I beam.

"I love stars and constellations and anything in space."

"Yes, we do. I know the night sky was first shown to you — to us — by dad. And your love of those twinkling lights is one truth that has not changed in all these years. In fact, the stars are an important part of your future. They will signal you to the important things in your life." I wanted to talk about her future partner Ryan and the stars, but it wasn't her time to know.

"I am an older, more experienced you. You could fill a universe still with what I don't know, but I have a feeling what I do know can help you. It can help us both." I think, *I am talking to myself.*

"*A-star-a.*" Lily tries my new name out drawing out the letters phonetically. "I love that."

I smile. "It feels good, hearing you say your future name."

"I guess that is easier than calling you Lily." She is letting her clever out and smiling. She must be more comfortable.

"Good point," I smile back.

Her smile flattens quickly and worry moves across the furrow of her brow like a cloud. She leans in and whispers, "How are you even here?" Lily looks around me to see if I'm real.

"I honestly don't know," I lean and whisper back. Having emerged from a family battle in the other room, I know she's emotionally exhausted. I choose words carefully. "I have ideas. It all started when I began reading from the same journal sitting right there on your bed. I was reading your writing from two days ago, and then I popped into your room for a moment. Do you remember seeing me a few days back?"

"Yes! I just assumed I was imagining it." Lily looks down, chin to chest, ready to cry again. "I imagine a lot."

My fingers reach out to gently lift her chin. I look at her until her eyes meet mine and say, "That was real. And imagination is a wonderful thing. It is one of your superpowers."

She looks in my eyes as her brow evens out and her voice builds in strength, "It is?"

"It is. Everything in the world begins in imagination. To be able to work with it means you are learning to be a powerful creator."

"So, my imagining all the time is a good thing?"

"Despite popular opinion, yes. Speaking of imagination, I'm still figuring out on my end how to connect with you here on purpose. So far, it's been a happy accident." I look around our childhood room, taking it all in. I remember the circular patterned metallic wallpaper so well, the orange paint, the journal, the stack of my reading books on the wood headboard. I ask, "Would you like to come to your future?"

She drops her diary and scoots to the edge of the bed. Color is returning to her cheeks. She stands up as if a weight melts off her shoulders. Her eyes widen as she says, "Seriously? How?"

I stand up. "It's our feelings which connect us. I think we follow them."

"Follow our feelings?"

"Yes. Instead of pretending you don't have them like you some-times do to keep peace with our family, I am asking you to *feel your feelings*. When you learn to work with your feelings, you learn how to direct your intention in the universe." I continue, "But there's more. You have to listen to your heart too."

"Listen to my heart?"

I smile, "Yes. Have you ever heard a ringing inside you that isn't from a sound in the room? Perhaps, a high-pitched tone or hum in your head? Close your eyes and listen for a beautiful note inside you. This is your heart."

Lily looks at me with a head tilt and states, "Sometimes I notice certain sounds in the air near me but, like, there's no music. Like, when it's super quiet. It's like, sometimes, when I'm at the piano and I'm trying to write a song. I like, hear a note before I play it. You know?"

I was the quintessential valley girl raised between the late 70s and the 80s. It's fun to hear my valley girl accent again. I grin and affirm, "That's it!" I lean in, "Your heart has a song and if you listen closely, you can hear the note that comes in your mind."

"*My heart has a song.*" Lily looks away thinking and repeats, "Heart song. I love that."

"Me too. When you listen to your heart, you're listening to the resonance of the universe." I beam. I wait a moment, then ask, "Are you ready?"

"Yeah. I think so." She looks at me.

"Good. We wouldn't be led to each other if it wasn't mean to be. Give me your hand. Close your eyes." I slowly say, "Feel me. Listen."

She reaches for my hand and closes her eyes as she slips her fingers into mine. I gently push my palm to hers.

"Can you hear that?" As I whisper the words, the tone gets louder. I open my eyes and the orange bedroom has faded. We are standing on a dark blue oriental rug on the concrete floor inside my basement.

"In the beginning was the Word. And the Word was with God and the Word was God."

– John 1:1[55]

The Power of Words

Lily opens her eyes and looks around at the white painted concrete block walls around us. Her hand is still in mine. We walk over to my computer. She looks wide-eyed at the journals on the wood desk before us. She recognizes her unmistakable little red book piled on top. It is laid open where she can see underlined notes and the plastic stickies colorfully tabbing pages.

She exclaims, "There it is!"

Lily looks around the basement at the details of her life yet to be. She's staring now at my laptop and its connected big screen. Computers were barely in existence in her world, and they did not look like this.

I begin, "Welcome to your future. You own this home and live here with your future partner Ryan. He is not here right now."

I hear the purr before I see the cat. Our orange tabby leans into Lily's legs with his loud purr. He knows her. Me. Lily smiles and looks down.

I wave my arms and announce, "This is your future cosmic cat, his royal kitty highness Orion." I take a bow before king kitty.

She looks back up. "Your cat is named Orion? That's my favorite constellation."

"Yes. It is." I chuckle and add, "For some reason when dad taught us about the stars, Orion stood out in the night sky."

I silently wonder, *How is this happening?* Out loud I say, "Orion kitty is the same age as you. Twelve!"

Lily's smile radiates. She bends to pet Orion who is pushing against her legs in approval and slowly swishing his tail.

"I'm going to read to you the words I stumbled across days before I arrived to you." I reach for the book, open to the page, and read, "*Dear Lord, I've been sinning a lot, help me not to.*" I put the book down again. "What do you feel about the word sin?"

Lily watches the cat saunter over to our long low gold velour couch, jump up, and begin cleaning himself. She follows him and sits down next to him. Orion kitty takes the invitation to step onto her lap. She relaxes as she slowly pets him. He's purring sounds like a didgeridoo.

Finally, she looks up and answers, "I don't like the word sin at all. I feel funny when the pastor says that word in sermons. I understand people do bad things, that they can sin. But they believe we are born sinners. I'm confused. How can they believe that?"

"Good question." I perch across from her on our brown antique rug ottoman, "I looked it up. Sin comes from the Hebrew word chatá and its Greek equivalent hamartia. Essentially both root words mean *missing the mark* or *off the mark*. The original root was lost and now most Theologians translate sin as an immoral act considered to be an offense against God or divine law. In Sunday school, we were taught original sin — that we're born sinners. You and I, we, look at sin differently than others. In time, we saw how our culture teaches us to aim for perfection. But we're here to mess up so we can learn. We're here to evolve, not be perfect."

"Do you think mom is a perfectionist?" Lily jumps in and adds quickly, "I do." She looks down as she pets Orion kitty. Her voice is distant as she asks, "What if I become like her?"

"Mom is a perfectionist. She lives in a culture that trained her to be one. You will repeat some of her perfectionism. You can't help it, you're taught by the same culture, give or take a generation. But you will learn how to soften it in time and help others do so."

Lily sighs, "I hope so. I like 'missing the target' better than we're born broken."

"It's a healthier translation." I take a big breath and let out a big sigh. Lily sighs too. I carry on, "All words are powerful. You might remember from Christian school years ago that in John 1:1, the Bible mentions, *In the beginning was the Word. And the Word was with God and the Word was God.* Just as it was written in that famous book, first there was the word. Which is to say, first there was sound or vibration. Sound is a primordial force."

"What is primordial?"

"Primordial means from the beginning of time."

"Sound was at the beginning of time?"

"Yes. Exactly. Sound or vibration creates the universe. Think of it this way: when two particles collide with each other, that collision creates sound. From that collision, or sound, comes the release of electromagnetism, which is what everything, including humans, is made of."

Lily looks around my basement like she's looking for particles colliding. "Particles make a sound?"

"I don't even think Orion kitty's keen ears can hear their collision. Our human ears cannot hear such sounds. A poetic way to say it is we're all made of music."

"Maybe that's why I like the piano so much."

"I think so too. Words like sin have a particular a vibration depending on how you say it. Vibration is up to us and set by our tone. Our tone is set by our belief and our intention; it is created by our thoughts or consciousness."

"What is consciousness?"

"I would describe consciousness as the working state of our soul." I stop to consider my words. I am not sure consciousness is something my 12-year-old self will understand.

"I have a better way to explain consciousness and vibration. Will you follow me?"

"Yes."

I get up from the gold couch and turn to walk up the basement stairs. Lily pops up and trails behind me. We walk through the kitchen, dining room, and into the living room where the family grand piano sits. She knows this piano well. Her lips curve up in recognition. I pat on the piano bench for her to sit next to me. My finger presses the C key in the middle of the piano. With my foot on the sustain peddle, the tone rings out in the room.

I turn to her, "This is called C4."

"I remember that from piano lessons!"

"Will you hit the other octaves of C above and below that note?"

Lily reaches across me and plays C1, C2, and C3, all the low bass C keys. I can tell the piano needs tuning again as each note rumbles through the room. Then she plays the higher C notes one by one: C5, C6, C7, all the way up to C8. I lift and press the sustain peddle with her and each note has its own suspended moment.

I continue, "Just like choosing which note to play on the piano, we can choose what octaves we communicate in. I could say the word sin in a myriad of octaves, lower or higher. Our consciousness is a lot like an octave. If our thoughts tend to stay in a certain low range, that may be all we know. As we learn and grow, we begin to discover other octaves. Other notes even. The tone, intention, and meaning of a word we use is up to you and me."

Lily pronounces, "There are some pretty low octaves being sung in our family right now. And in the world."

"True," I offer. "As sound makes up all things, words are creation in action. We each speak, write, and even think our universe into being through the words we use. Words — in all their expression — hold a frequency."

"What is a frequency?"

"Frequency is the number of times an event repeats in unit of time. Frequency is the speed of the sound vibration."

"I'm not sure I understand."

"It's okay, you don't have to worry about the technical words. You'll understand them later in life. What's important is that the octave we use when we say a word shapes its impact. Words have the power to harm, destroy, confuse, control, and manipulate. The reason you were crying when I found you before was because you were witnessing the toxicity of words used in fear. You or someone in the family kept saying words in the lower octaves."

Lily sits for a moment, thinking. "Ugh. Really low octaves."

"I'm so sorry."

Lily looks up and into my eyes, our eyes, and I feel her receive my words. It's like aloe on top of a burn. The burn still stings as the aloe soothes — both exist at the same time. Slowly Lily looks up at the sheet music resting on the piano. "Hey, it's like you said, words can do great things too. Right? Maybe that's why I've loved words for as long as I can remember. And singing."

I was always looking for the silver lining. I guess it started young. I reply, "Yes. Words and music shape our creations and our thoughts. Deep in your heart you know this without even having *the words* for it."

Lily laughs out loud at my emphasis. I give her a knowing glance. Our family loves word play humor and puns.

I laugh and keep going, "Sound is the powerful fuel of our life. Sound is a great teacher too. Deep inside the gooey center of your pain resides the learning. What some call grace. Imagine it like the sweet caramel center of a Rolo that takes a little longer to chew." I remember one of our favorite candies at 12 and continue, "Even the most painful moments that come from low on the piano, they bring you lessons that will help you grow. We gather those gooey sweet centers in our adventures across the years, chewing until we get to the tasty center. Playing and hearing low notes until we pick higher octaves as we learn. Creating with better words."

We sit together for a while doing nothing. We're both looking at the piano keys. Lily reaches over me and hits the lowest C1 again with her index finger and then presses each C octave in succession all the way to C8. I work the sustain peddle up and down with her to keep the notes resonating again. After each note rings out, she sighs. "I wish mom would learn to be more aware of the words and sounds she uses. I don't like what she creates so much of the time."

Before I can answer, we hear a sound. It isn't from my living room.

Somewhere in the distance, the sound emanates across the gap of time between then and now.

"Lily!" came a distant call, dim yet strong. I hear it.

"That's mom! It must be dinner time!" Lily gasps and looks behind her. She squeezes my hand and is gone.

I hold my breath. I hope she'll return. All I hear is the thump of the furnace in the basement below me. Orion's paws make dim thuds on the wood floor as he walks toward me. He jumps up on the piano bench in Lily's spot and leans into me as if to say he approves of our visitor.

Contact has been made. Now, to learn how to repeat it.

"Discovering the truth about ourselves is a lifetime's work,
but it's worth the effort."

– Mr. Fred Rogers

Soul Esteem

It is Tuesday October 10, 2017. I am at my writing desk reading out of my small red time machine. In Lily's timeline, it's been weeks since our first meeting. For me it's only been a day.

Dear Lord, I hope nobody gets mean. Thursday, January 20, 1983.

Today's Sunday. And as you know I don't like Sundays very much. Sunday, January 23, 1983.

So much said in few words. Sundays were a day of tension release for my family. My mom and dad would regularly fight before church. I sense it was leftover feelings from the week that needed release. Dad had busy work weeks. Mom had an internal pressure to impress the church community. The energy had to move somewhere. Without their awareness, it usually moved sideways at each other; they were each closest and safest to take it out on.

Sundays often meant church, which for me meant a double header of family friction paired with awkward attempts to fit in to social groups. My soul longs for authentic intimacy and expression, but instead I had to navigate social posturing that to me felt like it valued aesthetics over depth.

My older sister Sierra, two and a half years older than me, enjoyed the church youth group and attended almost every meeting. She found solace in the group energy. My older brother Tim, six years older than me, stopped going to church the same year as I wrote in the red diary. He told me he met his girlfriend in youth group, and they would listen to Pink Floyd and Tom Petty albums together that coming summer.

My oldest sister Maribel, almost 17 years older than me, was out of the house by the time I was three. When I was five, she became a wife. When I was seven, she became a mother. Her family went to church each Sunday in San Diego a few hours away. Way before I was born, she found solace in a church community where she met kids her age and felt supported by adults other than mom and dad. She wanted that for her kids as well.

My mom and dad went to church before we were born, and they continued even after we left the nest. They were active in the choir and enjoyed the ritual of their Sunday commitment. I respected the viewpoints of my siblings and parents.

But I felt different.

There were inspiring moments during a sermon where I'd look up from doodling on a tithing card to hear an interesting idea. I enjoyed messages of self-reflection and humility that encouraged us to understand ourselves so we could become better humans. Still, I had a measure of skepticism as I listened. By age 12, I had been used to adults making promises without follow through. I wished people around me would try for spiritual ideals on other days besides Sunday. I wanted understanding and kindness to be practiced beyond the walls of the church.

I reread Lily's words.

Today's Sunday. And as you know I don't like Sundays very much.

I can feel her healthy doubt with Sundays, including the sadness after family fights. My heart is heavy with her hurt. Along with the click of the furnace duct above me, I hear a high drone sound within me. I close my eyes and focus on the familiar sound. I wrap my arms around my torso as if to hug her.

I open my eyes. It is night back in my orange Los Angeles bedroom. I am standing next to Lily who is laying on the bed writing about her day. She feels me, looks up, and smiles, "Hi!"

I smile back at her. "Hi! How are you?"

Lily sets the journal and pen down and rolls to sit up. "I'm good! Today was unexpectedly nice."

"I'm glad. I just read your words. I could feel you, and I think that's what brought me here. You said, I don't like Sundays very much."

Lily looks down at her lap. She taps her fingers a few times on top of her legs as she thinks. Her gaze turns up to mine as she replies, "It's true. Like, they're so much pressure, you know? But today went well. That surprised me. I spent the night at my friend Dawn's, so I didn't have to go to church this morning. And my family seemed to make their own fun today. It's like, well, a miracle!"

I laughed. "Miracles are the best." I leaned in with more seriousness and whispered, "Your heart pulled me to you for a reason today. Do you want to talk?"

"Well, since you're here…" Her voice trails off and she looks away.

"The floor is yours," I offer with a smile and a bow. I sit down next to her.

Lily begins, "I've been thinking about what you said the other day about sin. Like, I can't stop thinking about it. At church, when the pastor asks us to bow our heads in forgiveness, I feel so uncomfortable. I mean, like, forgiveness for what? It's like, we're not born sinners, we're here to learn and grow and do our best."

"That's a big shift from how we were taught."

"Yeah. Last Sunday, when the pastor said, 'bow your heads,' I didn't. I sat straight up and looked around to see if anyone else joined me. Mine was the only head looking up. I felt relief. Then, I felt uncomfortable. I keep thinking about it."

"I think I remember that moment. Our refusal to bow our head is a very authentic act. It comes straight from inside us. You listened to you rather than others."

"Right? It felt big. But without anyone to see or share it with, I wasn't sure if it was even real. Or okay."

"I understand. It's hard to not have a mirror or reflection to con-firm what happened."

Lily nods and says, "At first, I felt relief. I also felt safe because everyone else was looking down. But now I just feel awkward, and guilty."

"It's understandable that you feel conflicted. The spark of you that I call your soul, your essence that is you, speaks to you through your heart and your body. When you listen to your heart, you are listening to your soul. The messages that come are often different to the instructions around you. So, when you listen to you, it may look a lot like you are disregarding others. Does that make sense?"

"I think so. I have felt this before. Like, usually, my doubt wins out, and I stop doing the thing that makes me feel weird. Like, I mean, ugh. I don't like that feeling."

"Me either. It takes courage to stand in your truth. If you do, you might feel rejected by the group around you. You are biologically hardwired for belonging." I stop for a moment to find my words.

Lily asks, "Hardwired?"

"Yes. It means that your body has internal biological signals that are with you when you are born to help you stay connected to the group at all costs so that you will be safe. Does that make sense?"

"I think so. Like, there's something inside my biology that makes me want to do what others do?"

"Yes! That's exactly it." I smile and continue, "Deeper down than that biological instinct to survive, a stronger part of you — what I call your soul — knows that once you see your truth, there's no going back. The thing is that change can be very uncomfortable. It's a big deal to say yes to your knowing like that. Every head down but yours! And then after that freeing feeling and joy at listening to your soul...suddenly, you feel separate. It's a tiny glimmer of *soul esteem* for you, for us."

"Soul esteem? Ohhhh, I like that. What is it?"

"People talk about self-esteem, but this is even deeper. More than the confidence of the personality, soul esteem is the confidence after listening and acting from your soul's knowing."

"Soul esteem. Wow. That's what I want. I'm so skeptical of people that talk about Jesus and love yet demonstrate favoritism and prejudice at church. Or anywhere. Even at church there seem to be cliques like the popular kids at school. Where do I find others that want soul esteem too?"

"Everyone does. Not everyone has the awareness, yet. For many the fear of change outweighs them listening to their soul. Discernment and critical thinking are fundamental for humans. They are of great value to you especially. Although you long to belong, you are not much of a joiner to any group, and it's like that for the rest of your life." I look at Lily to see how she's doing. I ask, "Where do you find God?

"Not in church. I find God outside. Always have I guess."

"Yes. We feel safe authentic connection outdoors, surrounded by nature."

"Totally! Like, in church, if people loved the way Jesus loved, maybe I could feel God there. But outside in the trees, it's just less confusing. God's just there."

"Yes. From family tension to church anxiety, church Sundays are difficult."

"Sundays are a drag. And Monday I'm recovering. That's why today felt like such a miracle. Dad's off to the races again not to be seen for most of the week. Mom's on me for my homework. And I'm often behind."

"I remember. Mondays mean school, yet school means freedom from tensions at home." Then I ask, "Am I right?"

Lily replies, "Yeah. That's true. School can be intense with friends and stuff, but it's a relief from fights at home. Most of the time."

"I want to tell you something I've learned. Freedom is core to our soul. Imagine if your soul had instructions for you, freedom would be on the list. In your future, I'm taking risks to free myself even more, so that we can step further into the life our soul wished-for. Choices around work, home, relationship, and even our name."

Lily stands up and paces back and forth waving her hands. "Freedom and my soul. Maybe that's why I get so annoyed at church.

Maybe that's why I see things others don't. I love feeling free." She lands on the bed with a sigh. "This is all so new. My whole body is…" Lily looks at me trying to find a word. Finally, she adds, "Vibrating!" She's looking at her hands as she turns them around and back.

"Good use of the word!" I laugh and say, "I have another big truth to offer. You ready?"

Lily smiles, "Yes."

"Okay, here ya go. You are made of energy." I smile back, "Breathe and enjoy that vibration you feel. Here's an interesting thought: even though my star name Astara officially came to me about six years ago, I didn't choose to share it with the wider world until a few months before we began to visit each other."

Lily's lips curve up even more, "Changing my name seems impossible. I like that there's magical timing in you coming and telling me about it. When I say our future name, it feels good." She stops and whispers, "Astara." She's tests it out again, "Astara."

The bed creaks. I lean toward her, extend my hand and turn my palm out. She puts her smaller hand there. We look each other in the eye. "I like it when you say Astara. A word is the act of creation. A name is a powerful vibration. A name calls something into being. Before I share about where the name Astara came from, it's important to share about where our name Lily came from."

Lily squeezes my hand back and says, "Really? Mom's usually so quiet about her past and her family. I so want to know."

Lily and I face each other on my childhood bed, looking towards the door to the hall that leads to the main area of the house. My hand gently holds hers. Quietly I tell her, "I will reach out to you soon. For now, get some sleep."

She squeezes my hand again. "Okay. I'd like that." She looks around and asks, "Do you think we can connect again?"

"If I'm here, we can do it again."

I drop my hand and smile. I close my eyes and follow the path of sound and feeling. I am home.

"We swim in mystery every day, yet we do not realize it."

– Astara

The Pool

It is Wednesday October 11, 2017. I savor my quiet. I use the solitude to process my meetings with young me. I walk five miles in meditation through my tree-lined neighborhood, tuning up all my energy centers one by one through my body. The blue sky is clear of clouds. The leaves are turning colors in the crisp air. Still, all the green hasn't left the landscape.

At lunch, I digest more of my conversations with Lily. After, I drive to the pool to swim. I park in the structure outside the downtown Hyatt. I have felt sharp pain and limited movement in my left shoulder since I left my corporate world. It's true what they say, the body keeps the score.[56] I tried everything from yoga to massage, from emotional healing to energetic unwinding, and swimming is the last layer successfully thawing my frozen shoulder. The water, the movement, and the buoyancy of this indoor pool have become my medicine.

In the locker room, I change into my swimsuit. I notice an older woman come in with a young girl. The young girl has long brown hair. Her height and her hair are similar to mine when I was her age. It's uncanny. I try to guess her age and laugh to myself, *wouldn't it be funny if she was 12.*

I adjust to their presence for I am usually alone this time of day. As the grandmother puts her bags on the bench across from me, her shy granddaughter seeks the privacy of a bathroom stall to change.

At the pool edge I sit and pull on my goggles and cap. I ease into the water. It's just below body temperature; it's not too warm, not too cool. I kick off the pool edge into my front crawl. The water is smooth against my skin, and I lose myself in the rhythm of the lap. Head turn, arm lift, and breath as my hand slices through the water and pulls back.

Suddenly, an inflatable ball bounces off my head as I swim. I startle out of the lap and pull my steamy goggles off. I look around as I tread water. The young girl is grinning to my left. She is treading water in the free swim area on the other side of the floating lap rope.

I grab the plastic white and blue beach ball and throw it back to her. I smile and call out, "Here ya go." I put my goggles back on and swim.

At the end of the pool, I do an open turn at the wall. I push off with my toes but stay longer below the water this time. I feel like a torpedo or a dolphin. Halfway across the length of the pool I remember how I used to do this when I was her age. We had a pool in our home in Los Angeles and I practically lived in the water. I would count how long I could hold my breath, pretending I was a fish.

The water holds me in its embrace. I feel the strength of my lungs. Peace washes over me. I surface for air and do the breaststroke underwater to the other side of the pool. I push off into the front crawl again. As I swim at the surface, her ball bounces in front of my head. I pop up and tread water again. My look alike is grinning again, floating to my right now. I smile back. I rush forward, scoop up the ball, and toss it back to her. She catches it and swims away. Her giggles echo off the walls and ceiling along with splashing sounds.

When I am done swimming, I climb out of the pool and walk over to the empty Jacuzzi. I slowly climb into the hot water and sit with the jet bubbles at my back. I lean my head against the concrete edge. Delight takes up space inside me as I remember the young girl playing with me as I swam. From a distance I watch her splash and play in the pool, imaginatively creating her own fun with a beach ball. I close my eyes and my body relaxes in the heat of the water.

Minutes later, I hear the gentle splash of bodies entering the

Jacuzzi. I am no longer alone. My look alike and her grandmother sit quietly on the other side of the hot tub.

I try not to stare. I close my eyes and then open them to glance at her. I close my eyes quickly and think on how she looks so much like I would at that age. Her build, face shape, length, and color of her hair. I open my eyes again and smile.

In the locker room as I get dressed, when they come back in to change, she slides into a bathroom stall to change in private again. I throw my bag over my shoulder and walk close enough to her grandmother to quietly ask, "How old is your granddaughter?"

She smiles at me and says, "She is 12."

I smile back. I walk out, thinking of my conversations with 12-year-old me and the synchronicity of this moment. I can feel Lily at 12 taking up residence within me. I walk to the car and breathe in the world around me the way she would breathe. I hear the rhythmic sound of my boots on the pavement. I take in every detail as her, for her. As I drive, the colors are brighter. I put on some music and sing along with the windows down. The wind is in my hair. She's smiling inside. I turn up the volume and sing louder.

At home, I make some tea. I head to the basement and sit down at my desk. I look at the red diary atop dozens of journals. So many time portals and I want to visit them all.

"Suddenly all my ancestors are behind me. Be still, they say. Watch and listen. You are the result of the love of thousands."

– Linda Hogan

Judith and Hannah

As I slowly sip my tea, I send a message to 12-year-old me. *Close your eyes and listen. Feel me.* I close my eyes and imagine our Los Angeles bedroom. The hum of my heart rings with its subtle high note. I feel warmth in my body; it is concentrated in my core. I feel a whoosh of energy through my chest. My lips and fingers tingle. When I open my eyes again, I can feel her. I turn around. Lily is here in my timeline. She's in my basement standing behind me.

"Hi," she says smiling. "I was just finished writing in my diary when I felt you. I totally heard you! I closed my eyes. I practiced listening and feeling like you said." Her words roll out fast, "I have so much to tell you! I had an amazing dream last night. I was flying. Like, over Los Angeles. At night. I felt so, like, free! When I connected with you just now, it had that same magical feeling."

I smile beaming at her enthusiasm, savoring her valley speak as I exclaim, "I love flying dreams! It's been a long time since I had one. And you met me this time! That's amazing." I pull up a chair and motion her to sit down next to me and confirm, "And yes, you were truly hearing me."

She walks and sits down, her back straight and tall. She exclaims, "That's totally amazing! Amazing! Like, like, I don't even have words." She's suddenly distracted and looking around at my technology.

I smile and say, "Good. We don't need words for a moment. I am

going to turn my fancy computer on so I can show you something."
I type into my laptop and pull up my family research onto the
bigger monitor attached. I talk as I type and click. "We joined this
world as the youngest of four children. Mom never told me why she
picked our name. Perhaps I forgot. My memory is we were mom's
last opportunity to pass her name. Do you remember her saying
anything about our shared name?" I sit back and look at Lily.

"Hmmm. I think she named us Lily because she likes it?" She states
with a questioning tone and continues, "I don't really remember."
Lily's eyes are riveted on my laptop as she watches me navigate the
website.

"I don't remember much either." I offer.

Lily blurts out, "Look at your computer! It's so small!" She gently
touches the edge of the laptop as if she's afraid to break it.

"It is small. If you can believe it, there are smaller computers out
now. They're called laptops because they're small enough to sit on
your lap."

"Wow. That's amazing!"

I agree, "Truly!" I take my hand and point to the digital family
tree on the screen. I continue, "Okay. Let me show you something.
Our birth name is not only mom's name. I'm pretty sure our name
came from her mom's mom, her grandmother Judith Lillian Torf.
Judith's maiden name was Bloch, she was known as Bluma, and she's
our great grandmother. Her exact date of birth is unknown, there's
no record I can find."

I zoom into the screen for Lily to the family tree on mom's side.
Her eyes get bigger. She cries, "The graphics are so clear. The colors
are so crisp! Totally amazing."

I concur with a smile, "We have advanced our computers quite a bit
since your time." It's thrilling to watch her take in her future world.

"I'll say!" She's leaning in and then sitting back. Then she leans
in again to look at more. She's so excited she's slightly bouncing in
her chair.

It's hard to remember what all this technology must look like to
me so young. We had large blocky computers, upright video games,

and heavy analog television sets. I'm still typing on word processors and typewriters at her age. I go on, "Although I don't know Judith's birth date, I know she was born Judith Lillian in Kovno, Lithuania in 1865 when her country was part of the Russian Empire."

"Judith Lillian! It's mom's name Lily Judith in reverse!"

"Yes! Mom was basically named after her. Judith died in Los Angeles, California in 1918. To give you historical context, Judith left this world just months after the global Spanish Flu pandemic started, nine days after World War I ended, and seven years before a physicist named Werner Heisenberg gave birth to Quantum Theory."

"Woah. What is Quantum Theory?"

"It's the study of the very small in physics. Some physicists study the very big like universes and gravity, some physicists study the small like particles. By the way, the small and large physics don't agree with each other because their math and their descriptions of reality don't match."

"Hah. Sounds like typical adults."

"Hah indeed!" I can't help but laugh out loud. I gather myself together again and continue, "Quantum theory is interchangeably called quantum physics or quantum mechanics. You're going to be very interested in this someday."

"I think someday is here." Lily is chuckling.

I laugh out loud again. It's fun to see my clever come alive in young me. I say with a giggle, "I shall share more then."

"Thank you."

I point to the screen where our great grandmother's picture sits in a circle and start, "Seven years after Judith died, in isolation on the island of Helgoland in the North Sea, a smart young man named Werner Heisenberg discovered a breakthrough that would change our understanding of ourselves and the universe. This physicist gave up trying to describe the small little electron based on movement, but instead focused on what he could observe: the light it emits.[57] Just like that, Quantum Theory was born and it begins to change everything in our world."

"Studying light sounds amazing."

"I think so too. It's that theory that may help us understand how you are even sitting here talking to me. Or how I meet up with you. How time isn't what we think it is."

Lily leans in to look at Judith and says, "I wouldn't have believed it before. But now that this is happening, I am starting to." She sits back again and looks at me.

"As we look at our name, we explore half of our blood line! This map to our family shows mom in relation to her family line. Do you think four kids is a lot in our family?"

"Um, yes."

"Well, mom's mom Hannah was the sixth youngest of ten kids. She was born into a poor immigrant Jewish family in London, England on August 14, 1898."

"Ten kids. I can't even imagine."

"The world was very different in Hannah's lifetime. Big families were common. Hannah died in Hollywood on July 28, 1965, five years before you arrived on the scene. You've got to see this." I get up and walk across the room. I grab a thick white manuscript sitting on our folding table by the laundry area. Its edge bound in black with a clear plastic cover. I walk back and sit down. "Aunt Leslee copied this for me in Los Angeles and sent this to me. It is a rare copy of our great aunt Eva Torf's unpublished memoir, *Stones for Bread*."

I hand the thick manuscript to Lily. She turns it over to read the cover. She whispers in disbelief, "I had no idea something like this existed in our family."

"Me either, until this year. Torf is our grandmother Hannah's maiden name. Eva's older sister and brother were born in Russia, and then as third in the lineup, Eva was born in London in 1892. Eva finished her memoir June 30, 1939, two months before Britain declared war on Germany. She finished her book at 47, the same age I am now."

Lily interrupts and says, "Really? That's totally weird. But in an interesting way."

"I agree. Tragically, two years later, she dies during World War II in a German bombing raid on Southampton in London. Her death was recorded on May 10, 1941. This memoir survives because she sent the manuscript to her sister Rose in Los Angeles before her death. It shares a little glimpse into Judith and gives me insights into Hannah."

"There are so many pages." Lily is quiet as she holds the manuscript and flips through it.

"I know. This manuscript is family gold." I ask, "Is it okay if I read you what Eva writes about her mother Judith, our great grandmother?"

"Yes. I would love that."

I take the thick book back find the marked page and read,

> *In the little Lithuanian village that mother came from, she was known as the 'flower Judith' or as they would say in the Yiddish vernacular, 'Die shone Bloom Yudeska.'*
>
> *Mother was a merry bright–eyed girl in those days. But as I recall her, the light had gone out of her eyes, and the gladness out of her heart. At 26, mother looked middle-aged and sad and tired. She was slightly below normal height and if she were not so sad looking, comely and buxom would describe mother exactly.*[58]

I set the manuscript on my lap and look at Lily.

"This is so wild." Her words come out like a sigh, "I'm trying to picture this woman I've never met that made my life possible." Lily leans in to look at Judith's photograph on the screen.

"According to Eva her mother was not demonstrative, but kind. Judith used to tell her children stories and sing songs from her Lithuanian village. Judith became agnostic due to the antisemitism in London and the immense pressure to become Christian. The whole family succumbed to religious suppression so they could financially survive."

"That's awful. It sounds like what mom dealt with in Hollywood."

"I know." I keep reading, "Listen to this on her first page."

> *Although we lived in a very crowded area, we were a very lonely*

*family. The neighboring Jews would not allow their children to play
with us because we were Christians; and the Christians would not
allow their children to play with us because we were Jews. A paradox
too complex for us to understand at the time.*[45]

Lily chimes in, "I think mom went through something like that.
It explains so much, but it's so sad." She stops for a moment and
adds, "Why are people so mad at Jews?"

"That's a good question. It's called antisemitism. Have you heard
that word?"

"I have, but I still get confused about what it means."

I explain, "Think of it this way. Our perceptions and judgements
of another reflect how we feel about ourselves. Our internal beliefs
stem from our own experience of the world. We then project those
beliefs. It's the same for a group! Imagine if a group of people are
unevolved, afraid, and think the world is limited in resources, they
will project and perceive the world is divided and full of scarcity.
They mistakenly think they must do everything they can to get
something or protect something. Throughout history such negative
projections eventually form stereotypes and myths that get passed
down. This deep-seated fear forms the roots of hatred. Inside a
culture, stories evolve over time both to justify and motivate dis-
crimination. Another word for it is bias."

"Bias."

"Yes. Similar negative bias exists throughout time for many races
and religions based on group misunderstanding, ignorance, and
fear. Antisemitism has been a convenient hatred since the dawn of
Christianity. It comes from fears that have been passed down family
to family, as well as through religious texts."

"Ugh. It's everywhere in the world. The news is so depressing."
Lily slaps her forehead and leans over. A moment later she sits up
straight again and offers, "And dad's mom, Hildegarde. She's so
bigoted, and so vocal about it! She's anti-Semitic. Amongst other
things. It makes me so mad." Lily grunts with anger and slaps her
hands on her legs in protest.

I sigh and respond, "Hildegarde's racism and prejudice make me mad too. Such negative bias can affect entire generations. Traumas are passed through genetics and behavior. Perhaps the perpetual strain of antisemitism Judith experienced eventually led to her early death. She died at age 53 when Hannah was only 20 years old. And in turn, I am sure that deeply affected Hannah too."

"So young."

"Yes. A shorter age span was not uncommon in those days."

"Wait. You said traumas are passed through genetics. How does that work?"

"Yes. It's a new field of genetic research that won't happen for about 20 years from your now. It's called epigenetics. In essence, you carry traumas that are not yours, but they affect your body, nonetheless. They use the word transgenerational trauma. We hold genetic markers in our DNA. Markers of intense events that didn't happen to us directly. They happened to mom, Hannah, Judith, and other ancestors, and yet we hold them in our blood."

"Mom's middle name Judith has new meaning for me now." She leans in again to look at Judith's picture. "I like her face." She whispers slowly, "*Judith Lillian.*" She says mom's name slowly with purpose, "Lily Judith."

It's powerful to know our own history.

*"I bow to my mother's bravery that allowed me to have
the life I have now. She instilled in me a passion for doing
the internal work she couldn't. That is my fierce."*

– Astara

Lily

We're still sitting side by side in the basement looking at pictures of our family. Our great aunt Eva's manuscript sits next to all my journals. Lily's head tilts slightly and she asks, "I wonder why mom didn't give us her middle name?"

"Our middle name Marie comes from our dad's side of the family, from one of his aunt's Olive Mary Livingston. I think she went by Mary. Dad told me she was his favorite. He first gave it to our sister Maribel as a middle name, then to us. I am grateful we have a different middle name from mom."

"Yeah. Thank God. I would have been Lily the second or Lily junior. I'm called little Lily sometimes and it's annoying."

"I smile and offer, "Here's good news: the nickname 'little Lily' stops after a while."

"That's a relief."

"As an adult, the name Lily has also suited me just fine. I enjoyed the association of being named after my own mother. I loved being the name of a flower. I didn't mind being named after mom."

"I don't mind either. It's like, I'm totally cool having a name that's a flower. Plus, the name Lily's unusual. It feels special. Unique."

"Yeah, our name was not common in your timeline. It gets popular again when you're older. But that's decades from your now."

"It does? That's hard to believe."

I pose, "Life is like that. Things have cycles and seasons." I swirl my hands in an invisible circle spiraling.

Lily looks to the side thinking about seasons. "I think that is why I liked living in Ohio with actual seasons. I enjoyed snow. At least in memory."

"You liked snow, huh? Do you remember in Ohio when you got all dressed up to go out in the snow and came back five minutes later crying for hot chocolate?"

"I do remember that! It's true, the cold is not my favorite, but I did enjoy being able to track the seasons."

"Speaking of seasons, I imagine mom coming into this world inside the heat of a Hollywood summer, on that fateful August 21, 1930, steeped in a fresher version of the same awful antisemitism and the financial drought of the depression. Just like her mom Hannah, mom was born into a poor Jewish immigrant family. But that didn't keep mom down. She's such a vivacious and expressive spirit, like the hum of a garden in full bloom in late August."

I'm careful as I speak, I don't want Lily to know that mom has been dead in my timeline for nine years.

Lily nods. "Mom is so expressive. I love that about her. But sometimes I get mad when she loses her temper and says mean things. And she doesn't even remember! Then I get sad."

"It can be confusing to navigate."

"That's it. Confused is what I feel a lot. But then I have fun with her! Then it starts all over and I'm mad again, and I forget the good in her. When she's in a good mood, we get along so well. When she's in a bad mood, I wish I was in another country. Or planet."

"I remember how hard it was. I'm sorry." I gently squeeze her hand resting on her leg.

"Thanks." Lily looks down at my hand and sighs.

My grief tugs at me. I describe mom in the present tense for the both of us. "I'm going to remind you of mom's magic for a moment. I'll share my perspective after many years of healing my relationship to her."

Lily turns her chair to face me. "I'd like that. Please."

"Many of the lessons of mom's life are about beauty, peace, and blossoming, so the name Lily is perfect. Mom is beautiful inside and out, she just doesn't know it. As a young woman, her passion for life was unstoppable, despite her circumstances. She has a shimmering quality, like an iridescent butterfly or a hummingbird. She shines brightly like she has a sun right there inside her. Her joyful smile lights up a room." I wait for a moment and say, "It was that very luster that brought a lot of attention when she was young, both wanted and unwanted."

Describing her this way, she comes alive for me again and I fight the threat of tears as I speak. I catch my breath before I continue, "I know that when it comes to her childhood stories, she's quiet. Yet, she'd often tell us of an ah-ha moment on a tricycle around age four. She rode her tricycle to the end of her street. When she looked back over her shoulder to look at her family home she declared loudly, *I'm meant for something better than this. I will make something better of my life!*"

"I remember that story!" The chair squeaks as Lily leans back fast.

"It's one of my favorites." I continue smiling, "For a woman who doesn't say much about her past, she tells that one often. She had many reasons to aim for something better. She was mostly silent about the past, which led us siblings elsewhere for family stories. Her oldest brother Dave had learning difficulties due to a high fever that affected his brain as a toddler. So, we turn to Uncle Sam as her younger and closest brother for stories. He was inseparable from mom as a kid. They both attended Vine Street Elementary and Bancroft Jr. High together. They stood up and protected each other at home, at school, and in the community. Sam told me a story about when he was 10 and mom was 12. At five a.m., in the pitch darkness of the morning, they held hands and walked, just the two of them, almost three miles from Melrose and Wilcox Avenue to the Hollywood Bowl, so they could be there for the Annual Easter Sunrise Services."

"Three miles is a long walk, isn't it?"

"It is for kids their age. Sam told us how his father Isaac was a bitter man. Sam shared experiences that would make my blood boil describing how cruel Isaac was to his wife Hannah as well as to mom and Sam and their older brother David. He was menacing in his unpredictability. Charming one minute, heartless the next. Angry words and meanness, physical abuse, and neglect. After years of listening to Sam's stories, a few of mom's, and the hints from extended family, I gather that mom and her siblings suffered a multitude of physical, mental, and emotional abuses, including whispers of sexual abuse."

"Oh no." Lily puts her hands to her cheeks and utters, "There have been hints of something awful. I always sensed something a bit off in her silence about her childhood."

"Me too. I believe that mom's claim on that tricycle succeeded. It's a great example of what the activating power of words can accomplish when coming from your heart. Mom focused on outward success. Without any emotional tools or support, she didn't tend to her internalized trauma. I believe inner ghosts have haunted mom her whole life, including the hidden silent legacies inherited by her parents. Just look at this family tree, there's so much beauty and experience. At the same time, there is so much pain and trauma. The advantages and the challenges, all of it is held inside her blood and our blood. Something that has reminded me of how connected we are is to look at her hands. Have you ever noticed you have her hands?"

"I haven't!" Lily looks down at her hands. I hold mine out and she looks at mine. I put my palms out in front of me like a game of paddy cake. Lily silently presses her hands to mine. I feel energy surge up my arms to my heart. Her fingers are the same but shorter, for now. She puts her hands back on her lap. "I'm going to look at mom's hands when I go back."

"Do it. It's powerful." I continue, "I think mom struggles to fully accept the success she's made for herself. She remains unsatisfied because her past holds her prisoner. I imagine her insecurity is like a vacuum in space, it sucks in all her sense of worth and love and throws away the key."

"You are giving me words for feelings I have that I have not known how to describe! Unsatisfied is a good word for mom. I wish she knew how beautiful and smart she is. I wish she knew how loved she is."

Lily's eyes get wet but there are no tears. She swallows and takes a long deep inhale and then exhales with a big sigh.

"I know sweetie. Me too. Me too." I lean against Lily, shoulder to shoulder, and put my arm around her. I say softly, "Her generation offered no emotional tools. They trained her away from her intuition and feelings. In her world she had to reject her feminine gifts — all of which would have helped her handle the trauma."

Lily inserts, "But mom is so intuitive. Sometimes it's scary how she knows something is going to happen before it does."

"Yes, her intuition is impressive, yet she doesn't use it to help herself," I say. "She's more comfortable helping others. Because she lacks emotional strength, facing the past is too painful for mom. Yet, that's what she needs to forgive, heal, and love herself to a new place. Instead, she finds self-soothing and escape in food."

Lily takes a big gulp of air and sighs. She knows.

I continue, "Growing up in the depression, in a broken home, mom's childhood was a place of emotional, physical, and spiritual poverty. We never got to meet Hannah, yet reading between the story lines, I sense her husband Isaac was unfaithful to her and abusive. Hannah got depressed and she was unable to shield her kids from their toxic father."

Lily sighs again and says, "That just makes me so angry and sad for mom."

"Yes. I can't imagine what she faced at home. As mom grew, so did the world tensions. Lily became a teenager during World War II. In the absence of loving guidance, protection, and stability from adults in her family, and in the face of a war-torn anti-Semitic culture, mom learned to fight. For everything. I shudder to think of the difficult life Hannah suffered. That is half of what mom and her brothers emerged from, yet I know that our life was positively shaped by all of it."

Lily pipes in, "Are you saying that even though it was super intense and traumatic, it gave us something good?"

"That's exactly what I'm saying. Abuse is not okay *ever*, but it does create a classroom of learning for a soul. Even mom's dad Isaac, who plays the scoundrel role in our family drama, had his reasons. When we learn to ask, 'Why was Isaac so angry?' we eventually find forgiveness and compassion. As an adult, I've learned that anger is one of the easiest ways to move energy and emotion. It's an attempt to feel anchored inside the body. He must have had a spectacular reason."

Lily stands up agitated and starts to walk as she says, "Ugh! Even so, if we soften towards him, I'm afraid we're saying it's okay that he hurt them the way he did." She looks me straight in the eye.

"Forgiveness doesn't ever make what they did okay. It frees you up from holding the burden any longer — which in turn helps end the legacy. I have heard stories that Isaac ran away from home. I imagine he escaped strict dogma associated with his father who was a high-ranking spiritual leader in the temple in Rhodes Island, Greece. I was told that our great grandfather on mom's side was as close to a Rabbi as you could get. The tale is that Isaac first ran away from Greece to America when he was six and was unsuccessful. He tried again at age ten and made it into our country. I am unclear as to what would provoke his need to run away so young and would create such seething anger in our grandfather's life. Nevertheless, his anger and rage dominoed into mom's world and on into ours."

"It sure did." Lily keeps pacing and states, "Grandpa Isaac scares me." She stops to look at me and continues, "He creeps me out. I feel bad, but it's the truth. Now I know why." Orion kitty has come down to the basement to join us and jumps up on the gold couch nearby. Lily goes to sit with him. Purring commences.

"I know. He can be cantankerous and unsettling." I make sure to keep my words in present tense, because I don't want to give away that Isaac will die three years from her timeline. "Although mom isn't as angry as Isaac, her abuses and hurts simmer below the surface. Anger is one of the only ways she knows how to move all that energy; it's literally in her blood. From childhood to adulthood, her life is a great battle: as a female scientist, as a Jew who became a Christian, as a multiple-subject teacher, as a wife, as a mother, and..." I stop. I was about to say, *eventually her battle for life*, but I can't. In my heart I know it's not time for Lily to know mom's health slowly declines, and soon.

Lily asks, "And?"

"And, well, a fight for just about everything." I take a deep breath and listen to Orion kitty's purr emanating off the gold couch. I gather myself again and add, "Despite the circumstances around her, and underneath all that fighting, in her heart mom is loving, spiritual, and has a deep desire to help others. She's drawn to the natural world with her passion for gardens and plants. She's social, has a vivid imagination, and as a scientist is perpetually curious about the world."

Lily smiles in recognition. "She's all those things. Thank you for reminding me."

"You bet. It's helping me as well." I take a drink of water from my water bottle and then carry on. "Lily was in a spiritual desert in her childhood home, so she sought love elsewhere. Mom discovers a Christian church nearby with kind and helpful people. That must have been big medicine for her."

Lily cries out, "Kindness! The most powerful medicine of all!"

"That's why she was deeply drawn to a different Jew: Jesus. She loved his teachings about loving others and kindness."

"She lights up about Jesus. I like what he was about too."

"Yes. His teachings offer her the first key to freedom. Imagine: the religious persecution of Jews during World War II was the backdrop of mom's adolescence! She was around your age when a war was going on that includes a decimation of our people. She grew up witnessing the world in battle and the Jewish Holocaust. She saw how she was the enemy according to many around her. She came of age in a strongly anti-Semitic Hollywood. She heard the news and saw movies. She saw how poorly Jews and other ethnicities were treated. She suffered cultural wounds daily. She also carried a Jewish/Christian paradox in her blood from a generation earlier. All of that along with her family struggles. No wonder she left Judaism."

"She must have felt it from all sides."

"Exactly. Just a few months older than you, at age 13, Lily liberates herself from her abusive home, converts to Christianity, and begins a new life. She got a scholarship to a nearby Christian high school for girls where she would live; she left home and never looked back. She gives herself the gift of freedom, yet it was a gift with a price."

Lily interrupts, "I totally remember mom telling this story. It's intense!"

"Very. Close your eyes, I'm going to tell you this story again. See if you can really feel being there with mom."

Lily closes her eyes as the sound of Orion kitty's purring fills the basement.

I continue, "Lily gets a science scholarship to a nearby boarding school to escape her abusive home. Isaac drives Lily to her new dormitory in her new live-in Christian school, Los Angeles Pacific College. She's riding in the backseat of the car. Abruptly, he yells, 'I've changed my mind! You are not going to this school!' He glares into the rearview mirror at Lily with his lips tight. He slows down to turn the car around to take her back home, but Lily is determined and audacious. She has what they call chutzpah. She is beyond brave, she is fierce. Fierce enough to jump out of a moving car to stay on her path. She opens the door and dives out. Instead of a Bat Mitzvah at 12, her rite of passage is this fateful drive with her father at age 13."

I halt briefly and go on, "Her teacher greets Lily at the door of her new school. Lily arrives young, sad, scared, lonely, bruised, bloody, scratched up, yet free. She's in pain from head to toe, inside and out. She stands there in too much shock to feel her bruised pride yet. The body eventually heals, but her insides reflect the state of her soul, torn apart and lost. Her strength of conviction and passion for a new life keeps her going."

I stop. Lily opens her eyes and looks at me. Orion kitty is no longer purring. He sits up on Lily's lap and looks at me. I have an audience. Lily quietly speaks, "I feel like I was there. It's so sad. I always knew that mom is strong but letting myself go there with her, I get it now. Mom is beyond brave."

"She is. It took me years to really understand that. Now let's travel through time to learn what happens to Lily, our mom, in college and beyond. Before I continue, can I get you anything?"

"No. I'm on pins and needles waiting."

My tone builds strength. "Lily's incredibly intelligent with a love of science, art, sports, and she excels in school. She's good at much of what she pursues. She's funny, kind, and makes friends easy. She's a jitterbug queen. As an expert basketball player, even at 5'2" tall she always makes the shot."

Lily laughs out loud. With her eyes closed she mutters, "Mom could even get a balled-up tissue into the trash can from the other side of the room."

"Always impressive!" I laugh and keep on, "Lily's earns a chemistry scholarship to Greenville College in Greenville, Illinois. She meets her future husband Carlyle Livingston working in the kitchen washing dishes with him. They get married in Greenville on August 23, 1952."

"Lily's next fight is as a smart woman coming into adulthood in an entrenched male-dominated world. Although her husband is an open-minded man, he can't protect her from the bigger societal truth. Lily discovers first-hand how men treat smart women in the world of science and academia. The story of female suppression is not a new one. Lily fights cultural poverty and narrow-minded conditioning, the kind women experienced in the 1950's. Like others of her generation, she tries in vain to push through the low ceiling of advancement."

"Lily the chemist has few allies. Even women are competitive, some buy into their oppression out of fear and are competitive for attention. She's judged her for her intelligence and beauty. Like many women of the time, Lily was trained that her worth and belonging is rooted in feeling attractive and desired by men and women. Remnants of that objectification remains in her world now."

I glance at Lily comfortably listening and state, "In the early years of her marriage, Lily works as a teacher to support Carlyle going back to school to become an accountant. It pays off. He eventually becomes partner of Arthur Anderson and Co. which garners her growing family an upper middle-class life. As a daughter of the

Great Depression, during her mid-thirties, Lily has manifested the "something more" her little four-year-old claimed from her tricycle. She is becoming more financially solvent each day and is surrounded by a family that loves her. Even with her incredible fight for the powerful new life she creates, Lily doesn't have the tools or skills to savor what she's made. She never fully receives her success. Her bubbly passion is dampened down by depression by the time she gives birth to her fourth child at 39."

Lily interrupts to whisper, "That's us!" She's grinning but her eyes are wet. She starts to fidget.

"Okay love. We're getting into the thick of it now as we enter the world. Do you want me to keep going?"

Lily looks up and says, "Yes. I need to hear this. Please keep going."

"Breathe deep as needed," I offer. "You ready?"

"Yes."

I continue, "Shoving her painful past down leaves her haunted and empty. Lily uses comfort food to fill the emptiness, soothe the memories of scarcity from the Depression, as well as an antidote for the lack of sweetness and tenderness she experienced as a girl. She's ashamed of her extra weight. That weight has a negative payoff — it keeps her from unwanted attention. Yet that attention equates worth, and so she although wants to be safe, she feels unworthy. Her need to feel beautiful is complicated. Her vitality swiftly shifts to volatility from the chemical swings of a sugar addict. It is a lose-lose-lose situation." I don't mention that mom becomes a diabetic, I can't remember what age it begins and don't want to upset 12-year-old me.

"Regardless of Lily's troubled past, she shines bright. As a matriarch, chemist, multi-subject high school teacher, gardener, party planner, family bookkeeper, wife, mother, musician, dancer, singer, and artist, she expresses an amazing combination of left brain and right brain intelligence. Life is the fight that keeps her energy moving. Even with all her struggles, she has enough passion and drive to power her entire family."

I pause long enough that Lily looks up. "Seriously. Mom is a rock star. After all she has been through, look at what she has been able to be and do!"

"I know! As hard as it is to live with her volatility, please remember this as you can throughout your life."

"I'll try. Can you tell me more about her relationship to food? It's overwhelming to watch her eat or even prepare meals. I feel funny around mealtimes. Nobody talks about it."

"All of us in the family watch mom suffer in her unhealthy relationship to food. Everyone feels powerless because we can't stop or help her. Yet, we can't prevent its influence on our lives. Mom's always dieting, so we're affected by her food patterns without realizing it."

"*So affected.*" Lily draws out the words slow and strong. She declares, "I even try her diets sometimes."

"I want you to know something. Your time with mom now, and in the years ahead, lay the foundation for your deep passion to learn about food, the body, and habits. You will learn to trust your own body, heart, and gut."

Lily crosses her legs and uncrosses them. She looks up at the open rafters and ductwork of the basement ceiling. "I would love to not follow her. But I can't help it sometimes."

"Be easy on yourself. You're caught in a strong tractor beam that pulls at you. A fancy word for that is entrainment."

"Entrainment?"

"The other night we discussed different vibrations depending on the octave you choose, like on the piano. When two beings meet, they begin vibrating into alignment with one another. Entrainment occurs when one vibration meets another; eventually it will sync with it."

"I think I understand. I'm matching her ways of being with food."

"To some extent, yes. It happens without thought. But we can make new habits once we know."

Lily crosses her legs and uncrosses them. She looks up at the open rafters and ductwork of the basement ceiling. "I would love to make new habits. For so many things."

"You can do anything you put your mind to."

Lily looks at me. She offers, "The other thing that gets me is how mom is so focused on looks. Yet, I also care how I look or how people see me."

I share, "Mom's lessons in food, the body, and beauty are based in fear. Mom watches us kids like a hawk, lost in appearances and tight perfectionism. It's a lesson you signed up for as a soul to learn about the truth of beauty and confidence. Beauty is not just surface beauty. And confidence is based in soul esteem."

"Soul esteem. I remember talking about that. It comes from listening to our soul."

"Yes. With mom in the room, we can't leave the house without combing our hair or checking our face. But deep in your heart you can hold the truth."

"I'm over-aware of being looked at, watched. I don't know how to say this. It sounds weird even to me. But."

"What?"

"I feel devoured by her."

"Devoured is a good word. She's hungry. Not just for food, but for love. For meaning and worth. Sometimes she does devour us in an attempt for that love."

Lily shakes the sound out of her, "Ugh."

"All of mom's brilliance disappears the instant she doesn't feel safe and loved. Inside her hurts, the world is against her. She comforts herself through food. That's why she can be all consuming sometimes. Mom's name Lily holds all these vibrations: her dazzling gifts combined with incredible unhealed pain and a lost sense of self. It took me decades to understand the name she gave us held all this complexity."

Lily sighs and looks around the room, processing. She looks at me. She looks at Orion kitty. Lily stands up and announces. "I am going to go home and take a nap. I have a lot to process."

"Perfect. Thank you for coming to visit and allowing me to share the epic story of mom." I bow to her with my hands over my heart.

Lily smiles and says, "Thank you for everything. I feel better knowing all of this. It is just a lot."

"It is." I suggest, "Before you go to sleep, I have a request. Connect with God, and ask for support and help while you sleep. Or angels. Or all of the above. Remember, you're not alone in the universe. God has your back."

"I'll try." Lily puts her right hand on her heart, closes her eyes and is gone.

I walk to the desk and sit back down. I grab the red diary between my hands like a prayer. I think about all I couldn't tell her.

Because mom did not tend to that deep father and mother wound, her life was filled with shame, unworthiness, and bouts of depression marbled with rage. Mom's coping strategy through food addiction lasted her whole life. Eventually her suppressed energy manifested as physical illness and led to an ongoing 20-year dance with diabetes. Multiple cancers and many hospitals later, mom finally died from pancreatic cancer on June 7, 2008, just 13 days before I turn 38.

My Depression-era parents worked incredibly hard so that my siblings and I could have a better life than theirs. Their efforts triumphed. Before the first day of summer in June 1970, born into an upper middle-class existence, I was afforded a completely different life — financially or otherwise — than either of my mom or dad.

Yes, I inherited the silent legacies of scarcity, abuse, and separation that were unhealed in my parents. But I also inherited all their magic. It was the journey my soul chose in the Earth classroom I came here to learn in. And learn I would.

*"And thou shalt be called by a new name, which the
mouth of God shall name."*

– Isaiah 62:2[59]

Astara

It is Wednesday May 13, 2011. I am 40. I lie on a massage table inside my Oakland flat as I receive an energy healing from my friend Atasiea.

Atasiea is a budding actor, model, dancer, healer, and channel. He's an old soul in his late twenties. He is a beautiful human inside and out; he is tall, slender, with dark skin and his reverence for life beams from his generous smile and kind gaze. His voice deepens in tone when he opens his channel to the cosmos, bringing in information and wisdom beyond his human personality and his years.

We met dancing within the Ecstatic Dance community in Oakland where we magnetized each other as soul family; a dancer friend recommended his Angelic Presence healing, and my heart knew I was to work with him. During our last session a few months back, I had spoken with Atasiea about my pull towards a new name. I sensed it was to express my own divine presence — the part of me not limited to my body, my personality, or my identity here on Earth. I was nervous. Yet I knew it was the next step on my path.

I was learning more about my intuitive gifts every day. Architect by day, I was now providing energy healing and tarot readings to friends and family on the side. Years before, Atasiea came into his star name and he recommended I read *Starborne*, by Solara, to follow a simple meditation to find my new name.[60]

I got the book and found the meditation. Solara recommends

you visualize a brilliant golden white star in the cosmos above, *the Star that We Are*, or Higher Self, and draw the cosmic energy down through to your toes until you become that light fully.

During the meditation I asked my Higher Self to give my star name to me. I heard "*Astara*" immediately. When I first heard *Astara*, I felt a kind of prickling energy from my toes to my scalp. When something is important, my heart sends signals through my body as if saying *this* or *take note*. Like when I stand taller and straighter than usual. It was so effortless I didn't believe it. My mind chastised, "*It came so fast! That was too easy. Of course, my star name is A-star-a. Seriously?*"

I gently reminded my small scared inner critic that life is incredibly easy at times. I claim it out loud.

I am Astara.

I become aware of my whole body from my hair follicles, my skin, my breath, to my pulse. It feels right and true.

I claim it again. *I am Astara.* I call in more of my vastness, merging heaven and earth inside my own skin.

I am Astara. The more I say it, the more I stretch into joy. And then awkwardness. Like wearing in a new pair of shoes, I know the more I speak my name out loud, the more comfortable it will become. I practice. Fear and excitement swirl together, but fear is strong enough that I only tell a few close friends.

Weeks later, now in my third session with Atasiea, he's one of the few I tell my new name. Atasiea's hands gently make Reiki symbols a few inches above my body. I begin to get visions and hear direct messages from the higher aspect of me that is Astara. With his guidance, I listen to my soul and begin to speak these words:

> *I am Astara. I am here. The heart is an ocean, a galaxy, and much more than you know. You can go deeper than you thought possible in this vast ocean surrounded by the flow of divine unconditional love. The heart is an expanding galaxy, more spacious than you can fathom. This world of existence, of presence — what you term love — radiates within and without. What you call co-creation in*

collaboration, is the truth of all creation, for all is one and there is no separation. Reality is a joint venture. Form emerges from the formless and returns back into the formless. Form and formless are the same — this is the truth of All That Is.

The secret is this: your heart is the center of the universe. Each heart is. As you live and love from your heart, you unlock the true source of power, of presence, of All That Is within you.

I am Astara.

Your body is changing, the energy work you have committed to is transforming you from a duality-based cellular structure to a new grid of unity consciousness. There is no going back. There will be more evolution of your body, grounding you in the new awareness of what has always existed. You are shedding the limitations that block the truth of oneness. You are remembering.

As I channel, my right arm lifts and moves. I hear Atasiea gasp from the energy building. In my inner vision, I have two solid arms, four invisible arms, and a pair of wings. My wings expand beneath me on the table. As I move my two arms, the arms in other dimensions move as well. Each arm is holding a tool. A scepter, a sword, a crystal, a drum, and my left hand is open receiving abundance, and the right hand is extending healing energy.

I watch old discordant energies that used to anchor me, trickle down my body and off my feet into the Earth as a waterfall of light. I place my hands over my heart and silently say *Love*. After years of therapy, my own muscle memory escorts old dense energies out of my body. I hear Astara silently say, *Yes. Do this. You are multidimensional.*

With each claim out loud of my star name, I tap into unexplored parts of my being. Every time I say *I am Astara*, I embody the limitless more and more.

> *"Somewhere a star emerges | from a fierce burning love |
> and although it may take | five lifetimes or more | for the
> light to reach us | like a spectacular firework, | I imagine
> that the sound travels faster | and emotion faster still. |
> Words reach me first | and a thousand poems | ask for you
> by name."*
> *– Astara[61]*

Reunited

It is a Sunday morning. November 9, 2014. I am 44. I wake with a smile and roll over in bed onto my back. Slowly coming to the day, a startling series of thoughts arrive before I even open my eyes. *I live in Omaha and I am content. Who knew? I am done looking for my beloved for now. I am going to stop dating.*

Searching for a partner has been my mission for decades. Or so I thought; this morning's internal decision is so clear and easy, it decides itself.

Over the years, contemporary movies and novels influenced my romantic-poet-self to want society's fall-in-love-then-family experience. A string of short relationships dots my adult life. They were all wonderful men who've taught me so much. Again and again, the timing was off — either I wasn't ready to commit for the long haul or my love interest wasn't ready.

I have known with clarity I do not want to do motherhood alone. I haven't met my partner, and as I approach 45, a baby is unlikely. In the bulk of my twenties and thirties, I was consumed with the desire to be a mother. My sister Sierra and Maribel each have three kids, and I've been an aunt since I was seven. I love kids, I love being an aunt, and I love my nieces and nephews with great enthusiasm. I have wanted a baby for so long that not having one yet was a point of discomfort and grief for the last two decades. Every baby shower, pregnancy, and birth I attended for friends and family fired up longing and grief all over again.

Forty-Four years old and I haven't met *him* or had a child yet. Still, somehow on this morning, I'm okay with all of it. In fact, I feel downright relieved. Relief like this does not come out of the blue. Still, it feels like a sudden, pleasant shock.

The savings account of energy I expended in the pursuit of mating starts to replenish. Palpable energy is returning in a tsunami of joy. I have a sudden urge to dance and cavort through the room. Instead, I lie in bed, grinning. After years of looking outside myself to fulfill my biological drive, is it possible I turned the corner on my historic yearning? *Yes,* says my heart.

In my dim bedroom, the only light is the soft glow around and between slats of closed blinds at my window; the lines of light bend across light blue walls. My eyes follow the sloped ceiling in my converted attic. As I lay in bed, a calm takes hold of me I've never felt before.

Somewhere between my heart and my belly sits my intuition. It whispers. *He is out there. You will meet him when it is time. Don't worry.*

Ironically, my morning's inner voice sounds like the advice given to me throughout my dating decades.

You will meet him when you are ready. You will find him when you stop looking. When you give up, he will arrive.

And so on and so forth. Advice that used to pester me has internalized as my own knowing. Just yesterday, I resigned myself as the perpetual single woman with a cat. One morning later, my fresh neutrality interrupts my infamous angst, and it feels strange.

Another thought arrives. *You will be fine, even if you meet him when you are 90.*

I giggle out loud and say to myself, "Ninety?"

I stand up and walk to open the blinds. I open the doors to the bathroom and garret closet with windows beyond. Fall morning light fills the room as I rub my eyes.

I jump back in bed and squeeze my face into my pillow and

squeal. Laying back down, I bump a stack of books off my side table as I stretch to grab my phone. I unlock the touch screen and start removing my dating app profiles. Every time I hit delete, I smile and breathe.

In slow motion, my mind whirs as bits of yesterday flickers through. My friend Leah came over for a visit. We talk for hours. We start at my living room couch, walk around the neighborhood, and end up at my long wood dining table sipping tea. At 29, Leah is an old soul. She has short black curly hair, olive skin, and big almond shaped brown eyes. Her lips gently pinch together and then open into a chuckle as she listens to my dating woes.

Her face sympathetically reflects my shifting weather report as I tell her about the ongoing comedic peril of my dating life. Her eyes open wide in supportive dismay or squint into laugh lines at the humorous pitfalls.

Leah met her partner the year before. Like a typical female friend, I look to her for clues and signs of how I might greet the same fate in the world. We laugh, cry, sigh, and exclaim together about the spectrum of our own awkward dating adventures.

Now Leah is silhouetted by the fading dusk of the sitting room windows behind her. She looks at her phone and back up. She says, "I have a text about a party tonight at the industrial art studio down-town. You should go with me. It will lift your spirits, and you'll love this place. I know it's late. Come on, let's go." Her lips curl in a grin and she tilts her head and winks, "*He* might be there."

She's referring to the hot topic of my elusive yet-to-meet life partner. It is 8 p.m. Around this time, I usually start a quiet night at home, reading in bed or watching a film. *I am content at home. I think to myself.* Another part of me offers, *What do I have to lose?* I was tired yet hopeful. Always hopeful.

I stand up and claim, "I'll go."

Leah stands up and yelps, "Screeee! Let's do this!"

The first cold night of the season greets us with a high of 20 degrees. We caravan there; I park behind her car and get out. My breath comes out in small clouds. A short two block walk feels like a mile when it's below freezing, at least to my newly transplanted California blood. My favorite dress warms me in the cold. The cream polyester holds a field of orange blossoms — a long Qipao style dress with a high collar. The front slit opens to brown leather boots and grey tights. I am walking myself into the world as an altar, and I feel good.

I am slender, average height, and have brown wavy hair cut just above the shoulders. I am told my face is familiar. My European American heritage crisscrosses from Spain to Greece, Germany, Russia to England, Scotland to Ireland, and on to America. Over the years I have heard more times than I can count, "You look just like someone I know," or, "I have a friend that could be your sister."

Leah and I walk through gates in a tall chain link fence. We weave through a sea of people outside leaning against art cars in the front yard of the warehouse. They are standing, talking, drinking, and smoking as the streetlights create stark outlines of the cars in various stages of creation.

We step through the front door of the warehouse into a large room. The strong smell of cannabis greets me, and suddenly, it feels like I am back in the Bay Area walking into an art party. A wave of nostalgia hits me from the smells, sounds, and diversity of people in the room. I haven't been exposed to such a scene since I moved to Omaha a year ago. My heart suddenly longs for Oakland at the same time pleasure fills me to be in such a gathering again.

Strange metal sculptures dot the large front room as people of all ages and backgrounds mill about. Paintings adorn the walls. Colorful blown glass on podiums. Artists, musicians, professors, yogis, and gypsy souls stand shoulder to shoulder sipping, talking, and laughing.

We walk into the next big room. I scan the collection of sights and sounds. Food is spread out over a red patterned tablecloth on a long table. At the back of this immense room, a man is painting to alternative music on opaque glass in front of a band. The colors he dances into place turn neon under black lights. More car art fills up the warehouse around his live painting performance.

My senses are blissfully on overdrive. Looking around, I know two people. It's exciting for me to know someone at an Omaha party. I greet one of them as they walk by. Leah introduces me to her friends. We lay our jackets and bags on the concrete floor in front of the band and painter. We're the first on the dance floor. I slowly dip, turn, and swing to the intricate sounds, mesmerized by the paint unfolding before me.

My body melts, and I hear a voice inside say *everything is going to be okay.* Every so often I look around the dark room. People are sitting at white plastic tables behind me. In front of me is the band. To my side others circle the long food table. Those standing around me are rapt listening to the music. I stop looking for *him* and just dance. I feel all the way down to my cells the truth of that inner voice. I wouldn't learn the root of this peace until much later.

After dancing awhile, I'm ready to leave. I lean into Leah's ear and talk loudly over the music, "I'm tired. I'm going home."

She turns to me in the dim black light, gives me a hug, and shouts. "Have a good night! Call me later."

"I will!"

I press through the people standing and watching. I step through the front door and work my way through those milling outside. I walk quickly to my car in the cold and drive home.

In the morning, lying there deleting my dating profiles, I suddenly remember it was the night before — at the end of that party — when the calm started.

What I did not know is the tall man with dark hair I didn't see behind me and never met was part of the reason for my new calm. He sat ten feet behind me at a table with another woman, on a date he wasn't enjoying. He saw me but didn't know his future partner was swaying to music before him in her favorite dress.

Neither of us knew we would meet in less than 24 hours or that our lives would change forever. We wouldn't realize for four more months that this synchronicity of us meeting and not-meeting happened at this art party.

I pull up Tinder, the last dating app on my phone. I tried many of them: Tinder, Match, and OkCupid. When I open the app, I see a missed message from a man named Ryan. I missed it three months before! I had no idea.

I instantly remember, *this was the man whose message made me laugh out loud!* I don't remember what he wrote, but I do remember the thrill of doubling over in laughter — it's a rarity in online dating.

I quickly text him a message: *I'm so sorry. Somehow, I missed your message from August. I'm not sure how!* I forgot all about not dating anymore and wrote without thinking, *Are you still available?*

He messages me straightaway, and butterflies do a polka in my belly. *Yes. Do you want to meet for coffee? Aromas Café? 1pm?*

I write back, *Yes. See you there and then.* My grin is wider than the plains.

That same afternoon, we meet at Aromas Café in my neighborhood. When I walk in, Ryan is leaning on a tall bar stool, his long legs in jeans crossed at the ankles of brown cowboy boots. His smile is a burst of light under his tan cowboy hat. He has brown hair, a short beard, clear brown eyes, and a kind face. When he walks towards me, everything begins to move in slow motion.

Grabbing coffees and a table is a blur. Somehow, we're now sitting and sharing deep conversation and easy laughter, with subjects spanning from art to quantum physics. In my absent-minded joy, I bend forward in laughter and touch his arm. I later find out that was when he knew I liked him. I excuse myself to go to the bathroom and do a happy jig in privacy. I had to actively move the burst of joy out of me or I would explode.

To spend more time together, we walk a block to Benson Brewery for a drink. We walk through the neighborhood, touring back alleys lined with colorful murals. Four hours later, we reluctantly part ways at our cars.

That night, after a dinner with work friends, I pull into my driveway. I get a text from Ryan saying, *is it too soon to hang out again?* I sit in my car and connect with the house. I ask the house if it is okay for Ryan to come over so soon. The house shows him standing in my living room looking at my artwork and piano. The house grins in response. I smile and text, *It is not too soon. Come on over.* I send him my address.

When he arrives, my stomach flip-flops. The first time he walks past the piano into the dining room, something in me says *this.* As I give Ryan a tour of my home, with my back to him, he can't see the cheer my face holds.

My orange tabby cat runs by.

I playfully warn, "Don't be startled if you see a streak of orange fur, that's my cat Orion."

Everything is happening in fast and slow motion, especially what happens next. Ryan walks to the kitchen counter and leans on it when he hears my cat's name. His head bends forward for a while. When he looks up, his eyes are wet. I stand silent, not sure what to say.

He admits, "I have always felt connected with that constellation." He composes himself and continues, "My mom says I was originally named after the actor Ryan O'Neal, but a part of me believes I was actually named after Orion. Hearing your cat's name reminded me." This moment tattoos itself in my heart.

"Really?" I smile and say, "My cat named himself."

Ryan asks, "He did?"

"Yes." I smile, "I was standing at the kitchen sink in my home nine years ago in Point Richmond, California. I was singing along to one of my favorite songs, *Orion in the Sky* by Shawn Colvin.[62] I was washing dishes, and he was such a tiny kitten. When he heard the song, he ran up my leg and sat on my left shoulder. I stopped doing dishes and looked at the feisty fluffball staring at me. I asked him, "Is Orion your name?" His tiny body ran down the length of me — thank God I was wearing jeans and a long sleeve shirt — and he ran in circles on the kitchen floor. I took that as a *yes*, and he's been Orion ever since."

Ryan says softly, "I love that."

"Me too. Even outside my experience with my cat, Orion was the constellation I first learned from my dad."

"I love that you have a connection to that constellation."

I smile as I make us tea. We work our way to the sitting room. He sits in the corner comfy chair as if it's made for him. It is. A voice inside me says *this*.

I couldn't bring myself to sit in that chair for a year, and I wasn't sure why. My *why* is sitting there now. I light candles. We talk for hours. When he learns I know tarot, he asks if I will give him a reading. He pulls cards and we talk about his spread.

After, a hush fills the small sitting room lit by candles. My nerves are sending signals as I sit quietly. Ryan stands up and sits on the ottoman in front of my chair. Time stretches. He looks me in the eye as his knees press to mine. The energy in the air builds. He asks softly, "Can I kiss you?"

I smile. I breathe and nod on the exhale. He leans toward me until his lips gently reach for mine. We kiss soft and slow. Time slows down again. The world is re-enchanted.

A crackling sound with a loud pop and sizzle interrupts our reverie. Our faces pull apart as we turn to see a three-inch wide beeswax candle is split open. The wick is on fire from the tip of the candle to the base. I nervously laugh and rush to put out the tall flame. Wax spills onto the wood bench beneath. The candle exploding felt like an exclamation point. *This*.

As the director of my own life movie, this night makes an indelible mark. *Take note*, my inner director says. *This. Him. Us.*

"Give up all the other worlds except the one to which you belong."

– David Whyte

Cliff Jumping

When I was 23 and still in architecture school, I was living in Alexandria, Virginia, and attending the upper division studies of an urban design consortium at Washington-Alexandria Architecture Center.[63] During a typical long stretch of all-nighters working on a design project, I kept strange hours which encouraged daytime naps. During one of those fateful naps, I had a dream that would stick with me for decades.

…

In my dream, I was at the edge of the Grand Canyon, and I saw a shiny beautiful air stream perched at the edge of the canyon a distance in front of me. The door faced the cliff's edge. If anyone were to open that door and step out, they would fall into air. Suddenly the door opened, and Stevie Wonder stepped out. He stood at the top of the metal stairs perched over nothing. He turned his head toward the sky, smiling into the sun. I was dumbstruck, for I knew that Stevie Wonder couldn't see that he was about to step off into the abyss. I screamed out "Stevie, no! Don't move! Don't do it!"

It was then that Stevie turned towards me. He smiled and said, "Girl, are you blind?" He stepped forward and as his foot fell off the last step, it hit solid ground. Where I thought there was a canyon, there was earth to meet him. I closed my eyes, rubbed them and looked back up. Was the canyon never there? Was I the blind one?

I was.

...

Over the years, I've told that dream to friends and family, as well as clients and colleagues. I call it the airstream of consciousness. This dream has become an anthem in my life. It is about the illusions of fear we carry to protect ourselves. And how, when we're willing to move forward into the fear, and past it, we find solid ground. Every part of a dream is an aspect of ourselves. Stevie was my wise inner artist showing me where I was blindly limiting myself.

I dove off many risky cliffs in my life since that insightful dream in my twenties, and I've always landed on both feet. One would think that the risk in 2013 to move away from all my California friends, family, and geographical roots to land in Omaha, Nebraska would have been the steepest cliff dive of all. In some ways, it was.

But there was a bigger cliff waiting for me in the shape of a 6'4" man with a big smile and an immense heart. Ryan and I were not only falling in love, we were falling into a new frequency. That frequency is love. To say yes to our deep reunion took lifetimes and plenty of leaps.

When we first met, our magnetic pull to each other distracts me from seeing how our lifestyles and goals were at odds. Within a week my comparing mind takes over. I'm a sustainable architect, I eat clean, I don't drink, and I'm devoted to my spiritual path. Ryan is working construction, smoking, drinking, and focused on the next fun adventure.

A week into dating, I cautiously let him know I'm turned off by his smoking and drinking and ask if he would be open to a cleaner lifestyle. Ryan is insulted and immediately ends our affair; he isn't ready to set his old world down and step fully into our story.

Yet.

Although I was sad, my head brain reminded me that it's logical to end our romance. A few days later, I wake up crying and my heart unequivocally whispers *it's him.* I'm startled. *Him?* I think. *It doesn't make any sense! Look how different we are!* My heart says,

Reach out to him. My thought goes out to my heart, *Reach out? But it's over!* My heart is persistent. *Reach out to him.*

I'm embarrassed to text him after we clearly ended it. Still, if there's one thing I've learned, I'm better off when I listen to my heart. I text him and invite him over to dinner.

Ryan says yes, and we set a date later that week. After dinner, we build a fire in the chiminea on the back deck. It's early December, and we're bundled up and huddled around its warmth.

I begin, "Although everything we said is true last week, my heart knows a deeper truth. My mind tells me to run, but my heart tells me I have deep feelings for you. It's not logical, but it's true."

Ryan is stunned into silence. He sits there for a while before speaking. "I don't know what to say. I'm moving to Minneapolis in January to help a friend get his house ready to sell."

I tell him, "You have an adventure ahead of you, and I have no interest in stopping you. I just want you to know where my heart's at. It is important to me you know."

"Wow. I've never had a conversation like this before. You're so honest, open, and transparent. So brave, yet unattached to outcome. I'm moved. I'm not sure what to say." Ryan looks at me. The fire colors the side of his face a golden glow.

"You don't have to say anything. Just think about it, and we will let time tell us what is to be."

…

The night before Ryan moves to Minneapolis, he asks to come over before he leaves. After dinner, we sit on my couch, and he plays my guitar. He asks, "Can I borrow your guitar to take with me?"

I smile at the thought that he will have something to return to me. I take it as a sign much louder than any words he could say. I answer, "Yes. Just bring it back."

He smiles and says, "I will."

He names the guitar Lily.

…

It is Saturday January 31, 2015. We'd gone our separate ways a month earlier, but my heart keeps saying *call him.* After a big snowstorm, I return home from a friend's birthday party and call Ryan late. As I wait for him to answer, I giggle at the words coming to me: I am *snowmancing* him.

Early on in our conversation he asks, "How are you? How's work?"

Suddenly, I have no words, and my throat is tight. I feel frozen, and I don't know why. When I open my mouth to answer, a sob pours out that I can't stop. I'm self-conscious because I called to *snowmance* him, and now I'm crying!

He gently asks, "What's wrong? Why are you upset?"

It takes me a minute to compose myself. Through my tears, I tell him about my work stress. I think to myself, *I never cry like this to someone I barely know!* I know tears come directly from the heart, so again my heart knows something I'm not aware of.

His voice sounds good. After he listens to my stories, he offers, "Come visit me in Minneapolis. Drop everything and come. You need an adventure."

I laugh through my tears and say, "I do. I wish I could drop everything and come now. I have a work trip tomorrow to Los Angeles. Maybe I can come after that."

We hang up. He texts me a picture of the guitar Lily by his fireplace in his house and writes, *she's safe.* I smile.

...

In keeping with the universal comedy, the only weekend that becomes available for my visit is Valentine's Day. I drive to Minneapolis on a Friday, excited and nervous. When I arrive, we pick up so easily where we left off that I forget my fears. Still, I have plenty of butterflies in my belly that last the entire beautiful weekend. It becomes clear to us that something important is happening.

Once I'm back in Omaha, we begin to have long phone conversations daily, sometimes up to four or five hours each time, covering philosophical ground and sharing stories. Our deep talks began to reveal incredible synchronicities.

We discover we were both at that art party the night before our first date, just a few feet away from each other. We just didn't know it at the time.

We learn that his second cousin, Mary, is a client of mine from one of my first sustainable design projects, a Welcome Center for a non-profit in the Santa Cruz mountains; she's family in California he's never met, and I will be the one to introduce them.

We eventually uncover that my best friend Kathy in California grew up in Nebraska, and she's close friends with his godmother's daughter. He's probably met my friend Kathy at a family wedding years ago.

We discover that we've both had the same vivid dream years before we met. In our dream, we meet at a party and start to play piano and sing together.

Story after story, we laugh at the synchronicity. We met on Tinder, yet here we are finding out just how connected we are. Ever so slowly, yet fast in the scale of lifetimes, we discover we have shared lives together in a multitude of roles. We're soul family.

Some use the term soul mate or twin flame. Comically, I remember the momentous candle flame explosion marking our first kiss. Twin flame becomes literal. The universe winks. The whole of the cosmos has a sense of humor. The remnant wax of that magical moment still sits on our wood chest in our sitting room, reminding us of how our higher knowing is revealing signs to help us find each other.

And then find our way back to each other.

And then stay together.

We estimate we've known each other for five lifetimes. When we refer to each other we say *you you you you you* as a term of endearment. One *you* for every life together. Yet, our Higher Selves know it's likely many more.

...

It is Wednesday, March 11, 2015. Ryan arrives to Omaha to see me perform in the Vagina Monologues. My sister Sierra flies in from San Jose to see it as well. I perform the monologue of a 70-year-old

Jewish woman who couldn't say the word vagina because of her past and her upbringing; she calls it *down there.* Exploring the role of an old Jewish woman got me thinking about my heritage. I felt this character could have been my mom or Hannah, the grandmother I never met. Ryan smiles in the audience at me on opening night, sitting next to my sister, beaming his pride. My heart is full.

Ryan drives north again to Minneapolis. After the typical *come here* and *go away* of a new relationship, we're successfully surfing the push and pull of our own tides. More long phone calls and texts later and we begin to surrender to the river of love. We decide to move in together in April after Ryan completes his friend's construction project.

· · ·

Cliff jump. It is Thursday, April 16, 2015. Ryan moves in. When he walks through the front door, the house smiles just as it had on our first date. I step off the moving-in-together cliff with Ryan and find there's solid ground yet again.

Ryan acts as both catalyst and bridge builder for me. Our first kiss last November burns through the veil and again my heart says, *this.* After he moves in, my heart says, *no more hiding.* I sense it's about time to claim Astara fully, to move from architect to whatever my next soul-aligned step is or else the universe will do it for me. When I had this feeling in the past, hesitating led to drama and friction in the world around me.

Still, I hesitate a while longer.

I thought my move to Omaha a few years ago was an epic leap. It was. I thought Ryan moving in was the big risk. It was. But it's my intimacy with Ryan that shows me the edge of a cliff offering the biggest leap of all. When you're with someone that loves you and is paying attention, they see into your life in ways you cannot. After a short amount of time together, Ryan dares me to question the credible world of corporate architecture that has held me so long. Ryan gives me a mirror to see how much it's affecting me.

As an environmental architect, I've been climbing the corporate ladder to transform the world through sustainability. I've been an active leader in the United States Green Building Council, first in Northern California and now in Nebraska. Perpetually on call at work and as a volunteer, I give most of my energy to my sustainability mission.

All the while, I connect with the swirl of stars within me and around me every moment I can. I've even been subtly bringing my metaphysical knowing to life in my corporate paradigm. I imagine myself as a metaphorical acupuncture needle in each conference room I enter. I stealthily create loving energetic containers everywhere I go to restore energy flow. I do the same in each city I visit for work, and I travel almost monthly.

Until now, I'm accustomed to being an architect by day and mystic the rest of the time. By climbing the corporate ladder to Omaha, I see behind the curtain of company leadership into the complex greed blocking the "greening" of our projects. I understand more and more each day why the sustainable measures I work hard to implement only reach a few projects. It's hard to wake up to the truth. I discover that my role is primarily used to make the company look socially conscious to get the next project.

I'm mildly depressed and anxious from the stress of work politics and the dark truths behind my paycheck. I start to have headaches, back pain, and stomach issues. Despite my energetic practices and tools, the split between corporate architect and clairvoyant is no longer working. The dichotomy is eroding me from below the surface and I am dis-integrating inside my architecture world.

By necessity, I'm crying most Saturdays — it's the day I emotionally process the energy output throughout the week to survive. Having my foot in two worlds for decades has been an important part of my journey, but my body and my partner give me important feedback — it is time for my soul to step into just one multi-dimensional world.

...

It is Thursday, August 20, 2015. I am 45. I stand at the edge of a new cliff and see something forming in the distance. The origin story of our company, Illuminating Hearts, doesn't really have a beginning. If it were to have a beginning, it would be this week. Every small step and glorious misstep have led us to the magic of what we're doing now. What feels like an exponential leap for two people who've known each other for just one year, has been in the making for lifetimes.

The idea of our company begins with the unlikely equation of a poison ivy break out, a didgeridoo, and some tarot cards. On this fateful summer day, Ryan unknowingly brings home the gift of urushiol, the oily resin from the plant poison ivy after brushing up against it on a landscaping job. He wraps his beautiful long arm around my torso as he curves into my body to sleep that night. A day later, we're both curious about the rash forming on our arms and torso. A few days later, I have the worst response — my entire torso is on fire with hives on top of the rash.

In the coming days, we first try an emergency room visit for me and then a dermatologist. Allopathic medicine prescribes me man-made pharmaceuticals, but they don't alleviate my discomfort. From his years of playing and studying the didgeridoo, Ryan recalls the ancient instrument was used by Australian aboriginal healers. Days into my pain, he asks if he can play the didgeridoo over me, hoping to offer healing and relief.

I happily say yes. I love the didgeridoo. I enjoyed the powerful instrument during my years attending Ecstatic Dance in Oakland; didgeridoo players would often circle the room as we laid out on the floor restoring our bodies after hours of dancing. I was to learn later that the didgeridoo produces multiple frequencies both heard and felt that have beneficial effect on living tissue and emotional well-being — promoting positive movement from cells to the flow of energy in the body.

I didn't know that with my head yet, as Ryan stands over me, circle breathing primordial sounds across my body. All I know is, I begin to cry. It's my body that knows what sound can do, and I experience my first itching relief in days. In time, I realize I'm accessing a deeper emotional knowing only my heart knows, not my head. I give over to it and let the healing release come through my river of tears.

I finally feel ease where the pharma can't reach; my healing release naturally soothes my immune system inflammation, expediting recovery. As the player, it had a powerful energetic effect as well — Ryan felt a burst of energy rise in his body from the base of his spine all the way to his head, what some call Kundalini. Our calling is activated. My heart says again, *this*. Our souls are ready to live a more soul-aligned life path, and our bodies and personalities are waking to our ripeness. As a powerful clairvoyant and ideator, Ryan hears his soul clearly that night and the vista from the cliff becomes clearer.

…

It is Monday, August 31, 2015. Ryan invites me to the couch in the living room then sits across from me. He asks, "How long can you live split across two worlds? When you retire, will you have the health to enjoy your 401k?"

Good question, I think to myself. I answer, "I don't know how long I can do this. My current work is already affecting my health and has for a while. My core tells me if I keep going like this, I won't have the vitality to enjoy my savings in less than ten years. I know this down to my bones, my cells."

He's smiling, and his eyes shine deep knowing. He takes me to the cliff edge, "Why not live your authentic life now? Why wait to live your dreams?" Ryan energetically stands with me at the proverbial cliff, puts his arms around me, and points to what he sees. In my dimension, he moves to the couch and softly shares, "I got the idea after I played the didgeridoo over you last night and watched you have such a beautiful healing release. What if we did healing sound for a living, combining your soul healing gifts?"

Without hesitation, I answer a resounding, "Yes! That would be incredible."

To make our new sound and soul hybrid offering in the world, we start with simple tools around us: Ryan's didgeridoo from Australia, my singing bowl from Berkeley, my voice, and my energetic soul tools such as tarot, dowsing, shamanism and soul retrieval, as well as Akashic records research. Based on my life-altering experience with listening to Dame Evelyn Glennie playing a large gong in San Francisco years before, I recommend we find one.

The gong finds us. It's less than an hour away at Gongs Unlimited[64], the world's happiest gong sellers in Lincoln, Nebraska. In our first visit to their warehouse, I have the immense joy to *sound* Ryan behind an 84-inch Nipple Gong. That is seven feet in diameter! A few days later, after that life-altering experience, Ryan quits smoking. Since then, Ryan shares how a didgeridoo and a large gong saved his life.

With the help of the feisty plant medicine of poison oak, our individual passions combined to reveal our soul mission: to empower people to remember and live from the intelligence of their heart. Within months, the simple idea expands quickly and effortlessly. Sound instruments and more soul tools fly to us. The vibration of a plant, a didgeridoo, and the heart brought medicine to Ryan and me. Their wisdom revealed a new cliff edge and invitation to bring our soul gifts to the world. Nature's Intelligence has spoken. We have listened. The authentic life beckons.

…

It is Sunday, March 1, 2015. I place my toes firmly on the cliff edge ready to jump.

We are now legal and official. Our lawyer files Illuminating Hearts as a Limited Liability Corporation (LLC) today. Yet, I still have my feet in two worlds. I am still working at the 9,000-person architecture engineering company I've been at for almost nine years. Creating Illuminating Hearts clarifies and reveals the dissonance of staying with the old.

I love my sustainability career. It has meaning and purpose. Yet, I'm not using all my gifts. There's a future calling that's more aligned, deeply fulfilling, and truer to me than I thought possible.

My body shows me first. I'm unmotivated to go to the office. I'm starting to add panic attacks at night to my physical symptoms. Work tensions are getting worse. Once subtle politics behind the scenes are fully seen and subtle no longer. Thanks to making Illuminating Hearts official, I finally see my pattern.

Almost every prior job or relationship, instead of leaving because I knew in my heart it was time, I unconsciously created a drama as the excuse to leave. A pattern of unconsciously vibrating myself out of the old instead of taking responsibility.

This time, I decide to vibrate into my new future consciously. Instead of making my old world spit me out, I took charge of my future and designed a path based on my soul's instructions. Instead of blaming the external world for the reasons to leave, I become accountable and leave because it's time. My soul knows. My heart knows. My body knows. Yet again, it was my mind that was the last to know, and now it's on board too.

I put my heart in the driver's seat. I listen to my intuition every day and act on its knowing. Empowered, responsible, and awake, I start preparing a heart-centered and soul-aligned exit plan and I walk to the edge of the cliff.

...

It is Friday, July 1, 2016. I am 46 when I leap.

I'm aware that the leap is not a choice, it is mandatory for my soul. If it is mandatory, is it really a risk? Yes and no. Yes, because I could deny such audacious change to stay comfortable. No, because my body tells me I'm not going to be well if I stay.

My soulful exit plan is put into place for almost a year with great care. The plan culminates when I fly home from London after speaking about biophilic design at the European Healthcare Conference. It is my last official speaking gig as a sustainable leader. Back on Omaha soil, I resign, ending the decades long split between my corporate paradigm and my spiritual transformation. In two weeks, I leave with respect for my co-workers and full transparency of my next steps.

Have I risked everything? Yes. I used my inheritance, then my 401k to invest in myself, our new company, and our dreams. I set down my steady paycheck. I'm in a new land with no familiar anchors. Truly risky business.

Am I ready? Not really. But I'm aware that the pull is much stronger than my fear. I take one step forward, which is off a steep cliff into the vast unknown. After leaping, I discover solid ground where I expected sky.

No longer using vast amounts of essential energy to survive the corporate life split, I begin the slow path of soul restoration after years of soul loss in a male-dominated profession. Both my feet are firmly and 100 percent placed in the solid ground of my own *heart-land*. The universe within and around me delicately arranges all that comes before and all that follows.

> *"Isn't this the ultimate risk, the willingness | and the capacity to carry it out | that galaxy, this universe, that star | this love."*
>
> – *Astara*[65]

Wedding Trail

It is Saturday, June 17, 2017. Still flying 67,062 miles per hour on this magic carpet called Earth, and I am three days from my 47th trip around the sun. Grief has me in such a tight embrace, I can't feel the magic. My dad Carlyle died on September 11th in 2009, and I am processing my seventh Father's Day without him.

Ryan and I are staying in a picturesque Earthship building — a passive solar home bermed into the mountain on the Kern Family Farm[66] in central California, at the base of the Sierra National Forest. We're on the first week of a 40-day Heart Fire and the Secret of Sound Tour visiting friends of ours who are WWOOFers[67] on this land. As a gift, we bring our Sound Alchemy to the farmers as one of our first stops on the tour.

This intelligent structure sits at 3,400-foot elevation. Tall glass lines the south side of this charming shelter with an abundant overhang to reap the benefits of the low sun streaming onto the concrete floor in winter yet provide shade in summer. The glass overlooks a patio that opens to a river carved canyon filled with pines, firs, and sequoias below. We're up high enough where it feels as if we're floating in our own cloud. I'm laid out flat on a brown velour couch against one of the windows, searching memories of my father.

My dad and I were not always close, yet we got along well. When I was young, my dad was my hero, and I longed for his attention.

Workaholism was his coping strategy for his marriage and life, which compounded into a cool remove between us, at least when it came to matters of the heart. For many years, I simmered below the surface with anger, feeling he emotionally abandoned mom and us kids.

Our relationship shifted one pivotal morning at age 27 when I called home to cry about a devastating breakup with my college friend and soul friend, Simeon. My family knew Simeon well; he and I had been close since college. By then, mom was in remission from her second round with non-Hodgkin's lymphoma, but her body was depleted from chemotherapy. My dad answered and let me know mom wasn't feeling up to talking.

I was scared to be vulnerable with him — it was mom who I typically sought out for nurturing conversations. I couldn't keep the sad from my voice, and he asked, "What's wrong?"

I decided to tell him. In this rare moment, he stepped up. He was tender. He apologized for not being a role model of healthy intimacy with mom and being so absent when I was young. His sincerity and accountability alchemized decades of bitterness on the spot, and I started to sob even harder. This time it wasn't about Simeon, I was grieving my father's impact on me all those years.

When I calmed, I forgave him. He gently reminded me to not give up and to trust that there are plenty of fish for me in the ocean of love. We both felt much lighter when I hung up. After his unexpected gift of reparation, my dad and I became close in the years ahead; I got to enjoy our deeper friendship for over a decade.

My dad was my first tour guide to the stars. He would take me outside to look at the constellations starting around five to six-years-old. The sky would've been filled with stars in our semi-rural neighborhood in Powell, Ohio at the outskirts of Columbus. After college, I took an astronomy course to learn how to use a telescope. I was good at it. My dad first brought the cosmos to me, it was as if his soul knew my soul. Missing my father heightened everything: my awareness of my dreams and my soul star name that I have yet to own.

Swimming in a puddle of heartache on a foreign couch, my inner wisdom whispers, *the depth of my grief reflects the depth of our connection and love.* I curl tighter into a ball as if by hugging me, I can hug him.

Ryan steps through the front door and stands over me, assessing the situation. He knows this is a hard day for me. He quietly takes my hand and helps me outside. He leads me on a short hike along a narrow trail within the farm property. We emerge through the oaks to a protected oasis with a creek running downhill over boulders and rocks of all sizes. It's hot and dry out, but the creek is full. We perch on a flat boulder and listen to the song of the water over rocks beneath us. I feel lighter after my emotional release. The water, sun, and blue sky, along with the green of the Oak, Bay, and Eucalyptus trees lifts my spirits.

Ryan turns to me, smiling like he's holding a secret in his pocket. He shimmies along the rock we are perched on to sit close. He takes my hands tenderly and says, "I have an idea." One of Ryan's superpowers is coming up with ideas, so I smile and wait for the magic. His smile is as wide as Texas as he asks, "Will you marry me?"

My mouth opens, and I turn around to see if anyone is behind me. I say, "Who, me?"

We both laugh out loud at my response.

The question was quite welcome, yet entirely unexpected. In our early years of living together, we talked about Ryan's three previous marriages. We talked about my not being married yet. We chose to avoid marriage. It was a cultural agreement we didn't need.

During our famous Valentine's weekend in Minneapolis in our first months, I comically used the line from the movie Four Weddings and a Funeral, '*Will you not marry me for the rest of my life?*' At that time, Ryan loved it and said, "*Yes.*" The playful phrase entered our relationship lexicon early on.

And here he's asking the question we didn't plan on.

"Yes you!" Ryan laughs and repeats, "Will you marry me?"

I answer beaming, "Yes. I will marry you." We hold each other by the water's edge, tears in our eyes and smiles on our faces.

Ironically, I think, *"We're already 'married' by our legal business partnership last year.*" Still, I know deep in my heart that our pending wedding will take everything to the next level.

Holding hands, we stroll back to the main farm for dinner with the WWOOFers. We run into our good friend Artemis[68] on our path and tell her the big news. Artemis and I became friends a few years before I moved to Omaha; I met her at a house concert where I fell in love with her singing voice. My soul recognized her as soul family.

Later, I introduced Ryan to her and her partner James who is the WWOOFer at the farm we are visiting. James[69] is in his mid-twenties, and although he's much younger than Artemis, he is an old soul. He looks like a young James Taylor but sounds like Billy Joel on the piano. Both are gifted artists and musicians; we love listening to them collaborate. When we first spent time together, it was fun and easy like we've known each other for lifetimes. And we have. James and Artemis are why we stopped at this farm along our tour.

Artemis could practically be my family for we both share Russian Jewish heritage. Similar hair, eyes, height, build, and when we sing together, it sounds like the blood harmony of sisters. Less than a year apart, there is a kindred quality to our connection.

Artemis jumps for joy and her curly brown-dyed-blond-hair bounces as her hazel eyes shine bright at the news. She gleefully yells, "Congratulations!!" She considers a moment and then asks, "Did you know the name of that trail you took is the Wedding Trail?"

Holding her hand, I jump like a kid as Ryan joins my hand. "No!" We answer in unison bouncing with her.

I stand back and exclaim, "I love it. The Wedding Trail!"

We walk to the assembly of tents and trailers the WWOOFers live in while working the farm. As we help to arrange dinner, I look up to the sky and there is a double rainbow in the distance. More signs announcing a beautiful *yes* to our impending wedding.

So many signs. So many angels.

"It only takes a few seconds or a minute to change your mind, connect to your heart, and fly yourself to a whole new frequency."

– Astara

The Donut

It is Thursday, October 12, 2017. It's late afternoon, and I go down to the basement to sit in front of the stack of journals at my desk. My little red journal has its own tractor beam; I can't seem to stay away. I grab it and read a tabbed page. My heart sinks at my words.

Dear Lord, please keep me from being bad. Tuesday, January 25, 1983.

I say out loud, "Where did we learn that we're bad?"

The hum of electricity all over me concentrates in my chest. My arm hairs tingle, my solar plexus is warm. I close my eyes, and when I open them, I'm in my orange bedroom again. My arrival interrupts Lily's frown of concentration as she writes perched on her bed. She looks up, drops the pen on the book, and runs to me.

I receive her embrace. I'm taller than our mom. In this timeline, mom is 52-years-old, just five years older than me. Although I look like my mom in many ways, I am slimmer than our mother would ever let herself be near my age, or for the remainder of her life. I wonder how I must look to Lily. She sees my familiarity as an adult, and yet I'm so different from her image of mom.

"You're back! You're here!" She stops to lower her voice and whispers, "I know we talked about the heart before, and sound." When we ponder, our eyes look up and around. Lily's gaze is on the window with a view to the hills at the edge of the San Fernando Valley. She finds her words and whispers, "Heart, sound, and *feeling*. But like, you coming here is so awesome. How's this really possible?"

"What I'm discovering is that we travel when our heart is activated by each other. For me, it's reading the diary you're writing this very moment," I answer. "From a physics perspective, when we feel and hear from our heart, we drop into the center of our electromagnetic field. This is where we connect to the zero point. And this is where time is infinite."

Lily asks, "Electromagnetic field? Zero point? Infinite? What does that even look like?"

I'm a very visual person and young me needs to see it. I do my best to explain complex geometry to 12-year-old me. I start, "Good questions. The shape of the flow of your energy is a donut-shaped swirl, called a toroid. First, imagine a donut or a big inflatable inner tube shape. Picture it as tall as you. Now imagine it is invisible and you are standing in the center. That's the shape of the outline of your electromagnetic field. It's made from a build-up of electric charges in your body and the environment. It's the energy that is flowing through you and around you."

"A big donut." Lily stands in the center of the bedroom and looks around to the corner of the room and down, imagining.

"This big donut is spiraling around you like water down a drain." I motion with my hands as I talk, "Nature makes this pattern for life at every scale. If you went to the kitchen and sliced an apple or an orange in half, you would see a cross section of that shape."

"Like the label on dad's Beatles album?"

"Hah! Yes! Now imagine it's invisible energy instead of an apple, and the core is your spine, and instead of fixed, it's in motion."

"Ohhh! Like spiraling apple donuts." Lily giggles and starts to twirl, which is not easy to do on carpet.

I join in and twirl-hop once. "It's more complicated than our brains can wrap around. It's called a double torus shape. Imagine two energetic donuts right on top of each other. They sit inside the bigger invisible donut we just imagined. The energy spirals from the center of the big donut in two directions at the same time around each smaller donut.[70] Our brains like things in a straight line, so it's hard to imagine two directions happening at once."

"Like, it's hard to picture, but I'm totally craving donuts." Lily smiles and puts her hand on her belly.

I laugh. I love how silly she's reminding me to be. I admit, "It's hard to imagine. I've seen videos of it, and I still have a hard time getting my brain around it."

"What I can picture is that bigger donut spinning. Like, I think I saw a waterfall in downtown LA like that once."

"There you go. Now picture this. You are part of a spiraling Milky Way Galaxy, on a planet with spiraling weather patterns, in a body with a spiraling energy field, with blood that spirals through your veins, with DNA that spirals in your blood. Every single scale of life has a spiral.

"Totally. Awesome."

"It is! Now, here is my theory on time travel. When we have strong feelings and hold a thought to connect, while we listen to our heart song — that hum we talked about before — our attention drops into the center of our energy donut, and we can access other dimensions. We can access the whole universe. And that center? That is what I mean when I say zero point."

"Cool." Lily takes a moment and suggests, "Are you saying my heart is a time travel machine?"

It's wild to see my fast brain in action, even so young. I assert, "I am. It's the center of your donut, which is your heart!"

She asks, "My heart is a donut hole?"

I laugh out loud and say, "I couldn't say it better myself."

Lily jumps and hoots. "Say it yourself! You are funny."

I giggle and say, "When I surrender to my heart, I mean, my donut hole, the combination of tightening and tingling in my chest builds and I'm able to visit you!"

Lily sits down on the bed and sighs. "Wow. My heart is a time machine."

"Eternity whispers in the breeze as trees listen between branches."

– Astara[71]

Willow Tree

I wink at Lily and say, "Now that we have time travel figured out." Lily laughs out loud and says, "Yeah, uh huh. Sure."

I smile and say, "Before my heart brought me here, I was reading what you were writing just now. What did you mean when you wrote, *Please keep me from being bad?*" I ask.

She looks down at her sparkly gold painted toes. She flexes them up and down to watch them shine under the ceiling light. I smile. I still love things that sparkle. It's all that star wisdom inside us and a little of our raven medicine peeking through. Ravens love sparkly things.

Lily offers, "I don't know. I upset mom and Sierra all the time. And then Dad and Tim are either gone or watching TV when they're here. They barely talk to me. There must be something wrong with me."

"Oh, my love. I'm sorry you doubt yourself. Their actions involve you, but they have nothing to do with you," I share. I sit down by her side. "Before I explain, will you hold my hand?"

Lily nods and reaches for my hand. She says, "I can feel heat where our fingers touch."

"Me too! Now, will you close your eyes with me?"

Lily closes her eyes.

I whisper in a low voice in her ear, "Now, think of your favorite place in nature and we'll go there together."

When I open my eyes, we are on a lawn beneath a tree canopy spilling over and around us touching the grass. A gentle breeze moves over me, not too warm, not too cool. I know this tree. This is the large willow tree of my childhood in our Ohio backyard! We moved away when I was eight. I smile to myself. That 12-year-old aspect of my soul is already integrating with me, and here we are together with shared thought and feeling. My eyes go damp with emotion. I remember the comfort of the willow's canopy that reaches all the way to the ground, a deep umbrella of green. This tree is the safest place in my Ohio childhood.

I turned three in our car driving across country from California. We moved from Los Angeles to this house in the Columbus suburbs when my dad was transferred for work to start the Columbus office. A snapshot memory pops in of colorful helium balloons rubbing against the car roof as we drive.

Under the bending branches, the air is humid and fresh like a summer storm has just blown through. Crickets sing to us. Stars wink through the dark silhouette of branches and leaves rustling in the breeze. A hint of cloud wisps move across a dark blue sky.

I think, *the stars of my childhood!* There's no light pollution yet and no fences. The yard is wide open, the grass is damp. Back then, children in the neighborhood could roam between houses and play in the creek that hadn't yet been culverted. I can hear the distant trickle of the creek down the hill. Lily is looking around too.

I whisper to her, "I love this tree!" I walk over to face the base of the trunk and sit down. I call out, "Come sit with me."

She walks over and sits against the tree, facing me with her legs crossed.

"I want to talk with you about feeling bad. The world is filled with parents using tools they learned from their parents. Mom and dad grew up hearing things like *"you are bad"* when they were little, so they say them to you out of habit. Those words are shaming."

"What is shame?"

"Shame would say that *who you are* is bad. Guilt would say *an action you took* is bad."

"Like, it's the difference between who I am and how I act?"

"Exactly. Actions are temporary. You at your core? You're infinite.

You can act badly, but you are not bad. You are a child of God, of the universe. Do you understand?"

"I think so."

"As a kid you like to test edges to learn. That is natural."

Lily looks at me, alert. She says, "It is?"

"Yes. When mom and dad were young, they tested things too."

"Hah. I could see that. Mom can be feisty, and dad is playful."

"That is why they get along so well!" I laugh and continue, "Actions we take have a result. Sometimes positive, sometimes negative. Some outcomes may inspire us and make us feel good. Some outcomes feel yucky. When we act badly, the consequences teach us. They inspire us to take a more loving action next time. Remember this: who you are at your core is infinite and doesn't change because of your actions."

Lily looks up through the tree limbs at the stars nodding. "Huh."

Her "huh" sounds like a goose honk with her head titled back. I giggle.

She looks at me and tries a second time, "Huh."

My head tips to the side and I look at her. I say, "Uh, huh," forcing it out as a duck sound.

Lily laughs and offers, "Is a feeling an action? Sometimes it's not something mom or dad says to me, it's what they don't say that makes me feel bad."

"Ah. You're talking about uncomfortable silence." I put my hands on the dark grass under the moonlight streaks coming through the branches.

Lily nods and says, "Yeah. Totally, like, sometimes, silence holds more than words."

"You are wise." I offer, "I remember how silence can feel uncomfortable. In our fear, we translate silence to mean someone is thinking badly of us."

Lily steps in and says, "Yeah. Like, that awful feeling when I do something and there is only silence. I think, *I'm a disappointment.*"

I interject, "Or, *there's something wrong with me.*"

"Exactly!" Lily is both stunned and satisfied hearing her future-self validate what she's feeling. There is a tone of satisfaction in her words. Something is shifting and settling in me as well. It's a non-linear domino.

I keep going, "When you get quiet and think about the big scary fights that go on around you, I know you think they're about you, but they're not."

Lily quietly looks up through the willow branches to the wink of stars. "Mom gets so mad at me, and sometimes it doesn't make sense." Her words tumble out fast and loud. "I must make her that mad. It must be about me. She even says so!"

I lean forward to take her hand and confirm, "I know. Adults can be messy with their own hurts. Especially parents. Especially mom. And even dad too. Just like you, mom and dad were kids once. They have a lot of confusion and pain about their parent's mistakes that spilled over to them when they were little. And on it goes down the generations. Without meaning to, parents project their pain from their past into the present in an effort to heal what is unresolved."

"Wow. I don't know if I ever thought about that." Lily looks at our hands saying, "Still, it totally hurts."

I sigh. "I know. I know. It really hurts. They probably don't realize they're working out their past with you and other family members. Their pain's so deep they block out the memory; they don't know that what they're putting on you is what they haven't healed. In a passionate moment, they convince themselves it is about something you did or didn't do. But here's the secret. Many times, it isn't."

"What about when I really do mess up? Or I'm mean?"

"When that happens, they're trying to teach you about conse-quences, yes. But it's never about you *being bad* at your core. It's only ever about an action that you need to learn about."

"I wish I could tell them what you're saying."

"Me too, but they might not understand. You get to practice learning and staying in your power and not believing everything an adult tells you about yourself." I remind her, "They want to help you grow into the woman you're meant to be. They love you so much.

They think the world of you! No one loves you as much as them. Except me that is." I radiate love in the dark.

I can see her smile flash in the dim light. She stays silent. She let's go of my hand and leans back against the tree.

I continue, "Learning is natural and sometimes involves disagreement. That conflict between you and mom and dad is natural as you grow. The rages you are used to seeing from mom, they're about her and her past. Those rages are not about you. Remember that."

"All of the fights AND the silences make me tired." Lily looks to the sky and says, "There's so much said that is awful. There's so much unsaid. And the worst is that the unsaid feels so heavy. I'm so tired."

I scoot over to sit next to her at the base of the Willow and put my arms around her. "I tell you what. You don't have to understand it all. Those kinds of arguments, that kind of shaming and meanness, it's crazy making. Even if you try super hard and say all the things you think you should, you cannot make it any less crazy. Remember, sometimes it's not about you, even if they say it is! It's their fear projecting onto each other and to you." I take my hand and say, "I want you to pretend there's an invisible pen and paper in my hand. We're going to write a permission slip out for you."

"Permission slip?"

"Yes. Like a permission slip at school. A permission slip given to you by your future self — that's me. A permission slip to not have to understand crazy and to let it go, because it isn't yours." I scoot back and look into Lily's eyes and put my hand over my heart, "Love comes from here. This is who you really are." I thump my palm on my chest a few times to mimic the *thump thump* sound of my heart. "We're here on this planet to practice love while releasing the grip fear has on our lives. To learn how to let go of *what is not you*, so you can *allow more of you*. More you than you know."

Lily giggles. "You sound like Dr. Seuss."

"I do!" I laugh too and chant, "*Let go of what is not you, so you can allow more of you. More you than you know.*"

Lily laughs until she snorts.

I roll on my back pulling my legs to my chest, giggling. My eyes are wet with joyful tears. I catch the low willow branches bouncing in the breeze as if they're laughing with us. As they bounce, they hit the ground gently, like a joke so good it is a knee slapper. I lean in to see my own young eyes up close and whisper, "Most importantly, how about we write you a permission slip to just be." I pop up and twirl, spreading my arms out above my head as if I am swirling the stars into place in a magical act.

Lily smiles watching me. She sighs and asks, "How big can you write it?"

I bend down to whisper into her ear, "As big as the moon! And we'll write it in gold! Just by existing in this big, beautiful cosmos, *you are worthy*. There is no requirement for worthiness. You were born worthy." I point to her heart and say, "You decide in every waking moment of your life who you are. You are worth what you say you are."[72]

"I am worth what I say I am." Lily emphasizes each word long and slow as she looks down at her lap and back up at me. "I like that." She calls out to me, the tree, the sky, "I want to feel like that every day!"

I twirl over to the tree laughing and land with both my palms on the bark. I motion for her to come stand with me and she puts her palms on the tree below mine. I bend to whisper again in her ear, "This tree is strong, like you. Like a tree, you are rooted. Your roots connect you to this Earth. Do you feel it?"

Lily nods, "Yes."

"As you notice the tree and the stars, that sensation in your heart and body — that's love." She stands to join me and wraps her arms around the tree as far as they will reach. I continue, "Notice the simple reminders of beauty around you every day, and you'll remember just how loved you are."

Lily continues to hug the tree and her words muffle against the bark, "What if I forget?"

"Don't worry. Because you come from nature, if you wander away for too long, its rhythms and beauty will always call you to return.[73] A bird will fly over you to remind you to soar above fear. Trees will remind you to stay grounded with their trunk and roots and reach for the stars with their branches and leaves. Dogs will teach you to about loyalty, especially to yourself. Cats will teach you how to be confident and ask for what you want. Dolphins will remind you to play. And so on. Pay attention and trust the messages you receive from all your nature friends."

We hear frogs in the distant creek and Lily asks, "What will frogs teach me?"

I giggle and say, "Frogs will teach you how to clean yourself of negative thoughts like meanness and doubt."

"Frogs are smart." Lily giggles again.

I laugh. "They truly are. Your human family will remind you too. Little gifts of love will show up through time they spend with you, words they share, and even strangers may bring you just the smile you need. The whole world sends you reminders every day. Even when times are hard."

Lily looks at me, and then back to the night sky. "I don't want to go home."

"Oh sweetie. Will you do something for me?"

Lily tilts her head, "What?"

"Next time you feel totally alone inside the chaos of mom and dad arguing, or Sierra picking a fight with you, or Dad or Tim's silence overwhelming you, or a tension at school, imagine sitting under this tree with me. Remember how held you are by nature and how loved you are. Future you will be there reminding you: You are worthy. You are loveable. Their pain isn't about you."

I was asking a lot of a 12-year-old. It would take practice. But I know me, and practice is my forte. Lily leans against the tree in silence for a while. At last, she sits forward and replies, "I'll try."

"That is all that's required. Things get magical when you remember you are not alone." I slowly whisper, "I'll tell you a secret."

Lily perks up and whispers back, "What?"

"We've never been alone, and we never will be. It takes practice to shift out of our habit of feeling alone, but it's worth it. If you practice believing in yourself, you just might have more fun." With that, I reach for her hand and say, "Close your eyes, listen to your heart. Think of home."

When we open our eyes, I am back in her bedroom, her hand in mine, standing at the edge of the bed.

"Thank you," Lily says and throws her arms around me.

I hug her tightly and say, "It's my pleasure. What a treasure to see our willow tree in Ohio again."

Lily nods against my chest and presses harder.

I ask, "Do you feel any better?"

She nods and pulls away to see me. "I feel hopeful. I feel different."

"Good. I'm going home. Have a beautiful rest. I'll see you soon, I'm sure of it."

"Goodbye!"

"Sweet dreams."

I close my eyes and breathe deeply imagining my basement and sitting at my desk. The warmth in my fingers remains as I look up. I am home.

"When you hold yourself sacred, you will know what to do."

– Lily Marie Livingston, age 35[74]

Flying at Night

I stand looking at the clip-on lamp attached to the exposed wood joist aiming light at the pile of journals in my basement. I imagine the young me I just left in Tarzana. In my mind's eye, she's in bed holding her small red-hard-bound-lined-pages-diary-time-machine thinking of me. I stand up to switch off the light and close my laptop screen. I go upstairs to the kitchen to make some evening tea. In my sitting room chair, I hold the steaming mug to my lips and sip slowly. I pick up a book to read to take a break from visiting my younger self across time.

My energy is increasing in the two days I have been communicating directly with my past self. Turning off the technological gadgetry of my world is also helping. It's as if I have turned up the dial and the volume is louder for all my senses. I hear more sounds inside and around me, even the sound of my breath. Colors are brighter. My sleep patterns are beginning to recalibrate with the sun and moon. I feel the air on my skin.

Although words are the portal to the past, the sounds of my voice combined with my strong self-love is also part of my bridge across time. I hear an internal voice say *continue to follow your feelings.*

My amplified senses remind me of how I saw the world as my 12-year-old self. She's looking through my eyes. We are doing more than building intimacy and sharing through time, I am integrating her into my life, and she is welcoming me into hers.

I feel joy beneath the surface. Like a kid in a candy store, I look at my home now with her excited eyes. Orion kitty jumps up in my lap and settles in for a good purr session.

She is not here, but I can feel her thoughts and emotions rush through me. She exclaims, *"My own cat. My own furniture. My own home!"*

To a 12-year-old, my world is a dream come true.

I hear her cry out, *"I am free!"*

My heart does a dance. With her looking in at my world with me, I feel at home more than ever before. Does she see differently in her world as well? I imagine, yes.

After reading a while, my eyes get sleepy and I head upstairs with Orion kitty to go to bed and fall into my dream's embrace.

...

In my dream, I am back at the willow tree of my Ohio childhood. Twelve-year-old Lily floats through the tree canopy. I try to grab her feet to keep her from flying away. It's a quick instinct, so I let my arms relax instead. I am floating too. I look back up at Lily now above the tree, and I am lifting with her, our bodies passing through the draping willow branches. Up we rise above the gentle motion of the dark green leaves in the moonlight. We both look back to our Ohio house where we lived from age 3 to 8.

A younger version of us stands at our bedroom window. I am not sure she can see us. As if on cue, we both wave at her in the window. Her face presses to the window as she bounces up and down, waving back. I send her a thought message, "We love you. We will be back."

Together, we rise. I turn my attention to the world above and below us. We soar together for a while amidst the stars and clouds, looking down on the sleepy suburbs of Columbus at night.

I am dreaming, yet I am lucid. The intimacy of self meeting self fills my awareness. Flying like this with Lily fills me with renewed joy. Connecting with my 12-year-old self is healing me in ways I hadn't thought possible. I can only imagine what will happen when I meet an even younger me across time. I fly free, yet connected.

*"E-motion is energy in motion. Choose to feel and know
all of you. By allowing the presence of the emotion
beneath the story, you transform yourself and the world.
In this direction lies your freedom. This path at first seems
to be shrouded in fog and you cannot see very far. This
mist, this fog, is the unknown enfolding you in its loving
embrace."*

– Astara & the Galactic Council

Piano Lessons

It is Friday, October 13, 2017. In the morning, I feel more refreshed than I have in years. I used to fly in my dreams, and I haven't in decades. My heart is light and happy.

I head back to the basement desk to connect with the journals. The sun is streaming through the high window onto the couch, rug, and concrete. Light reflects off the white concrete masonry wall. Our basement is partially below-grade; I feel hugged by the Earth. I open my little red book and keep reading.

I came home and went to piano lessons, I didn't have much fun.
Wednesday, February 2, 1983.

The tragedy of that statement catches my breath. Where the willow represents support and safety to the 12-year-old me, the piano is my safe place in our future.

I set the diary down on the wood desktop. The cognitive dissonance between my young self's frustration at the piano, and the current me that delights in the piano, forms a strange pressure on my chest. The weight turns warm and moves down to my arms and hands. My fingers long for the keys. I go upstairs to my piano and begin to play and sing.

My dad dies 25 years from my Los Angeles living room, when I was 39. He passes a year, three months, and five days after my mom's death. But who's counting? As my siblings and I go through the estate, we make decisions together about what we want. One day, we sat and talked about the big emotional items. I got my courage up to ask for the two treasure's I most covet: Aunt Sylvia's grand piano and grandfather's typewriter. Sierra, Tim, and Maribel generously allowed me to take both. I cried in joy when they said yes.

Sylvia's piano became our family's a few years before she died, around when I was 10. Decades later, at age 42, the piano arrived to my Oakland home. Now it sits by the front door of my Omaha home. Perhaps because of its rich family history, or perhaps because I love playing it, this grand piano has been a recurring actor in my waking and my dream life teaching me a great many things and bringing me hours of joyful serenity.

It wasn't always this way. Piano lessons in my adolescence frustrated me with the structure of classical music: sight reading, metronomes, and the pressure of practicing.

Sitting at my heirloom piano, I speak words out loud to my young self across time, "I know the lessons are no fun. I also know this: the piano is your great love."

Suddenly, I am sitting at the grand piano in my living room in Tarzana in 1983. The house is an open floor plan with sleek lines, curved kitchen counters, recessed wood-panel hidden cabinets, and high ceilings.

Our house sits on top of a short hill overlooking the San Fernando Valley below. This whole north side of our 1950's ranch home is floor-to-ceiling glass with an impeccable view. In the peak of summer with 100-degree heat, all that glass is an ordeal to keep cool. My mom complained about the heat, yet loved the view. Behind me, daylight floods the room through the expanse of glass.

In front of me, the room is open and spacious. The dark

wood-paneled ceiling angles up high to a center beam connected to a wood column at the middle of the room. The thick glass coffee table lays low on a curved metal base over orange carpet. As a little girl, I would lie down on the floor to look through the side of the thick glass table. The room extended infinitely in all directions, up and down. My own multi-dimensional kaleidoscope.

Sitting on this piano bench again with this view, I silently laugh at the thought of this grand piano in my now small Omaha living room. I float my hands across the grain of her pitch-black satin finish. My fingers lightly touch her keys without pressing down. The piano is in better shape, she is 34 years younger than the piano in my current timeline.

Originally my aunt Sylvia's piano, this black beauty arrived just after we moved to Los Angeles. It sits in the place of honor at the farthest corner of the house with the best view.

Sylvia hung herself at 40, just four months before I wrote the first entry in my red diary. Sylvia's piano was not a witness to her death; it sat waiting for the somber news, a sentinel facing the valley below. My dad's only sibling, gone so young. The shock of her swift exit ricochets through our family. Suicide is epic for any family member to digest, let alone a 12-year-old.

After Sylvia's death, an unasked question perpetually hovers. *Why?* Mom and dad avoid talking to us kids about it. The silence takes up more space than words. I only remember a numbing shock and confusion.

When we lived nearer to Sylvia's home in Cincinnati, we spent more time with her. After our move west, Sylvia visits once. Still, I knew so little about her. She was quiet, beautiful, and her playing was effortless. I would sit listening to her and marvel at how fast her fingers moved across the keys.

Sitting at my piano, I can feel the thoughts of my young self across time. *Did our family contribute to Sylvia's suicide? Were we too far away? Did she feel alone?*

My adult self knows Sylvia is responsible for her own death, yet 12-year-old me does not understand any of it. My mom's brother, uncle Sam, blamed Sylvia's mom, Hildegarde, for her death. He felt she was a victim to Hildegarde's need to control Sylvia through religious stringency. For years, I suspected that the dominating style that Hildegarde brought to her family negatively affected Sylvia. There were rumors that Hildegarde would force Sylvia to pray for hours alone in a dark closet. I never asked my dad what he felt or thought about his sister's death; I was too afraid to broach the subject.

I remember Sylvia the way you squint at an abstract painting. As I focus on her memory, I get an overall feeling of the pattern and color and tone. No matter how awful her death, I felt softness, warmth, and a wistful longing when I thought of her.

I want so badly to play the piano, but I don't know if I will be heard. I don't know how real my visit is, and I don't want to stir up any excitement. To the right of where I sit, the view along the back of the house is unobstructed all the way to my parents' bedroom door. I do not see or hear anyone. I savor being reunited with the terrazzo floor, the glass walls, the dark wood paneling, and the orange shag carpet.

When I lived in this house, my authority was outside of myself. Everything I did was my young attempt to slowly bring my authority inside. As a young girl I had to do what my piano teacher, Lura, and my parents told me to do. Lura was a family friend and I liked her. At the piano with me alone, she behaved as any traditional piano teacher would, by insisting I practice more. I was more interested in improvisational creations and spent my time writing songs instead of practicing. I thought I had to decide between practice and creating, I didn't know I could have both.

My young thoughts pour through me, *I don't want to be a concert pianist. I don't want to practice the classics. When I play, I like to feel the piano play me. I only want to write the songs that come through so I can sing.*

I turn around on the piano bench and look through the tall window. The wood deck with its metal water fountain juts out above the concrete patio around the pool. Beyond the deck, the view of the San Gabriel Mountains and the valley lies in all directions. The sky is clear blue. The sticker bushes burst forth their sticky red blooms at the perimeter of the house. I used to have the darnedest time getting those out of my hair. The Camelia bushes, my mother's favorite, have dropped their soft-petaled coral-colored blooms all over the ground like a pink-red carpet.

I turn back around as Lily walks through the swinging door of the kitchen with her head down. She looks up and stops, smiling. "Woah, you're back!"

"Hi!" I beam as my heart rate picks up. "In your journal entry today you wrote, *I came home and went to piano lessons, I didn't have much fun.* Those words brought me here. I have been sitting here waiting for you, happily reacquainting myself with our house." I make sure I don't mention Sylvia. I take a breath, "So, you went to piano lessons with Lura today?"

"Yes." Lily is not smiling.

I comment, "You are not smiling." I wait and ask, "It wasn't fun?"

Lily breathes in deep as she walks towards me and exhales a breathy, "No. Like, I… Well, I… I hate my piano lessons." She comes and drops next to me on the piano bench in a huff.

"Hate is a strong word. But you don't hate the piano?"

Lily looks up and says more quietly, "No. Actually, I love it."

I offer, "So do I." We both smile at the obvious. I continue, "Lura means well. Her approach at teaching just may not be for you. Regardless, the piano is an important part of your life."

"All she seems to care about is my practicing. She doesn't care about my songs."

"Oh, love. She just doesn't understand how you learn, what motivates you, what makes you tick. Can I share a future dream with you? It might help give you a new perspective on this piano."

"I love dreams!"

I chuckle. "We do." I explain, "When I was 23-years-old and living in Alexandria, Virginia for college, I had a vivid dream. I was miles away from this piano and miles from this Tarzana house, but still this piano appeared in my dream. It told me how important our piano is to our soul." It's exciting for 47-year-old me to tell a 23-year-old dream to 12-year-old me.

...

I sit at the piano outside at the back patio by our pool. It is night and the lights of the San Fernando Valley twinkle in the distance, what mom calls the jewel box. What an unusual location for the piano. I think, 'How did it get here?' There's sheet music in front of me. The dim light from the glass walls of our house illuminates the music. I see my mother's handwriting faintly. Although I have excellent vision, for some reason I can't read the music. I lean in and squint. I am frustrated I can't play my mother's music.

A tall man walks up to the piano and looks at me. He has light brown skin, dark pants, a white buttoned long-sleeved shirt, and a leather collar tie with turquoise rivets. His brown hair braids down his back. He looks like a Native American medicine man. His face is older, kind, and he's smiling gently.

"What are you doing?" He asks.

I groan, "I'm trying to play this music, but I can't read it."

"Why are you trying to play this?" He points directly at my mother's writing with his index finger.

"I don't know," I shrug. I hadn't questioned it until now.

He takes the music and tosses the pages off the piano. They scatter on the breeze in the Los Angeles night. Some fall in the pool. He doesn't care. He sits on the bench to my left and his fingers begin the bass notes of the song Heart and Soul. I forget about mom's music. I slowly come in with the right-hand melody notes.

The sound of our playing is beautiful together. Effortless. Easy.

I can play!

And then I wake up.

...

"That's what fun looks like," I declare.

"I love that dream." Her eyes are closed. Lily lifts her shoulders, smiles, and inhales deeply as if to hold it inside her.

"Me too. Can I show you something?"

She opens her eyes and answers, "Sure."

"Give me your hand."

Lily touches my fingers, and a current sparks between us. We are off.

. . .

We are standing on the other side of the living room. It seems to be a different timeline, for we are silently watching an older 14-year-old version of Lily talking with Mom.

Mom stands at the side of the piano, resting her hand on the curve of its lid. Mom is at her heaviest during these years, but she has a lot more vitality than she will in a decade. Her face is relaxed as she watches Lily.

This is a calm moment for mom. She's still coloring her hair, so there's no grey. Her hair's curled and set, the brown waves laying neatly. Mom says, "We promised you when you turned 14, you could decide a few things for yourself. You can choose if you still want to go to church or take piano lessons."

Fourteen-year-old Lily sits quietly on the piano bench. She asks, "Really? I don't have to keep going to church or keep seeing Lura?" she asks.

Mom offers, "Well, we would love it if you joined us at church, but no, you don't have to keep going if you don't want to. In terms of Lura, she is our friend, and we will see her at family gatherings, but you don't have to keep taking piano lessons if you don't want."

Lily stands there still silent. She is afraid, but she stands taller as she says, "I want to stop going to church." She waits bravely.

Mom offers, "Okay, sweetie. If that's what you want."

Lily's relief is palpable. There's no fallout. Mom's calm bolsters her to continue, "I also want to stop piano lessons." Lily doesn't leave the piano. She's afraid if she leaves, she won't sit back down and play again. She is holding her breath.

Mom pats Lily's hand and then waits. It seems like she is not sure what else to do, so she offers, "Are you sure?"

Lily finally exhales and says, "Yes."

"Okay, love." None of the parts of us know how to read mom's face, she so adequately hides her emotion. Lily looks up for guidance, and mom says, "I understand, you won't have to take lessons anymore." Mom walks out of the room.

Twelve-year-old Lily squeezes my hand tight. We look at each other. Then we look back at 14-year-old Lily. I can feel how we both wish she could see us. She looks towards the spot in the room where we stand, I can tell she senses our energy. For some reason she doesn't see us. Our hands channel the energy between us.

…

We're back at the piano bench again, back in late winter of 1983 in 12-year-old Lily's timeline. No one else is around.

"Wow." Lily says. "I don't have to go to church soon? Yes!" She pumps her fist in the air in victory. Relief washes over her whole body. I can see her face soften. She bursts out, "Wait, quit piano lessons? Are we sure that is a good idea?"

"Not going to church anymore is a wonderful relief. In terms of piano, we aren't sure at all. It's something I've revisited over and over in my mind in years to come. I think that's why I felt you so strongly before I came here. Perhaps what's more important than piano lessons right now, is how you decide to relate to this instrument. I've thought about this a lot."

She's thinking deeply about all of this. Her forehead squeezes and reveals the subtle indent right in the middle of the forehead. It's a scar after falling from our highchair as a baby.

"It's important to look at who you give your authority to. Ask yourself, who decides for you? Who decides you are a piano player? Them or you? Do not give Lura, or mom, or anyone else the ability to decide who and what you are. Regardless of disliking the lessons, you love the piano. What if there's a better teacher out there who understands you? What if you had a mom who encouraged you to keep up with lessons and practice and found a way to help you enjoy the learning?"

"But I don't have those better lessons, or that mom who encourages me to keep going. We just saw what happened," Lily adds.

"I know, love. But you have *you*. And I am here to remind you, you have *me*, an older wiser part of you. No matter what you decide now, or how many years you turn away from the piano, you come back to it. The piano will visit your dreams, it will haunt you, until you embrace it. Later, when you're an adult, you'll find a piano teacher who gets you. Someone who shows you how to play the way you want to!"

Lily quietly digests all my words. "I will? That's awesome!" And then she asks, "No matter what I do, the piano gets to be in my life?"

I confirm, "No matter what." I lean forward so I can spread my arms and drag my hands silently across the width of the whole piano keyboard, "It seems you are meant to love this big, beautiful instrument. It is a part of your life classroom, but don't pressure yourself. Music is the language of the universe. And you will seek, research, and build as much understanding as you can about the universe. How you speak that universal language is unique to you, and that is enough. And it is beautiful." On a whim, I propose, "Want to play together?"

"You want to?" Lily beams sideways at me.

"Yes!" I invite, "Just listen to me, to your heart, and trust yourself."

We start to play. Tentatively at first and then our notes start to coalesce. We are drawn to the chord of C, making improvisation easy as we move across the white keys. I explore deeper base notes. Lily explores higher octaves. My fingers find their way up the octaves and lightly reach for Lily's left hand. When we touch, I am back in Omaha, at my desk.

The morning light is streaming in, and only five minutes have passed.

> *"I have heard that youth is not a time of life, it is a state of mind. My heart knows this as my mind begins to catch up."*
>
> *– Astara*

Ohio

Later that day as I make dinner, I think to myself about 12-year-old Lily and now 14-year-old Lily. How young was the me waving in that window in my flying dream?

That night, lying in the dark, sleep isn't coming. My mind reaches out to the various ages of my youth. I call out a mental *"Hello?"* to myself, waiting to see what parts of me are there ready to connect.

Thoughts and sensations wash over me, as if there is an answer waiting. I eventually fall asleep.

...

In my dream, I am barefoot in the lawn behind my childhood home in Columbus, Ohio. I hear a quiet voice in the distance whisper, "Hello?" I look up and see my young self in the window above, face pressed to glass, looking at me. I am standing two stories below her, barefoot in damp grass.

"Hi!" I think back to her.

Her thoughts float to me across the night, "Who are you?"

"I am your future."

"You're my future?"

I reply, "Yes. I'm you, just older."

With that, suddenly young Lily is standing on the lawn next to me.

She squishes her bare toes to feel the coolness of the grass. What little feet! She looks happy to be closer to me and says, "Hi!"

"Hi!" I smile back. I ask, "How old are you?"

"I'm five." She holds up her hand to show me all five fingers outstretched. She asserts, "I just turned five last week."

If I just turned five, it's late June, a week past summer solstice.

She can't stop staring at me, at herself as an adult. She asks, "How old are you?"

"I'm 47-years-old."

Lily looks intently over my face and my body. Even in the dark I feel five-year-old me look me in the eyes. It is then her face shifts and softens. I sense she feels the familiar connection of our soul.

I assert, "You and I are both the same, just different ages. Do you like stars?" I know the answer, but I am excited to hear what she'll say.

"I love stars! Daddy takes me outside at night and teaches me their names! I love saying their names."

"You will always enjoy looking at the stars. Because of that, you change your name from Lily to Astara when you are my age. Your connection to the sky grows stronger as you grow." I bend down to her level and smile saying, "You can call me Astara."

"Astara." She tries the name on. "A-star-a. Ohhhh."

I wink at her, "It's late, even the fireflies have gone to sleep."

"I couldn't sleep. I came to the window and saw you." Lily looks around, "I'm not sure how I got down here."

"You fell asleep after all." I smile. "This is a dream. We're dreaming together you and I, meeting across time."

Lily's expression shifts and she looks at me, the sky, her house, and the trees behind us. "It looks so real."

"It is real in a different way. You can do anything you want in a dream. You can ask me — your future self — anything." I ask, "What do you want to know?"

"How do I stay happy? It's hard to stay happy when everyone is sad."

"What a great question. First, you don't have to stay happy. You get to have the full spectrum of feelings that are a part of life. There are many times when your feelings are different from those around

you. That's natural. It's also natural to be affected by your mom, dad, sisters, or brother's feelings."

Lily walks closer to me. "Mom gets mad if I am not happy. She gets mad if I am mad too! She gets mad a lot."

"Mom is uncomfortable with emotions — hers and others. Out of all the emotions possible, mom sometimes chooses anger over sad. Feelings scares her, so when you feel sad or mad she gets uncomfortable. Anger helps her move all that energy bottled up inside her; it gives her a sense of protection and power when she feels unsafe and powerless. Still, mom loves you very much and has much to teach you about life. You need to be connected with mom and dad right now to survive in the world, but you will grow up and have a separate life someday."

"I will?"

I remember that I tried to run away from home at age four with my sister Sierra, who would have been six at the time. Five-year-old Lily doesn't trust adults to look out for her and wants to be free of their big mood swings. I tell her, "Yes, you will. When you feel overwhelmed by the emotions of adults, or even friends, you can go outside and be with nature."

"What if it's snowing? Or raining?"

"If you can't go outside, just look out the window and dream and imagine playing with nature. If the weather is nice, go to your favorite willow tree and lean against it. Tell the tree your fears. Or play down by the creek. Talk to the birds, bees, bunnies, frogs, and bugs. Play in the garden and make the snapdragon flowers sing. Watch worms crawl. Get your hands in the dirt and bury seeds that will grow later. Learn about light from the fireflies. Nature, fairies, angels, and God always surround you in support. Connect with them so you can feel it!"

She walks around me in the damp grass, "Maybe that's why I love playing outside!"

"Me too!" I giggle and walk through the grass with her. We both stop and smile. I say, "Your mom, dad, sisters, and brother love you very much. Sometimes their souls are working out some important and scary lessons that you may not understand. Turn to your heart in those

moments and trust your own feelings. When you feel overwhelmed, go outside and let the blue sky and fresh air blow your hope back to you."

"I sometimes feel hope. I sometimes feel happy, but I can't stay there because someone else is angry or sad."

I point up to the stars dancing in a clear dark sky. "The sky is your teacher. You, your mom, your dad, your sisters, and your brother's feelings are like the clouds, they come and go. Yet the bigger truth, the core of you and all of us, is like the sky above the clouds. That sky is always there, it is steady. Day turns to night and back to day again. When the sun is out, you cannot see stars, but they're there. Sorrow clouds or even joy clouds will eventually pass. The stars are always there, loving you all day long, even when you can't see them."

"Feelings are like clouds?"

"Yes! They come and go." We both look up.

"The sky is always there." She repeats while stepping forward and pointing up.

"Yes!" I ask, "Did you know you have a superpower?"

Little Lily says, "No. I do?!" She bounces and tilts her head.

"You do. Your superpower is your feelings!"

"My feelings? But I thought they get me into trouble."

"Your superpower is your amazing ability to feel. You feel things others can't or won't. You feel so big and so brave. You can feel other's people's feelings too, even they don't know what they're feeling. Someday, you'll understand your power and why you're here on Earth. Mom has this power too, so does Sierra, Maribel, Tim, and dad. They might have a different path than you, and that's okay. Feeling those yucky emotions is important so you don't keep them in your body. If you keep them too long in the body and don't feel them, those feelings can hurt your health."

"I like the clouds. I like the stars. I like that the sky stays there as the clouds go by." She walks closer to me and quietly whispers, "I sometimes get angry like mom, so I don't feel sad too."

"Anger is a natural part of life. It's okay to be upset. It's important to listen to what is making us mad and ask for what we want. Remember, that anger cloud passes easily if you feel it and let it go."

Little Lily stops and looks up. She seems to be remembering something.

"My family tells me I'm too sensitive. That I should lighten up. How can that be my superpower?" Lily kicks the grass with her right toe.

I remember a similar conversation with my 12-year-old self. I imagine that other ages need the same message as well in ways that each age will understand. With such an old belief, it takes repetition and practice to transform. I imagine that as five-year-old Lily and I talk, the gift goes out to all ages.. I reply, "Ignoring feelings, or pushing them down inside you, or trying to make them go away to please others — that only blocks the good that you are. Someday, when they say 'You're so sensitive,' you will respond with 'Thank you!' instead of feeling bad about it."

Lily stands still. "I wish I could be funny like that instead of so sensitive."

I look down from the starry sky to see Lily. Her face is sad. I say, "You are allowed to feel a whole bunch so you can get to know your superpower!" I add, "And, you can also be playful and confident."

"Maybe." Lily sits on the grass.

I walk to her and sit down. "Did you know mom has a feeling superpower too? She doesn't like it or know what to do with it. Without trying, she not only feels her own feelings, but she feels the feelings of others too — just like you. She's trying to love and care for others this way. The biggest gift you can give mom, is to have your own feeling, really feel it. Does this make sense?"

"I don't know. Mom doesn't like me to get angry or have big feelings," Lily looks in the direction of our house.

"Your feelings are yours, and they are important. Go somewhere alone where you can feel it. You could grab a pillow and yell into it. Or go outside and run hard. You can tell all your worries and frustrations to nature and God." I turn to see if this is sinking in.

Lily looks back at me, "I like that."

"Just as mom takes on a feeling that is not hers, you hold feelings that are not yours. You're trying to help, love, and protect the other people in your life. For you, it comes easy to feel things. I'm going to ask you to try not to take on feelings that aren't yours. It's going to take

practice to learn what feeling is yours and what feeling is someone else's. That's the challenge of your feeling superpower."

"I'm sad a lot. And sometimes the sadness feels so big, so scary! I don't even know what it's about or where it comes from. Is that what you mean?" Lily's eyes are big as she looks straight at me.

"Yes. Exactly. A great way to see if that big sadness is yours or not, is to ask, 'Is this mine? Is this somebody else's?' Then listen inside yourself for the answer. You will hear a 'Yes' or 'No.' Trust what you hear."

Lily looks at me. She stands up and starts to walk in a circle muttering, "Is this mine? Is this yours?" I can hear her repeat it a few more times under her breath. "Is this mine? Is this yours?"

"You'll practice this for years. This is how you get better at your feeling superpower. You don't have to practice alone. All the ages of you past and future, are here for you whenever you need, just ask for us. You'll know we're here when you feel a warmth in your body and your heart says yes to the information that comes." I stand up and walk to her.

She repeats to herself, "A warmth in my body." She stops, looks up, and grabs my hand. My whole body tingles. "I love this feeling!" Lily jumps up and down, pulling on my hand. Her hand squeezes tight in joy. She's starts to dance around the lawn under the stars, so happy, so free for a moment. My heart relaxes in relief because I know how difficult this age was.

She stops dancing, her breath fast, "Hey, I think I saw you before flying over the house. Was that you?"

"Yes."

"I also saw someone flying with you. Who was that?"

"That was you at age 12. She's here with you in spirit, even though you can't see her right now. Your soul and your angels will help you practice standing strong in your feelings. Being sensitive and feeling your feelings is a brave superpower."

"Brave superpower." I can see her teeth in the moonlight giving away her smile. Her eyes wander and she looks at the stars for confirmation.

I affirm, "Everything is going to be okay. You are loved. You are not alone. You are amazing."

Lily runs up, grabs my hand, and squeezes tight. We stand there under the stars together, looking at the steady sky on soft supportive ground. The warmth begins again in my fingers and my heart. I can feel the love in the air, brighter than fireflies, it makes the stars wink some more.

I hear little Lily say in a high-toned whisper, "A-star-a."

...

*"We are not a culture that has built into our way of being,
our way of thinking, our civic imaginaries — contemplation, mourning, working through difficult contradictory
emotions. That's not part of our society; and therefore,
where society leaves off, we need to take up."*

– *Junot Diaz*[75]

Out of the Blue

It is Saturday, October 14, 2017. When I wake up, I am grateful.
It's as if the night vision with five-year-old Lily took me finally into
a deep rest. I hope it did for her too.

When I head down to the basement, I turn to the entry of the
next day in my 12-year-old timeline. Lily writes,

*Dear Lord, Grandma is very selfish. I know I should understand
cause I'm her granddaughter and she's old and Christian, so am I,
but I just can't. Thursday, February 3, 1983.*

My dad's mother, Hildegarde, was an eccentric woman. In 12-year-
old speak, she wasn't nice. I didn't like her much while she was alive.
No matter her circumstances as a child, which I eventually learned,
she evolved into a bigoted narrow-minded human. She hated anything different; she would say it smacked of the devil.

Regardless of my mother's conversion to Christianity — her
attending a Christian school, marrying a Christian man, living a
Christian life, and raising her children Christian — in Hildegarde's
eyes, my mom would always be Jewish. Since Hildegarde perceived
Jews as killing Jesus, my mom was looked down upon from day one.

This was decades before I arrived on the scene. My mom was in a continual battle with her anti-Semitic mother-in-law. To us kids, mom's anger had good reason. We saw what was happening.

Twelve-year-old Lily sends me a memory. Grandma waits until mom leaves the house before seeking us out. We hear the telltale sound of the hose on her thighs rubbing together as she walks down the hall to our bedrooms. We run and hide. She inevitably finds us and makes us kneel in our room to pray for hours until mom returns. Later, when mom finds out, the battle resumes.

For us kids, if mom's yelling wasn't aimed at us, it was oftentimes still scary. If it was aimed at Hildegarde? It was sheer pleasure! We would go in the other room and silently root my mom on. Go mom go! Tell her where to shove it! It was like watching a movie from afar. Or an exciting game of sports. We pretend to be a commentator and make popcorn.

For this reason and so many more, Hildegarde is deeply disturbing to young me. I alternate between frustration and fear; I pray for the feeling to change. She's my only living grandmother, and I long for the textbook doting and warmth that comes with having a grandmother.

Years later, after my aunt Sylvia dies, I hear whispers and hints from mom, dad, and my uncle Sam, that Hildegarde was a primary influence in Sylvia's suicide. My uncle would blame her outright.

I heard she made Sylvia pray too, but worse. The story is that it was for hours, shut in a closet, in the dark, for many years. Could such a horrible thing be true? I didn't know what to believe; I couldn't wrap my mind around such a thing. Still, it added fuel to the fire of my dislike.

Hildegarde died at 93 when I was 25. I remember the funeral. It was just my dad, Sierra, and me that flew to Milwaukee on a red-eye flight to honor her life. It was odd to see her dead body in a casket. She wore a dress as she laid there in the retirement home basement chapel. They applied theatrical level make-up to her lifeless form — blue eyeshadow, pink rouge, and red lipstick. Hildegarde never wore make-up; it would have been un-Christian in her eyes.

My mom couldn't attend; she was lying in Cedar Sinai Hospital back in Los Angeles, fighting for her life against non-Hodgkin lymphoma. My brother and our other sister couldn't attend either. My dad sat in the front pew, with me on his left, and Sierra on his right.

When they started to sing the first hymn, my dad began to shake. At first, I thought he was crying. I leaned in to comfort him and realized he was laughing. Sierra leaned in as well to see. He whispered for our ears only, "Your grandmother hated this hymn." As with most tragic situations, comedy is inextricably linked. My dad's quiet laughter was contagious, and Sierra and I huddled in with him as our shoulders began to shake as well. I pulled my long hair to my face, so no one would see me laughing. Please God, let them think we were crying. For dad, the laughter eventually turned to tears. I was glad. It was the only time he could surrender to his grief in front of us.

We flew back home on a red-eye that night. I was exhausted from the whirlwind. My sister Sierra was upset at the airport about our flight arrangements, price, time, and she let the airlines know it. I can't remember the details. I was strangely calm. We boarded the plane. Once in the air, I fell asleep in my window seat and dreamt of Hildegarde.

...

My grandmother sits in the seat next to me. She has grey hair yet exudes vitality. She looks so calm, peaceful even. Not a trait I would ascribe to her while alive. She asks, "Can I show you something? I want to help you understand my life."

"Sure." It seems the right thing to say.

"Look down there." And she points through the airplane window, to the Earth below. The sky is cornflower blue, like the crayon. It is dusk. Lights are emerging from the cities below.

Out of the blue, the world shifts below; we are flying over her life. She points out the window to different life stories as we fly over them, showing me her world. Her father and mother, siblings she knew while she was alive, and those who died young. How she was treated, what she felt, how her life evolved. Everything below us whizzed by in a blur. Rather than being left with any details I could grasp, I was left with this heated rush of understanding, and compassion bloomed in me. I looked anew at Grandma sitting in the airplane seat next to me.

"Thank you." I reached for her hand, and she held mine. She never did that in life. She always held my wrist as a child. I disliked that, it outright spooked me. For the first time in my life, with her hand in mine, I felt love for my grandmother.

"I have to ask you; how do I explain this to others? They won't believe me. There are a lot of people that are mad at you. You were a difficult woman in the world for many. Some blame you for Sylvia's death."

"This is for you, not them. I am sorry. I love you."

…

I vividly remember that dream of Hildegarde even decades later. When I come out of my memory reverie, I look up to see a 12-year-old Lily leaning her elbows on my desk, looking at my laptop.

"Hi!" I exclaim.

She stands up grinning. "Hello."

"I'm glad you're here."

"I could feel you!" She's declares. She admits, "I also wanted a change of scenery."

I was just reading your words you wrote today, *"Grandma is very selfish."*

Lily nods and says, "She is."

"I've felt the same. I learned some things since your timeline that might help you see Hildegarde differently."

"I feel bad about my feelings toward her. I think, like, why is my one living grandmother her? She's like, awful."

"Years from your timeline, she visited me in my dreams and shared her life story. She showed her difficult life, which influenced her intensity. Just imagine having siblings that you love die young, having parents that are not kind like mom and dad, a strict religious upbringing, and the challenges of being German in a country that doesn't like Germans all that much due to the World Wars."

"I hadn't thought about all that."

"How could you know? Be easy on yourself. Then you can be a little easier on Hildegarde when you're with her. You don't have to like her beliefs. It's okay to set boundaries. Still, see if you can find it in your heart to love her and be kind."

Lily hangs her head down and mutters, "I will try." She is shyly bumping her toes into the side of her other foot. She looks up at me.

"Thank you. You don't have to pretend or force it. Just be open. That's all that's needed."

"Okay." Lily looks around the room for a minute and then back at me. She declares, "I should head back. I have tons of homework to do."

"Alright you. Good luck with your homework."

Lily leaves and I feel bare. I wanted to talk with her longer. A part of me wishes I could talk about Hildegarde's and Sylvia's death, but in my heart, I know she isn't ready. I go upstairs and cook breakfast. I take a break from the journals for the rest of the day to process so many conversations with myself. That night, I sleep heavy without dreams.

*"Love is never lost. If not reciprocated, it will flow back
and soften and purify the heart."*

– Washington Irving

Law of Thermodynamics

It is Sunday, October 15, 2017. I wake up and go to the pool to swim.
I slept well and it shows in my body. I have the pool to myself this
morning, and my shoulder thaws out even more as I surrender to
breath, water, and movement.

When I arrive home refreshed, I see young Lily in my mind's eye,
but she's not connected to any passages I read today from the red
diary. I can't shake her emotional tug across dimensions. My intuition
nudges me to take a shamanic journey. I sit with my drum and let
the repetitive rhythm take me, as I entrain to the theta brain wave
state. I close my eyes and connect with my spirit guides, my High
Self, and my animal spirits. I ask for guidance from my generous
inner-verse and soul team to show me what I need to know.

…

*Standing in Lily's orange bedroom, she's laid out face down on
her bed crying. She doesn't sense me. I assess the space and wait to
approach. I walk up to the bed, and Lily feels my presence. She turns
over but doesn't seem to recognize me. She isn't responding with her
usual warmth. Lily stops and asks through her tears, "Who are you?"*

"I am future you." I answer.

"Future me?"

*"Yes. I'm an older version of you visiting from the future to bring
you love."*

She's so sad as she looks at me with confusion. She says, "Love sounds good right now."

I stand next to her bed and sit down. I ask, "What day is it?"

"It's Wednesday."

"What's the date and year?"

"August 11, 1982."

It's months before she starts writing in our red journal. I ask, "Why are you sad?"

"I just found out. I just…" Her smile fades and her voice trails away and the tears start again.

I wait for her to gather her breath.

"I just…" Lily finally finds words, "Aunt Sylvia died. I just found out."

"Oh love." I understand now, this is a big day. Our Aunt Sylvia killed herself at age 40 the day before. I offer gently, "I'm so sorry. Do you want to talk about it?"

"Yeah." She looks down and says quietly, "Nobody else will."

"I'm sorry no one's talking with you about it."

"Why? Why would she leave like that?" She turns over and sobs again, muttering between sobs, "She hung herself." She moans into her hands, "She was so young."

I lean over her and sigh. I put my hand on the back of her heart. I tell her, "Death is a mystery. Especially suicide. Sylvia's leaving the world as she did, torments all of us. It is especially painful for dad; she was his only sister. He may not show it, he has a hard time processing emotion in front of us kids. He gets better at expressing emotions in a few decades."

"Really?" She sniffles and wipes her nose. "I can't imagine him comfortable with emotions."

"I'm here to help you with what you can't imagine. Yet." I keep going, "In physics, the laws of thermodynamics help us understand death from a bigger perspective."

"I think Tim has talked about those laws, but I don't know them."

"You don't have to worry about the details, I'm going to keep it simple. According to the first law, energy isn't created or destroyed, it just changes form."

Lily questions, "Nothing is created or destroyed?"

"Yes. From an energy perspective. From a physical perspective, when someone dies, their matter is gone. It feels final. Even if we're lucky enough to know the law of thermodynamics, we miss them and grieve them. Yet, death isn't a final ending."

I know this is a lot for a young girl in grief. Lily is wiping her eyes. I check in, "This is a lot, should I keep going?"

"Yes. I want to know more about death."

Who am I kidding? This girl is me. I love this stuff. I go on, "From a spiritual perspective, there are many versions of death. Some believe we die and go to heaven or hell. Some believe in nothing and think we just die and turn to dirt again, no meaning, no purpose, nothing else happens, except maybe if we are lucky, we become tree food."

I peek at Lily again. She's listening and staring at the ceiling; a single tear is streaming down her face. I continue, "I personally believe in reincarnation — meaning after we die, we are born in a new body, in a new family, in a new life. But our soul is always our soul. Our soul's purpose is to learn through lifetimes. Each soul is an individual spark of God."

It seems my voice is relaxing her. Lily stops crying for now. She asks, "Do you think Sylvia is going to reincarnate again?"

"Yes, I do. From this perspective, the body dies, but the soul endures. In Tibet, bardo is a term for the state we enter when we let go of one condition before we enter the next. Bardo is any state of transition where our lives become suspended by a major experience. Bardo occurs throughout life."

Lily is still now. She looks up and says, "Bardo."

"Yes. In Tibet, there are six states of bardo. The first is the bardo before birth. The second is the bardo of the dream state — which is where we are now. The third is the bardo of meditation. The fourth bardo is the moment of death. The fifth bardo is between death and heaven — some call it the astral. The sixth bardo is the moment in-between heaven and rebirth. Some believe that when we become aware of the concept of bardo while alive, we can prepare for a more aware life and death."

She curls to her side to face me on the bed and asks, "We are in bardo right now?"

"Yes. We are."

"Cool."

"Now imagine that time doesn't exist. Kind of like how you and I are coming together across time in your dream. For them, it isn't reincarnation, it's just multiple lives, in parallel timelines or dimensions, all happening at once. You pick one life as the focus and voila, that is your dimensional reality or lifetime. All of it is mind-blowing. The mind isn't essential here. You must follow your heart to know what's true for you. Trust your intuition."

Lily rolls on her back and looks at the celling. "Mind blown is right. Death isn't what we think? Dreams are bardo? Time doesn't exist?" She looks straight at me and says, "I don't know what is real, but like, when I listen to you, I feel better. What makes me totally sad is suicide."

I offer, "From the reincarnation model, all souls come here to learn. We chose this life, our family, and all our experiences. When a soul wants out early, that soul leaves before the learning they came to do is complete."

"And that is suicide?"

"Yes. Many souls have a dark moment in their life, which can be so painful it feels like an eternity. They might believe the illusion that they will never feel better. In their deep pain, they're tempted to see death as the only way to escape. They can't see their pain as temporary, that tomorrow will bring a new feeling."

Lily sighs, "I wish Sylvia knew it was temporary."

"Me too. Sylvia's soul came here to learn as a part of our family. Her lessons are teaching us. When somebody leaves early, at their own choosing, they discover to their dismay that they left the classroom early. In their own soul timing, they get back in line, re-enroll in the same life course, and start over. Sylvia got lost and scared in her pain place, and for reasons we may never know, decided to escape the pain. The good news is, she'll be back. One way or another, she will repeat her lesson here. It's inevitable."

Lily adds, "I like the idea that Sylvia will return to live out what she was meant to. In church they talk about suicide so negatively, with such shame. I don't like when they say sin. I don't believe in hell. I believe in second chances, and third chances."

"In the eternal game of life, we get a zillion chances. You are right. Hell doesn't exist as religion conceives of it. Hell is a state of mind. It is the extreme case of denying God in everything. Hell happens for so many right here on Earth."

"I think mom goes to that mistaken place a lot. I think I've seen it myself after the scary places I've gone with her."

"That's it. We can leave hell anytime; we have to choose to go back to our power and reconnect to love and remember our divinity."

"How do we do that?"

I smile inside because I know Lily will more conversations with me in a few months. I offer, "Everything is more beautiful, amazing, possible, and filled with love than we can fathom with our limited brains. Our hearts give us a clue to the expansive nature of the universe. Many moons from now, when you are much older, you will teach about this. All you need to remember now is that when you commit to living, learning, and listening to your heart you can't go wrong. I promise."

Lily rolls over and stands up from the bed. Her color is back in her face. I stand up to face her.

I ask, "Can I give you a hug?"

She grabs me and holds me tight as our embrace reshapes the fabric of our lives for the better.

I whisper in her ear, "I love you. Thank you for reaching out. I'll return whenever you need me."

We stand to look at each other, younger me and older me holding hands. Before I can satisfy my eyes, a warmth moves up my arms and Lily is gone. My fingers hold air.

. . .

I set my drum down. Months after this interaction, I start my first journal. And only a few months later I stop journaling for years. I try to theorize why I stopped writing. I sense it is more complex. Perhaps life gets busy for young me. School and extracurriculars, friends and boys, and the family dynamics during all of it. Perhaps I was thrown by Sylvia's death and grief. Perhaps it is something else. Either way, my writing doesn't start again until I leave for college.

It doesn't matter. I'm grateful another 12-year-old soul part has returned. I feel a new peace about Sylvia and death with my young grieving self.

I head downstairs to make an organic banana-date-vanilla-almond-chocolate smoothie. I drink it joyfully, for all the ages inside me. I also drink in all the nourishment of wonder and curiosity I have gotten from my young selves these recent days.

*"Do we ever really let go? do we revisit something
eternally until it changes shape and form in our psyche
and soul? We revisit it until we can hold the depth and
breadth of it in our own hands and hearts."*

– Astara

The Secret to Life

It is Monday, October 16, 2017. Morning comes. I wake up and
Orion kitty's staring at me. It's still dark out, but he's decided it's time
to be fed. A month past the fall equinox and the Earth has turned
to longer nights and shorter days.

I take my typical long walk along our streets lined with old trees
and brick Tudor homes built circa 1930. I walk out of the house
under a navy star-studded sky and return home beneath a baby
blue sky with the sun winking over gabled rooftops. After juicing
cucumber, beet, celery, carrot, I eat a light breakfast. I am ready to
meet myself again.

Down in our cozy basement, I settle at my desk to read the final
entry in my potent month-long diary.

*I waited an hour for somebody to pick me up from school. Wednes-
day, February 9, 1983.*

I remember the waiting. Mom was notorious for not picking us
up on time. She even forgot us at times. All my siblings have more
than one anecdote about waiting for mom to get them. She was
teaching me uncomfortable, yet important lessons. Lessons on how
to be patient, how to wait, and what it feels like to not be the priority.

Our mother never meant us harm, and she was there for us every day. She loved us deeply and truly. And when you are emotionally hiding inside yourself to survive, how can you be emotionally available to others? Such unavailability eventually spills out to other arenas of life. Adult me knows this, but young me doesn't.

I feel Lily's distress as mine again. The memory zings through me and my heart hums all the way through my head. I close my eyes, and the frustration fills my body with renewed freshness. When I open my eyes, it's daytime, and Lily's sitting alone outside Egremont Junior High in Encino, California. She's perched with her backpack on the low wall by the entrance, below jacaranda and valley oak trees. She looks down the street in both directions for any sign of a car. She looks down and continues to write in her journal.

I walk over and sit down next to her. It's early February in Los Angeles, it feels like 70 degrees. Lily's hair is pulled back into a French braid. She's wearing a thin sweater with thick rainbow stripes over blue jeans. I loved that sweater. I remember taking my school pictures in it.

"Hey, you," I call gently.

Lily looks my way and a smile starts. She stops her lips from curling up and says, "Hi." She looks down and kicks asphalt rocks and a fallen acorn.

"I read in your diary how you've been waiting and the feeling of frustration whooshed me to you. I'm so sorry you have to wait," I offer.

"Like, I'm used to it." She says with a sigh. Lily looks down the street both ways and then back at me.

Smiling I say, "What if I told you this was building your character."

"Hmmmm," is the best I get from her.

Still smiling, I offer, "What if I told you, you are learning patience. One of the most important lessons in life."

"Hmmmm. What if I'm learning what it feels like to be forgotten." Lily looks away.

"Yeah, it sucks. I know. I've *literally* been here. I'm so sorry mom is bad at being on time. There is a songwriter that we fall in love with when you're 22. Her name is Tori Amos. I believe she's correct in one of her songs when she says she found the secret to life. You want to know what it is?"

Lily straightens her spine until her whole body lifts a few inches. She asks, "What?"

I begin to sing, "*Well, I found the secret to life. | I found the secret to life. | I'm okay when everything is not okay. | Yes, I found the secret to life. | I found the secret to life. | I'm okay when everything is not okay. Is not okaaaaaayyyyyy.*"[76]

Lily finally looks at me. The slightest hint of a smile tugs at her lips again. She's not able to resist my song. The smile pulls harder. Now it's in full bloom.

"Good." I add, "Now that I have you smiling; you know it's true, right?"

"I like the song. Too bad I have to *wait* to hear it."

Lily's grin feels like success to me. So much waiting! I laugh out loud at our wit, "Haha! How about this, visit me again, and I will play it for you. In the meanwhile, you have this superb set of pipes at your disposal," I point to my throat and bow.

Lily giggles and then admits, "You have a nice voice."

"Thank you. It's our voice. The voice you hear is thanks to your willingness to sing often and everywhere. In the car, in the shower, at the piano, with friends, with family, on road trips, on the bus, on a bike." I grin and wink. "You get the idea."

Lily's smile doesn't quit this time. She asks, "Really? I always thought I was just singing."

"Singing is an incredibly powerful tool. Not only is it pleasing to the ear, but it inspires different states of thinking. It is even like a massage inside you. The benefits of singing are too many to count."

"I didn't know that singing was so good for me."

"It is. You will sing no matter what, just because of who you are. Now that you know that singing is in your future, sing with all the joy and confidence you can."

"Well, if that is the case, like, that singing is so good for me, I'm going to try more. I'll try for more confidence, but I feel uncomfortable singing on my own. Still, like, I'm excited to imagine that in time that could change. Someday."

"With time and practice it will. Possibly sooner than you think."

She looks down the street again and back to me and sees my joy. She asks, "Wait. Like, I can come see you anytime?"

"Anytime. I hope you do." I assert, "I have two requests. First, keep writing. There are journals upon journals you fill in your future."

"That's easy, I like writing." As if on cue, Lily takes her backpack off, unzips it, and puts the diary and pen away. She asks, "What's your second request?"

"Remember the secret to life. You can be okay when everything is not okay."

"Like, that one is hard. I like it though, so I'll try." Lily looks down at her feet.

"Also, after I leave, know that I'm not far away. Come visit me as often as you need. Feel for me and I'll be there. You can sing with me or get support of any kind. I'm inside you, and you are inside me. Trust our connection. Follow your heart, the center of your donut." I smile in memory of our donut talk.

"Mmmmm donut."

"Mmmmm. Remember, the mind has thoughts, the heart has feelings. If it's a negative thought or you're spinning on that thought for a long time, your heart isn't involved. It's a subtle distinction, but important."

Lily doesn't know that we have reached the last entry in her journal writing for six years. Lily turns to face me. Her heart seems to know we have turned a corner together, and her hands reach for mine.

She says, "Okay. I'll do my best to follow my heart." Her face is much lighter since I arrived. In fact, she's shining. She's no longer looking up and down the street.

"I'm so glad. Your heart is where all the magic blossoms."

We sit there, fingers entwined, smiling at each other. Same eyes. Same smile. Lily. Astara. Bonded.

I close my eyes, and when I open them, I'm back in my basement. My desk is still a hodgepodge of journals. I can feel them waiting for me. I feel wistful. I know more of 12-year-old Lily is integrating within me this very moment. Her hands are mine. I can feel her smiling through my smile, sitting in some other dimension of time no longer waiting but just being. I sense this is just the beginning.

"I am practicing holding the tension of knowing and not knowing at once. I inhale the unwritten and exhale out the unanswered."

– Astara

The Void

I grab my small diary and turn it over in my hands. What a compelling time portal this red diary has been. I had first dismissed my short adolescent entries, not realizing the potency inside one simple sentence. When I began, I knew the power of soul return. Still, I hadn't realized how much I needed this threshold into myself, until I was inside it, inside me in a whole new way.

As I integrate my journeys within these passages of my first journal, a thought persists, *Why did I stop writing between my 1983 diary and my journal in 1989?*

For a soul that has writing in her blood, and over 30 more journals waiting to be filled in the decades ahead, this thought won't leave. I set the diary back down and go upstairs to busy myself in the kitchen making lunch.

Later, I go upstairs to my attic bedroom to journey and find out more. I sit on the bed and form a silent intention. I ask my inner child to tell me what I need to know to understand the gap in writing between 12 and 18. I connect with my Higher Self and ask for clarity. My fingertip scrolls to the shamanic drumming track on my phone. I tuck my earbuds into my ears and lay down. I surrender my intention, hit play, and close my eyes. As I entrain to the theta brain wave state, I connect with my spirit guides, my High Self, and my animal spirits again.

...

I have become raven. I am flying over my home, circling the roof, the decks, the pool, and the driveway. It is night and the only light is in my bathroom window. I see mom helping young me into a bath of ice. She is sitting by my side.

As raven's eyes blink, the next day comes. As raven, I fly in closer. There I am again. Mom's helping me into an ice bath. Raven jumps me through time. Sun sets, sun rises, and I see young me through the bathroom window. She's laying on the bathroom floor moaning.

Mom leaves to get something. I fly into our adjacent orange bedroom and become human again. I walk to look at the kitten calendar on the wall. It's 1983. My inner knowing whispers I am here just a few weeks after my last visit with Lily. I walk to the bathroom where 12-year-old me is lying out on the cool terrazzo floor, covered in hives. Lily's rubbing her arms with her hands trying to soothe and trying not to itch at the same time. There are ice cubes lying in the bathtub melting as the gurgle of the water draining almost finishes.

I sit down next to my young self and put my hand on her heart. She looks up at me and starts to cry. She is weak and can barely speak. She mutters, "Help."

I hold her hand and say, "I am here." I now remember the rash, the itching, the pain, and the fear. I had forgotten this. I start to cry too as it all comes back.

After young Lily writes the last diary entry, I got an ear infection. I got them all the time as a girl; it was my body's creative solution to protect me from hearing mom when she shifted to toxic words and criticism. This time, the doctor gives me a new antibiotic. Big large pills that are hard to swallow. What a metaphor. I take all of them.

A week later, feeling healed from the infection, back to school I went. In good spirits, I start to notice my belly feels tight and uncomfortable, and my face feels warm. I go to the bathroom to splash my face with cool water to soothe the heat. I look up and see hives across my 12-year-old face, neck, and arms.

I blink and my memory shifts. I'm at home. Mom is taking my temperature. It's 102 degrees.

I blink again. I'm shivering in an ice bath as my mom rushes around the bathroom gathering things. She's trying to get my fever down. I'm at 103 degrees.

I blink again and I'm on my bed whimpering from the pain, itching, and fever. The next day, I'm at 104 degrees now.

All this rushes back to me as I sit next to my young self on the floor. Lily's passed out and still hot. Her body is rejecting the medication. Mom is not back in the bathroom yet. I remember that years later my mom casually shares how I almost died during this allergic reaction to sulfa-based antibiotics. So, this is the memory I had blocked out.

I kneel at her side and move my hands over her, from head to toe, scanning her body while passing loving energy to her young, scared, and overtaxed body. As I do this, I commune with my helper spirits in all forms and ask for their assistance. I feel Archangel Michael stand-ing at her feet. He is passing violet light throughout my little body to systemically remove the foreign substance to reduce my inflammation.

My guides stand in a circle around young me, unwinding the toxins out of our young body and field while beaming healing energy. The spirit of black bear is next to me, radiating cool blue light over young me somewhere in another dimension. The blue soothes and quiets the remaining inflammation.

A deer spirit now stands in the bathroom and gently places her hoof on Lily's chest. She lifts her hoof and sets it back down, tapping soft tender love and grace to my young heart, like an electrical reset for her circulation and nervous system. Lily's heart is filled and surrounded by love. I see a healthy light returning to her core, instead of the physical fire trying to burn out the toxins.

Lily begins to stir. I feel her forehead and the temperature seems to be dropping. She opens her eyes and looks at me and our soul team gathered. I grab her hand again and say, "We've got you. Everything is going to be okay."

Lily tries for a smile and blinks her eyes at me in response. The bright red tone of her splotchy face and skin is lessening, she's starting to come down from the systemic inflammation she's been suffering through.

She slowly mumbles, "I'm so glad you're here."

"I am too." I move to sit cross-legged next to her and take her hand again. I state, "You are strong. You are amazing."

"What happened? Like, I don't remember much."

"Your body was rejecting the medication you took for your ear infection."

"Oh my God, those pills were awful. They were big and blue. I hated them. Like, they had the worst aftertaste. I took the whole bottle. Blech."

"Blech is right. Your body had quite the work out fighting the medication in your system. You've had a high fever for days. You had Mom scared; she's been working hard to care for you. Do you remember the ice baths?"

"Sort of. I remember feeling hot and cold at the same time. It was awful. I've been scared too. Why don't I remember?"

"You went deep into that in-between place we talked about last year after Sylvia died. Bardo. The void. You were here, but not here. You were in between the two. In fact, you almost died. In your future, you'll learn about something called shamanic deaths — this is a metaphor of what you went through this past week. You died to an old part of you. This is a threshold into a new world for you. In the coming days, you'll feel different. Pay attention and notice what has changed."

"I almost died? Totally crazy. I do remember feeling awful. Like, really really awful. It was horrible."

"Yes. While this is significant it's also overwhelming. I'll sit with you awhile. Rest."

"Okay." Lily closes her eyes and whispers, "Thank you."

I put my hand on hers as we sit there in silence.

I feel mom's energy coming down the hall. I remind her, "I'm just a thought away. Reach out when you need me." I wait until mom is closer before I fly home as raven.

• • •

I emerge from my vision. I lay there for a while, feeling a big energetic return in my body. Energy stuck and displaced is coming home. I breathe it in and feel it filling me up from head to toe. My fingertips and toes tingle. My nose and scalp tingles too. I feel rested. I roll out of bed and stand up. My whole body feels different.

A return of self brings vital energy, clearing my mind. My clarity reveals the domino of events: Sylvia's death, my near-death experience, adolescence, and a new interest in boys.

I silently thank young Lily for coming home and for all her hard work in those years. I imagine her soaring into my heart. I hold my hands over my heart and hug her invisible self to me. She sends me a smile across the dimensions. She's stronger in her timeline too.

I take the night off and go for a long walk, letting the cool air and silence of the trees help me integrate the return of so many lost parts.

I can't wait to explore the next journal.

*"It's all good and well to have something in the future, and
to hold on to something in the past, but if you don't live
for today, you don't live at all."*

– Lily Marie Livingston, 19 years old

San Diego

It is Tuesday, October 17, 2017. I wake up and immediately go to the basement to jump into the next journal. The hardbound cover is white with a floral print and lined pages are coming loose at the binding edge. I wrote in clean cursive, compared to my messier writing now. The journal starts April 10, 1989. I am 18.

From the front to the back, every single page is full of words. I am glued to the journal reading entry after entry, memories slowly return. In college now, I'm free of my childhood home. I no longer expend my energy to exist in a house with the unpredictable storm that is my mom or the politics of high school. I miss mom and dad, and I'm in the discomfort of beginner's mind, yet I'm relieved. I have space for writing again. I'm ready to take on the world.

In my first year of college, I go to the University of California San Diego, in La Jolla, California, for eight months. When I lean out far enough on the balcony of my dorm suite, I can see the Pacific Ocean. I look down to the volleyball courts and lawn three floors below.

Lily writes a dream from an afternoon nap.

I am on a boat. Not just any boat. It is square and white with stained wood. I am on this boat with Aidan, my current boyfriend, and other people I don't know. Carra from high school was there, and we were all going to another boat to watch her perform a routine. I got up my nerve to tell Aidan my decision, and it didn't go well. He wanted to be alone. Then I went and sat on the deck looking at the ocean. It was wavy, a silvery grey-blue with a touch of lavender. The horizon was peach with no sun.

The phone rings and it is Duston, my high school boyfriend. He asks me, "Who is there?" He was making sure I was alone on the ship. Which was impossible, there were so many people. My mind was on Aidan, as if any final decision was up to him. I began describing the beautiful ocean to Duston. Suddenly, a large dark creature is swimming below the surface towards us and disappears underneath the boat. I gasp, frightened. I forgot about the phone and Duston.

I yell to everyone on the boat, "Did you see that?"

It was a killer whale. It was zipping fiercely back and forth. I began directing the movement of the boat by yelling "Left!" and then "Right!" so that everyone could see the whale. Nobody could see it but me.

We almost crashed into the ship my friend was going to perform on. It was named "Anastasia." An incredible wind started blowing people off our ship. I kept hanging on to sturdy parts of the ship. I had to keep moving along to stay ahead of each piece of the ship railing braking off in the strong wind.

I search for Aidan. He is with other people. A woman he is with suggests we all climb into the water onto the ice. She and Aidan crawl onto a piece of ice. I crawl alone onto another. I am whimpering and sad. The woman asks Aidan, "Why is she whimpering?" He replies, "It is because she doesn't understand my silence yet." Monday, May 5, 1989.

Many years later, instead of experiencing silence as tranquil, I still translate the quiet company of others as cool, removed, judging, or critical. My father was often stoic, my mother was often critical. I introjected both, internally weaving them. I'm amazed at my insight at that age. Converting others' silence — which is most likely benign — into a reflection of my inner critic, has generated unnecessary anxiety for decades.

Eighteen-year-old me sends off a flare across time. I close my eyes and hear my heart song; I connect with the center of my toroidal field of energy. When I open my eyes, I'm standing in my dorm room. Lily at 18 is perched on the twin bed, writing down the dream. I can feel the ocean air through the open window. The dorm walls are white. My bed is covered in a white and teal floral bedspread with matching sheets. I remember buying those sheets with my mother. I hesitate, not wanting to startle Lily.

Young me turns and sees me. She drops the journal on the bed. The pages flip shut by gravity and the pen rolls off the bed onto the floor.

"Wha? What? Hello?" Lily stammers.

"Hi." I offer sheepishly, "I'm sorry to startle you."

She is groggy from her nap. She has the most endearing mark pressed in her cheek from her pillow.

I softly state, "I am you. I am your future. Don't be scared. I'm reading from that journal you're writing in." I point to the floral book resting on the floral bedding. "The strong feelings from the dream you just wrote brought me to you. We met years ago in a similar way. Do you remember?"

What a moment to wake up to. She steadies her breath. Lily eases to the edge of her bed and looks at me. Again, it's our same eyes that calm her. She's trying to place something in her mind as she looks at me and then up at the corner of the room and back to me again.

I offer more information. "In my timeline, I just visited your, our, 12-year-old self yesterday. A few nights ago, I visited our five-year-old self. I'm on a mission to connect all our ages and bring us home to each other. Our writing is a time portal. The journal of you at 12-years-old began this reunion, and now the journal sitting right there on your bed." I take a breath and continue, "You're writing after a six-year hiatus. I'm so glad you're writing again."

"Six years. I didn't even think about it. I just got this journal for an English class. I love writing every day." She bends to pick up her fallen pen and shifts back on the bed. Lily looks at her diary and says, "Well, almost every day." She's watching me now and says, "You do look familiar."

I keep talking in hopes my words will help her remember our

meeting from years before her timeline, "Let's talk about your amazing dream."

"My dream just now?" She looks down my body; when her eyes move back up to meet mine, her body starts to relax.

"Yes. You are on a boat with Aidan and others. There is a killer whale that only you can see. It ends with Aidan telling another woman you don't understand his silence."

Lily's eyes get big, "That is my dream! Like, you read the whole thing?"

Her valley girl inflection has diminished, yet it lingers subtly. I affirm, "Yes. This is not a new concept to you, this ability to leap across time and space. You know the Richard Bach book you're reading, *Bridge Across Forever?*[77] Just like the time travel in that book, you are co-creating this with me." I assert, "I wouldn't be able to be here without our desire and consciousness for something like this to be possible." That book was pivotal in our life, showing us a new way to view the world.

"This is totally cool." Her lips curve into a smile. "You know, there *is* something familiar about you. It feels like a dream I can't quite remember."

I grin, "It's all a dream. When you were 12, we talked about how life's a waking dream, just as much as we dream when we sleep. I'm thrilled to see you, me, at 18. I remember our roommate Clara, this room, the smell of the ocean. The ever-distant sounds of waves as white noise through the window. Walking through extensive groves of Eucalyptus trees across campus to class. Bike rides at night singing James Taylor songs with our dormmate, Jessani. Have you done that yet?"

"Yes!" Lily's jaw has dropped.

I continue, "Long conversations about architecture with your roommate Clara. Hiking down to nearby Black's Beach surrounded by surfers and nudists alike. Solving calculus problems in your dreams. The small group English class, your favorite Biology professor and his fantastic teaching style, and falling in love with modern dance. So many hours dancing. All of it."

"Wow. That's amazing. It's been great to be so close to the ocean. Like, there are so many amazing things here." Lily's smile now takes up real estate, and she asks, "So, what do you think about my dream? I love talking about dreams." She shifts on the bed to make room for me.

I sit down next to her. "I do too. Okay, so I think the whale represents the unknown hidden hopes of your future. It's coming, hunting for you, and about to change your relationship to life and everyone around you. Only you can feel it and see it. No one else knows your deepest desire or is able to advise you."

Lily moves to her pillows and props herself against the wall. She states, "That makes sense. The future and my desires are exciting to me, but exciting is also scary."

"That's it. The unknown is a lot to contend with." I scoot and lean against the side wall to face her at the foot of the bed. "Aidan is a main character because you're processing him in your life. What to do, how to talk to him, stay with him, or leave. You fear leaving the ship of your relationship."

Lily slaps her hands on the bed beside her and exclaims, "The ship of our relationship! I love that."

I chuckle. "At the end of the dream, Aidan says, 'She doesn't understand my silence yet.' That is such a potent moment. It's something we still struggle with, and I'm 47!"

Lily is looking quietly at me. She's afraid of leaving Aidan, however irritating he is at the time. After all, I'm a hopeful romantic. She states, "You don't look almost 50."

"Why, thank you."

"How exciting to see what I will look like! You give me hope." Lily looks away shyly and slowly looks back at me, "And it's true, I don't like silence."

My chin bounces in agreement. "It's okay that we have a hard time with silence." I ask, "What does silence mean to you?"

"It means I'm invisible, unwanted, or not important. Sometimes it means I'm being judged or criticized. I feel it sometimes with dad, Sierra, or Tim. I don't know why I don't feel it as much with mom.

Her silence I just take as her sadness or depression. I also feel it with friends. It's hard to describe, it feels unsettling."

"Very unsettling. That's because we make assumptions about what silence means based on our insecurities and the past. Silence could mean peaceful contemplation, or someone is so comfortable with you, they don't have to speak."

Lily asks, "What does silence mean to you?"

"Silence to me can still be scary because of our powerful inner critic. Our inner critic takes the quiet and uses it as fuel to convert all that space into criticism."

"That's exactly how I feel."

"Yet, with practice I've learned over the years that I often misunderstand silence. You can ask good questions to check your assumptions, like asking the person with you how they're feeling. Knowing we typically have an incorrect assumption about silence is the first step. From a place of awareness, evolution flows. It's going to take practice to create confidence inside of silence. You'll practice this with others; it's usually only triggered when you're with someone else." I wink at her. "And you can start now — earlier than almost 50."

"What about the ice and that other woman? What do you think that means?"

"I sense the ice represents our fear of silence and that familiar feeling of being *ice-olated* — alone and emotionally frozen in an uncaring world. It's a play on words, *ice-olation*. The woman represents your fear of Aidan rejecting or not wanting you anymore. The woman is also the confidence you wish you had or that confidence when you met Aidan for the first time and hadn't felt your insecurities yet. Most of all, the ice is how you *ice-olate* yourself to stay safe. Ultimately, such *ice-olation* keeps you from the intimacy you desire."

Lily sits in silence. She's hunched over her crossed legs thinking, folding, and unfolding her hands. She sits up. "I heard recently that all the parts of dreams are parts of ourselves. But sometimes I think they're actual premonitions too. I like what you're saying, because then the dream gets to be both a reflection of me and a vision at the same time."

"That's beautiful. I'm so glad you get this." I move so I'm fully facing her to ask, "Would you consider telling yourself a new story when next triggered by silence?"

"Yes. I want to."

"The new story is you're enough, you're loved, and you're supported. I know at times it appears to be the opposite."

"I do feel alone sometimes. And criticized."

"I know. It's a lifelong journey. I struggle with it as well, but what I've learned is the belief in being abandoned or criticized is an emotional habit. We're used to it from our childhood, so we manufacture that experience again and again because we identify with it. Will you close your eyes for me? I want to take you on a thought journey."

"Okay." Lily closes her eyes.

My voice is low and even. "My sitting here helps you know that you have *you*. You might see me, or you might hear me in your thoughts. You can call on other ages of you as well." I wait a moment and say, "You have loving allies everywhere: in nature, your dreams, family, and friends. Even trees can support you; listen when they talk to you and trust what you hear."

Lily's eyes are still closed and her lips curl up slightly. She pronounces, "I do love trees. I forgot I used to talk to them."

"Trees are smart, and they have a great sense of humor. You have other allies that you can't see. You have soul guides that have been with you for lifetimes, and they come whenever you call. You have angels around you, but they can only help if you ask. You have God. At my age, I call God the Presence of All That Is, or Universe, or Source energy. You can have conversations with your guides, angels, or God. They listen deeply and have great wisdom. Start to notice their presence and communicate with them on purpose."

"I feel tingly all over listening to you. My heart feels warm and good, like I can breathe deeper."

"Good. Now, open your eyes and look around the room. Does anything feel different?"

"Everything feels different. I do feel less alone." Lily opens her eyes and turns to me. "Like, for a while at least. You mentioned the ice in the dream could be *ice-olation*. I love that play on words. Maybe I isolate myself because I'm expecting to be abandoned. Or I abandon myself when I'm hard on myself."

"That is gorgeous. I agree and think they both exist simultaneously. Our biggest fear is abandonment. It is so big we believe in it. So, we keep seeing it and expecting it. Ironically, we abandon ourselves when we turn our inner critic inward and that important aspect of us starts to really beat us up."

"That's it! I am afraid of abandonment yet doing it all the time — to me!"

I sigh with relief hearing young me so aware. I offer, "Let's look at the ice further. Think of water as being a lot like emotions. *E-motion* is energy in motion. Ice is frozen emotion or held energy. If you are isolating yourself to keep your emotions safe, there are feelings you need to melt."

"Like, the floating pieces of ice could be certain emotions I ride on to get where I need to go! Or something like that."

"Ohhhh. That's brilliant. Here's another cool perspective for you. Feelings, even intense ones, are temporary. If you don't shove them down or hold them as thoughts — if you allow yourself to feel them fully — you will move through them faster. In time, what used to take you weeks to process, will take days, then hours, and eventually minutes. Find a safe place and just feel. You can feel your way to the next best choice. It works, I promise. For men, career, friends, family, and well, everything."

"Feeling everything is like not fun."

"During, yes. But ironically, it's your ticket to fun on the other side. Doubting your feelings, looking outside for validation, suppressing feelings to protect others, and *ice-olating* — it creates less fun. Leaning in to the not-so-fun-stuff, frees you up. Fun is on the other side of difficulty. Plus, some feelings, even anger and frustration can be downright pleasurable. Stomp around. Hit a pillow. Sob. Roar. Just move that energy! A good cry thaws out our *ice-olation*."

"Wild!"

"Every year or so look back and re-read your journals, you'll notice a pattern. You write about some of your sad days and frustrations, and then a day or two later you write about all the good of your life and how happy you are. The waves are a natural part of life. Get to know them. See success as a process. Success is found in both the inhale and exhale. Success is embracing both the tide coming in as well as going out. The ebb and flow of sad and happy makes you, *you*. All of you, the dark and the light, belong. This is the key to peace inside and ultimately peace on this planet."

"Totally awesome! Phew, like, do I have a lot to practice."

"I practice every day in your future. It's a life practice but you'll get better at it in time." I stand up grinning. "How about a hug?"

"I'd like that." Lily stands up and walks to me; we're the same height now. I wrap my arms around her and hold her close.

"Astara," Lily whispers in my ear.

"Yes?"

"Where does that name come from again? Did you tell me when I was 12?"

"I don't think we talked about it in depth." I lean back and look Lily in the eye, "It comes from the stars."

I see Lily's smile as I close my eyes and follow my heart home. I'm sitting at my basement writing desk, and only five minutes have passed. I'm amazed that reunion with my 18-year-old is giving me clues of wisdom for my present timeline. She's given me a new attitude about silence, not leaving myself, and feeling my feelings. I spend the day spaciously, not doing a lot. The space gives me plenty of feelings to flow through to the other side. I lean in and stomp around when needed, cry, laugh, and dance around the house.

Day shifts to night. After dinner, I go out back to stand on our deck. The treetops are swaying in the evening breeze, playing hide and seek with the almost full moon. Thinking of my advice to 18-year-old me about connecting with my allies, I ask the trees, *what advice have you got for me tonight?*

The trees whisper, *Do as we do. Where do our roots grow? In the dark. Where do our leaves grow? Towards the light. We support and extend at the same time. Do as we do.*

Those trees are so smart.

"It's fun to close our eyes and in the dark, say to ourselves-
...I am the sorceress, and when I open my eyes I shall see a
world that I have created, and for which I and only I am
responsible...slowly then, eyelids open like curtains lifting
stage center. And sure enough, there's our world just the
way we built it."

– Richard Bach[78]

Architecture

It is Wednesday, October 18, 2017. In the morning, after breakfast, I head downstairs to the wood desk and sit down. I grab my 18-year-old's floral journal and open it.

Poring through my entries over the years, the men I date are a main focus as I seek a partner. Pages and pages of writing my philosophies and poetry are fueled by my search for love.

In my 18-year-old's timeline, it is late spring and I'm days away from summer break after my freshman year of college. I'm only two weeks from turning 19 and moments away from moving up north. Do I write about that? No.

I write about my boyfriend Aidan again. At 18-years-old, I brood as I try to make sense of relationships. I giggle quietly yet I also feel for my young self. I remember the angst.

Whatever it may be, I know there is a reason for all things. Aidan's bad moods are all a product of something. The first law of thermo-dynamics applies to life itself. You can't get something from nothing, and that's true for all problems.

I pride myself on trying to be different and making a good change for the better. Being different doesn't mean wearing different clothes, listening to different music, or having different colored hair. It means going against what's (taught and seemingly) natural and (comfortable) easy to be an honest, good, and healthy individual. In that way, the final means becomes a way of life. Sunday, June 4, 1989.

Decades later, I know what young me doesn't: my soul mission is to learn about connection and intimacy. Because of that, there's a lot of relationship processing in my journals.

From ages 12 to 18, my language evolves in leaps and bounds. I'm emerging into the philosopher poet I'm slated to be. My inner 18-year-old and I have much to teach each other. Does she know she's onto the truth? From this passage, I'm in joy that my talk with her about thermodynamics at age 12 took hold. My skin prickles in acknowledgment.

My boyfriend Aidan was a study in contrasts, vacillating between connection and withdrawal. He fit right into my push-pull-mood-swing-familial-legacy of what I thought intimacy was. I was drawn to him like a moth to the flame. Somewhere in the automatic pilot of my subconscious I thought *this is what love is.* Aidan and I were friends in high school; his loving attention provided comfort and familiarity as I leapt into the beginner's mind of college.

In my first year living away from home, I move to a familiar city — San Diego — where my sister Maribel lives. I hadn't even visited the college before I apply, get accepted, and decide to go. To me, it was a chance to get away, yet it was close to a beach and at least one family member. Being near Maribel anchored me against the awkwardness of being a freshman. Plus, I wanted to get to know Maribel better.

I thought I knew what I wanted life to be like when I grew up. Once I got to college, it became clear I didn't know. I wanted to fall in love, get married, and make a family. Yet, I wanted more than marriage and a baby. I wanted to dance, write, and make art. Yet, dancing and writing my life away didn't feel like it was enough for my credibility in the world. I internalized the expectations I picked up from my parents and the culture around me. I defaulted to wanting a responsible life that would be impressive in others' eyes, especially my parents.

I was "undeclared" as a major during my first year in college, and now it was time to choose. I took a career test. It's four hours long, spread over two days, and spits out a large printout. At the end it lists possible careers for my personality with potential incomes. From lowest income to highest it lists: Dance Teacher, Writer, Lawyer, and Architect.

At that time, I'm dancing 18 hours a week, auditioning for dance roles in college performances, and landing some roles. Yet, I didn't see myself making a living as a dancer. I convinced myself, *I can always dance on the side.*

At that time, I can't see how to make a career out of writing. I convinced myself, *I can always write on the side.*

Lawyer is listed as the one with the highest potential income. I'm a good communicator and researcher. Why not Lawyer? Something about being a lawyer felt uncomfortable and sad.

In that moment, 18-year-old Lily's thoughts and questions about her future weave with my memory and start to pull at me across time. I invite her to come to me with my heart and mind. I think, "I am here. I love you."

Eighteen-year-old me stands by my writing desk, blinking, and looking all around. Her eyes land on me and she says softly, "Hi."

"Hi! Welcome to your future."

"That's where I am?"

"Yes, you're in the basement of your future home. Your future partner isn't here, but your cat Orion is." Orion kitty comes strolling in and weaving a figure eight between Lily's legs.

"How did I get here again?"

"You may remember from when you were small that time travel involves emotion and sound."

Lily's face tightens in concentration as her brow raises. She says, "Emotion and sound." She places her hand on her heart and says, "It's starts in the heart, doesn't it?"

I affirm, "You got it. Pretty cool, huh." I point to the journals piled high to my left. I stand up and show her the one I have open from her timeline and close it.

Once she sees the cover and the inside writing, she stands still staring. "Um. Wow. Like, I don't have words."

"Well, actually, you have quite a lot of them." I smile and point to the journals.

She laughs, "I do."

I say, "I want to take you to a pivotal memory when we were 15. Will you come with me?"

"Yes!" She seems excited now.

I put my hand out, and she puts her hand in mine. I say, "Close your eyes, feel me, listen to any high tone you hear. It is your heart." Hand in hand, I feel where I want to take her and follow the high tone of my heart. Lily squeezes my hand tight as if to emit joy.

We're in our Los Angeles home. We stand on the white terrazzo floor holding hands at the edge of the great room by the kitchen where we ate most of our meals. The rest of the family cannot see us. Fifteen-year-old Lily cannot see us — yet.

Younger Lily sits at the kitchen table. Our sister Maribel is visiting and has joined us for dinner. Someone asks Lily what she's thinking about studying at college. Lily answers with enthusiasm, "I'm considering law. I love words and talking. I like the idea of advocating for others' rights."

Lily opens her mouth to say more, when Maribel, with a playful eye roll, chides out loud, "Lily? A lawyer? Hah!"

The table is silent for a moment. Before anyone can see her upset, Lily runs from the dinner table past us and down the hall to her room. We follow her. We hear soft laughter in the distance. Everyone keeps talking. No one comes after her.

Crushed, sad, small, and feeling dismissed, some of Lily's power leaves the table with her.

I can feel 15-year-old Lily think, *"Maybe Maribel is right. Me being a lawyer is laughable."*

My eyes lock with 18-year-old me. It seems we can both hear

younger Lily's feelings. She turns the corner from the hall into our orange bedroom. We release our hands and walk into the room after her. She slumps onto the bed. We both walk near the bed on opposite ends. She feels us and looks up. She looks at 18-year-old Lily with wonder. Older, but not much older.

Eighteen-year-old Lily takes her gaze as recognition. She steps forward to face younger Lily and says, "No wonder I can't imagine myself in law school. That memory got shoved way down so, like, I didn't remember. How amazing that it influences me nonetheless."

I answer, "Yes. That is why I wanted to take you here." I turn to 15-year-old me on the bed and ask, "How are you?"

"Bummed. But it's good to see you."

I am glad she remembers me. I enjoy watching her watch her slightly older college self. I sit down on the bed and affirm. "We saw what went down at the dinner table. I'm sorry."

Fifteen-year-old Lily looks down at her lap and says, "Yeah. It's typical."

Eighteen-year-old Lily sits down on the bed as well. "I'm not sure Maribel was right to poke fun, but like, I understand why she'd laugh. We would technically be good at being a Lawyer. But now, like, a few years later, I see that I wouldn't be fulfilled in the long run."

Younger Lily looks up at the slightly older version of herself in wonder. She gazes at her and admits, "You're probably right. Still, that totally hurt back there."

I offer, "It's no fun to be laughed at."

Eighteen-year-old me agrees, "Yeah. It totally stings when others laugh at us." She offers, "But maybe Maribel didn't mean it to be hurtful?" Her inflection both asks and states at the same time.

I pile on, "Maribel means well. She gets much better at being your sister and friend in the years ahead. You guys will get closer." I stop and say, "We came to give you love and remind you that you're magnificent. You can do anything you want in this world. Don't worry. Once you decide, if you don't like it, you can change your mind again."

Both ages of Lily look at me and then each other.

I stand up and suggest, "Would you guys be up to try something?"

"Sure," says 15-year-old Lily.

Eighteen-year-old me nods and stands up. The youngest Lily stands up from the bed and meets us in a circle.

We hold hands and I say, "Repeat after me."

They look at me, curious.

I claim, "I can do anything I want to do in this world."

And in unison they claim, "I can do anything I want to do in this world."

There are three equally strong smiles and the same eyes looking at each other. Youngest Lily giggles. And then we all do. I turn to youngest Lily and ask, "How do you feel after making such a claim?"

"Better."

"Good. Would you go back to dinner and give Maribel another chance?"

"Yes."

"We're here should you ever need us. Just reach out."

Fifteen-year-old me says, "Okay." She walks to her door and turns to look at us before she heads back down the hall. She's smiling.

I walk over and grab 18-year-old Lily's hand and say, "Close your eyes, feel me, listen deeply."

We are standing back in my house in front of my desk. Eighteen-year-old Lily's eyes are big. "How amazing. I could feel our younger self. I could feel her disappointment."

"At the dinner table, she was experiencing what I call power loss. We helped her find her power again, which means you have more energy inside you now, so does she, and so do I. Every time you heal, you give a gift of healing to me. That applies for all our ages. And even our entire family."

"I can feel it." Her eyes fall upon the long gold antique couch in front of the ottoman. Lily walks over to the gold couch and sits down. "So, I've narrowed my choices down from my career list."

"Oh, do tell."

"Well, after dance, writing, and law, I'm left with architect on my career test list. I've been thinking about it — I do love math and I also love drawing. It seems a logical conclusion to do something that combines them. So…"

I nod and insert, "Whatever you decide, don't let the memory of Maribel's unskilled moment or the pressure you put on yourself from others sway you. Make big life decisions for you."

"Well, I do feel a lot of pressure inside."

Lily looks around at a small slice of her future for clues. I love watching her take my world in. She's in a basement surrounded by art supplies. She notices the artful ottoman upholstered with a brown, blue, and gold floral rug on casters in front of her.

Afternoon sun streams through the high basement window onto the dark blue Asian rug under the couch. A modern cherry wood TV stand holds a books, VCR, DVD, and pictures of mom and dad when they first met in college.

Her eyes glance at Ryan's woodworking power tools off to the other side of the basement, the hint of masculinity and her future partner. She doesn't recognize his grandmother's painting leaning on an easel.

Her eyes rest on my drawing tools and paintbrushes right in front of her, and the large black portfolio case leaning against the wall. The same portfolio filled with many of the drawings that she'll start within the year.

I reach for Lily's hand, and she takes my fingers between hers. With my hand in hers, she shares, "I am not sure what I will do, but this has been amazing to meet our 15-year-old self. And to be here. Thank you."

"It's my pleasure. Literally."

Lily looks around again, soaking it in. She closes her eyes. "I'm so content here. It's hard to explain."

I'm smiling. I confirm, "I feel the same. You are amongst a world that is all yours. A world made by you. No wonder you feel good here."

Lily asks nervously, "Will I see you again?"

She can feel the energy fading and the summer of 1989 pulling her back.

I say, "Absolutely. Any time you want. Just reach out and so will I." I lean in and whisper, "Our connection works in both directions."

Growing up in Los Angeles, with family in the movie industry, we have seen so many films. A part of her wants to be in the future already. The urge to skip the scary parts is in all of us. I can feel the pressure she's putting on herself for the choice she is facing, as she begins to carve her world out of the clay of the universe.

I squeeze her hand. She looks me in the eye. I impart, "Trust in what you decide. You can always change your mind." I take a deep breath for us both adding, "You got this. I love you."

"I love you." Lily claims into the air for all our ages. With that, she's gone.

Hearing "I love you" from my 18-year-old mouth changes me. My heart feels as wild and powerful as the Pacific Ocean, right here in the middle of the prairie.

The universe will offer neon signs to help 18-year-old Lily's decision. Our roommate Clara has a dream of becoming an architectural engineer and becomes someone to talk about it with. Across the dorm hall, on the boy's side, my dormmate Robert is dreaming of becoming an architect and talks about it with Lily. Between the career test, the prestige of the title "architect," as well as having two college friends headed in that direction, signs accumulate.

It is a decision that changes the trajectory of our life. I know with all my heart that my adventures are not to change the past or alter big decisions because each one is a part of my soul classroom and necessary to my growth. I show up to younger me only to help me see a new perspective and to love, support, and sing any lingering or lost ghosts of myself back home. This is how I can influence the world from inside out.

Architecture is not an option at the University of California San Diego, so I leave the southern beaches and vast eucalyptus groves in La Jolla for the shimmering bay and redwoods of Berkeley, California. My older sister Sierra is attending Berkeley, so it's an easy decision to head north.

Sierra generously extends an invite to stay with her for a few days to figure out my next steps. I crash out with Sierra and her roommates for a while and then decide to move in. I take a Berkeley architecture summer design course to feel out the new career direction. I buy a large black portfolio case. I start to draw those drawings I just saw in my future basement.

I head upstairs and make lunch.

> *"Time endures, the past does not wholly disappear. The future is forever showing itself in the present."*
>
> – J.T. Fraser

Berkeley

After lunch, I sit down again at my desk to read more. I pluck the ripest entries. I look for signs of change. I notice a note I wrote in a different color pen.

This is the first entry in my room at Oxford House. Berkeley, it is. Next stop, Architecture. Thursday, July 13, 1989.

A slightly older 19-year-old Lily has decided.

I knew our brief meeting wasn't going to alter our decision. Yet, as I read, her words come alive for me. I see signs that she remembers our meeting, that she feels me with her. Quotes about time and the heart occur throughout the journal. She mentions, "There's a certain spirit that has returned to me," echoing of the soul return and claim with 15-year-old Lily.

I move to Oxford Street in North Berkeley, California. I live upstairs with Sierra and six pre-med students in a large Arts and Crafts bungalow with a big porch that first summer. The landlord divided the 1910's house into three student apartments. The entire cast of roommates in Sierra's upstairs flat were pre-med. A focused and demanding education makes for stressed roommates. In spring, the scent from an old Wisteria vine would rise into our upstairs windows as the porch is consumed in lavender and white blossoms.

After my first summer course at UC Berkeley, I move to a small apartment on Hillegass Street in south Berkeley on the other side of campus for a short while. One of my favorite things about that place: it was only a block from the famous Berkeley Baptist Divinity School designed by Julia Morgan. As the first licensed woman architect in California, and one of the first female architects on the planet, she was a hero.

Her design is a brick and concrete Tudor building with a slate roof, and just off the sidewalk, a grand cloister of arches leading to a garden within. She got her design influence for this building from Oxford University, England. I feel regal pretending I'm in London when I walk by on my way to class. As I amble through the arches, I fantasize I am the next Julia Morgan.

Freshly ensconced in a new apartment, 19-year-old Lily writes in excitement.

Well, I'm back! It is yet another month I've survived. I seem to live this life, holding my breath. Pleased [and surprised] as each month, year, decade, passes by and I'm still a normal functioning human. I've learned with each day, more and more, especially this summer, with the big decision I made to move up north and pursue architecture. It was scary, and I must say, I'm still very much scared.

Yet, there is a certain spirit that has returned to me. One that I've missed. A certain confidence that has let me take chances and make choices that have shaped my future. One that I feel will bring knowledge and wisdom with each passing moment of time.

I feel as if this past summer I was blindfolded and then I ripped off the blindfold to expose myself to the bright light of reality, where dreams take root and grow to beanstalks in the sky.

Instead of blinding me, this light is nourishing me. I feel a center to my being; my soft tummy holds my "well" being. My body is a sanctuary for my soul, my heart the guide to lead the two down a path to the many wonders of the world.

I've been reborn this summer, and I can't wait to do it again. The morning walks, the silent time to think, the schoolwork, the "work"

work, the thoughts of love, the essence of my life has taken on a whole new meaning!

Now I can throw my head back, look the sky straight in the eye and admit to it: "I'm scared." In return it just seems to keep still except for the one cloud that winks back at me in understanding. Saturday, September 2, 1989.

In my basement, I shout spontaneously, "Whoo hoo!" with a fist pump across spacetime. Young me is feeling into fears and finding the joy on the other side. Lily's looking to the sky as her mentor, with a new understanding of winking thought clouds. It's thrilling to understand our multidimensional meetings have woven into our very being in that timeline. And now mine.

As I read, I feel Lily hear my whoop and cheer. Sound has done it again. As my enthusiastic heart hurls me towards her in time, I feel the whoosh of air at a cellular level and my ears feel a pressure differential like I just jumped in water or climbed higher in elevation.

I open my eyes and stand above Lily sitting on her roommates' bean bag in her new apartment. She's smiling.

"Astara!" She exclaims.

"Hi!" I'm thrilled and words start pouring out, "Berkeley! And architecture! I am so proud you made this leap north."

Lily beams, "It's been so strange and overwhelming and new." Her face changes. She leans in and whispers, "Still, I'm freaking out."

"That's completely normal. You are going through a lot of change and fast." I look around the room for a place to sit and choose a spot on the floor in front of Lily. I continue, "I love what you wrote just now, *'There is a certain spirit that has returned to me. One that I've missed.'* I believe that is thanks to meeting up with our 15-year-old self." I say smiling.

"Like, that was totally life changing." She's wiggling in her bean bag, and I hear the crunch of the beans inside with each shimmy. "I'm so glad you are here!"

"Me too, love." I read more back to her, "I also love, *'my body is a sanctuary for your soul, my heart the guide to lead the two down a path to the many wonders of the world.'* We've talked over the years about the heart as a time travel machine. Your words are so poetic."

"Thank you. I had fun writing that."

"Would you be up for a tour of the heart?"

She leans back into her bean bag with a crunch and says, "I would love that." The sun peeks at the edge a tall window facing west with a limited view of the bay in the distance. Her day is beginning its slow wind down to dusk.

> *"The scientist knows that in the history of ideas, magic*
> *always precedes science, that the intuition of phenomena*
> *anticipates their objective knowledge."*
>
> – *Michael Gaugelin*[79]

Black Whole

We sit facing each other in the living room of her South Berkeley apartment. The brown carpet, the white walls, the aluminum windows. A plain modern 1950's apartment building, without ornament. Aesthetically minimal, but to Lily, it's her first apartment away from family of any kind and aesthetics are not her priority right now. She exudes freedom from every pore.

I lean in and say, "I traveled in time and talked to our five-year-old self the other day and we talked about our superpower. Do you remember what your superpower is?"

Lily looks up, thinking to herself. "Superpower. I'm guessing it's something to do with my sensitivity. No matter how I try, I can't seem to get rid of it."

"You got it. Sensitivity is your superpower."

"It seems to drive my family and other people crazy."

"Sensitivity takes time to understand and build skills for. It also makes others uncomfortable if they're scared of feelings — theirs or yours. When you feel, it's an invitation for them to feel. When you understand their feelings and they don't, that causes discomfort. When you don't understand your feelings and they are near, they feel discomfort. All of the above scares them."

"I hadn't thought of it that way."

"The wisdom of the heart is planted beautifully inside us. You want to know why you can never get rid of your ability to feel deep, big, bodacious feelings? The Earth needs you to live into your superpower. We are in desperate need of humans who understand their feelings so they can practice intimacy and relationships better. At a soul level, you know you're this sensitive for a reason. We lose faith because it's not an easy superpower. You don't shy away from difficult, challenging feelings that many people do not let themselves feel in their lifetime."

"But it makes me sad. I wish there were more people that wanted to understand feelings."

"There are more old soul sensitives on this planet now. No matter the soul age or the feeling skills, each soul is here to do important work. First, you need to make friends with your superpower. That will magnetize those like you."

She breathes in deeply, then exhales loudly and says, "It's a doozy of a power. Where does it come from?"

"Your heart."

Lily laughs and rolls her eyes, "Well, duh."

I laugh, "This concept comes naturally to you." *If only she knew that the eye roll activates her visionary pineal gland and higher brain center,* I think to myself. I say, "The heart is how you and I are sitting here together. Yet, you live in a world that ignores the elegant simplicity of our heart and denies the intelligence of intuition. There's new science just about to emerge in a few years, right in your backyard, that will demonstrate the power of the heart."

"In the Bay Area?"

I smile and sigh, "Yep. It will be called the HeartMath Institute." [80] Oh, how I miss the Bay Area.

Lily grins as I sigh and says, "Totally amazing. Right here."

"You will literally live on the pulse of that science. As you grow, they will grow in their heart research. The heart is the key to *every-thing*. It's a compass to help you navigate your life: your joy, purpose, knowledge, direction, and soul learning. Your heart holds all the knowledge of your soul across lifetimes and dimensions. Your heart *is* the bridge across forever, like the title of your favorite Richard

Bach book. In that book, his love connected him to his beloved across time to explore lives they live in other dimensions."

Lily nods, "In that book, I found a writer who thought like me. It opened my mind."

"It's a mind-blowing read! Maybe it opened up our mind enough to drop us in our heart?" I smile and raise my eyebrows a few times for significance. "It's your love and your heart that allows us to connect. It's what pulls you to write in your journals. Now and for years to come, we're leaving each other breadcrumbs to find and love all the parts of us — lost, alone, or scared — into wholeness again."

Lily slowly rocks side to side in her bean bag. I hear its crunch as she says, "When I came to you, I couldn't believe it. All I had to do was close my eyes, listen, and *feel* you."

I smile and rub my hands together, "Exactly. The heart is, literally, the center of your universe, it's a black hole. In the future, a physicist Nassim Haramein discovers that black holes are not points of singularity that devour light ad infinitum. Instead, a black hole is an infinite point of singularity that generates life. There's a black hole inside of every atom and subatomic particle inside you, in the center of our universe and out into the largest scale of multi-verses into infinity."[81]

Lily sits up straighter. "When I was young, I can't remember which science fiction book gave me the idea, but I sensed black holes were not the "dark" force others described! Even though I couldn't prove it, I knew they created life." Lily's breathless with excitement and quickly adds, "In physics class, our professor talks about what you told me at 12 — how the physics of gravity, the big, and the physics of the quantum, the small, are at odds with each other in the science world. They agree to disagree for years now."

"I'm glad you got confirmation. Even in my day, many physicists disagree with Nassim's cutting edge theory, mostly because he connects science to the spiritual, saying we're all connected in our infinite nature; it's the way we're made."

Lily replies, "I just got a book on Chaos theory and fractals. It's difficult to read; I'm skimming through to learn about fractal patterns. I've loved pattern games since I was a kid."

"I still have that important book on my shelf," I wink. "Chaos theory shapes the quantum evolution. By the way, our pattern-seeking mind will make you a great architect." I smile and lift my eyebrows a few more times. I keep going, "Patterns and fractals. They're critical to Nassim's unification theory. If you want to find something that connects all things, what would it be?"

Lily asserts, "Patterns?"

"Yes. Patterns *and* space. Our atomic structure is made of 99.99999% space. What we call reality is not what we think, the material world is only .0000001% solid. Given that we are more space than anything else, space is what connects all. Other physicists focus on particle acceleration to find the 'God particle' — the smallest particle as a key to creation — but there's no such thing because a particle is made of infinity. How do you measure the smallest piece of infinity? You don't."

Lily giggles, "Duh."

"Instead, Nassim focuses on patterns and space — a fundamental pattern of division. *If we find the pattern in which the universe divides, then we have the key to creation.*" Now I am breathless with excitement.

"It makes sense. We can't measure infinity, but we can identify patterns."

"Nassim's discovers space defines our material world, rather than the other way around. The vacuum, or space, is extremely dense. It's not empty — it's infinite, it's full. He harnesses the gaps in present day quantum field theory to reveal his theory.[82] He ultimately finds the Fibonacci sequence[83] as the pattern of division everywhere from shells to trees, to flowers, to your fingers, and veins in your body. Everything in nature has this fractal pattern."

Lily confirms, "Nature's so intelligent."

"Heart swoon," I sigh and continue, "Nassim discovers that our biology, you, we, all of us — we're the event horizon of a black hole universe. He eliminates the 'strong force' math of quantum mechanics in the way of the small and large physics coming together; he thus unites the quantum with relativity." [84]

Lily is leaning forward. She claps her hands once and lays back into the bean bag with gusto. "Seriously? He like, unites the big and the small physics? It solves the age-old tension you and my professor mention."

"But wait, there's more, hah hah!" I rub my hands together like a comedic evil villain. "Nassim finds the mathematical pattern or structure of the vacuum, is radiative *and* contractive."[85]

Lily offers, "Like an inhale and exhale?"

"Exactly. The grid can grow in perfect three-dimensional fractal octaves from infinitely big to infinitely small. This 64-tetrahedron, when extrapolated as flat geometry, is called the Flower of Life." I lift my finger up and show her a gold flower of life ring I wear. "This is what a two-dimensional representation of the flower of life looks like."[86]

Lily leans forward again and looks at my ring. "I've seen this pattern before. So that's what that is!"

"Now put on your dancer hat. Nassim furthers Einstein's field equations to discover a torque and Coriolis Effect in the way the structure of the vacuum moves — the universe spins at every scale."

"I see a whirling Sufi dancer in my mind."

"The universal feedback structure is a fluid dual torus structure in a black hole with this dynamic spin at every scale, like water going down a drain. The inhale and exhale, or expansion and contraction, is in all of life, at every scale. A Sufi dancing or the spiral of water."

Lily pops up from the bean bag and starts a slow twirl on the carpet as her hands swirl.

"Do you remember when we talked about donut shape of your field when you were young?"

Lily rubs her belly. "Mmmmm. Donuts." She stands still and looks at me. "Yes. We talked about two donuts on top of each other inside a bigger donut of energy."

I laugh because she did exactly that at age 12. "That's it. The top one has a vector up from the bottom and around. The bottom one has a vector down from the top and around." I stand up in front of her and move my hands as I talk. "In nature, this fractal shows up in weather. Hurricanes spin in one direction in the north hemisphere, and spin in the other direction in the southern hemisphere, and then meet at the equator. They go back to the poles and then repeat and meet at the equator again. Just like your energy field."

"Ohhhhh. My heart as the equator." Lily puts her hand on her heart.

My poet self has already started at her age. I put my hands on my heart and nod, "Uh huh. Now let's reduce the double torus fractal to an atomic scale. This is when it gets weird because things start to disappear. In an electron and positron exchange, they disappear and reappear, again and again. The electron carries information from the material world to the vacuum, informs the vacuum, and then the vacuum informs the material world when the electron comes back out."

"So, wait. It's like we're flashing in and out?"

"Yes, just like the electron and positron, we are constantly appearing and disappearing at an extremely rapid rate, at the speed of light." I take a breather. I sense this big, beautiful information I'm sharing with myself is building power in my body. I guess she's feeling it too. I add, "It's simple and complex at the same time."

"We're each a magic trick and we don't know it."

I guess that's my answer! Lily's smile tells me she's also feeling the power of the moment. I declare, "That's a poetic way to describe it!" I continue, "Half the time you are the vacuum. So, who are you when you're the vacuum? What are you sending to the rest of the universe when you inform the vacuum?"[87]

Lily's eyes get big as her arms scribe the air left to right with her words, "I'm the vacuum half the time." Now her arms wave right to left as she says, "And I inform the vacuum half the time. Mind blown, again."

I go on, "It explains it so much to me. The double torus, or donut, helps us scientifically understand consciousness. Consciousness demands feedback. For you to be self-aware, you must know you exist. This double torus allows for critical feedback. What comes from the outside goes inside to inform the vacuum. Next, it comes back outside, and the vacuum informs us of the information inside. The relationship of all the understanding put together in the vacuum effects yours and vice-versa. You are co-creating your reality with everybody else."

"Oh my God. I Love it!!!" Lily walks to the window and looks out. "Have you ever thought about how that could explain relationships?"

I watch her and reply, "Absolutely I have. I love it too. Love being the operative word. I often think about how this explains the physics of intimacy. I'll connect the dots in a minute for us. First, it's important to understand that black holes are not only the center of all galaxies, they exist *prior* to galaxies. Black holes are a fundamental pattern of the vacuum that produces matter which eventually becomes visible to us, like stars. They absorb and radiate information. There are black holes and white holes. If you are on the inside, they appear black; if you are on the outside, they appear as super bright white. Seen from above, it resembles the double torus structure in the universe. Much like the swirling yin yang symbol."

"I know that symbol!"

"It's meant to indicate the infinite swirl of duality. You live in a black hole universe, from the quantum, to the cellular, to the galaxy. Life is an eternal dance of contraction and expansion, invisible and visible."

"This is epic."

"Indeed. What we call reality is not as fixed as we think. It is a co-created story or a joint venture. When we talk about intimacy, imagine all the aspects of the black hole. Communication happens inside the vacuum as much as it happens here in the seemingly solid three-dimensional world. The unknown or unseen is the point of creation. The swirl of masculine and feminine energies — not so much gender types — but rather the qualities of being a human where feminine is receptive and masculine is active."

Lily walks back from the window. "It seems to me that there is a mystery inside of intimacy that people may not know about. So many of us, including me, see the world as solid and see the surface."

"Yes. But I think you see more than the surface of things. Just look at your journal entries! If we learn about the infrastructure of the universe, we see that intimacy is much more informed by what we can't see than we realize."

"Wow. Yeah."

"The fractal spiral. The swirl of the yin yang. The Flower of Life." I extend my ring again, "this sacred math of creation, geometry, and meaning is embedded across many ancient traditions: Egyptian, Mayan, the I Ching, Kabbalah, and so on."

"Kabbalah too? I have always wanted to learn more about these traditions, especially Jewish mysticism." She doesn't know that in just a few years, Sierra will be moving to Israel and claiming more of our Jewish heritage for herself.

I assure her, "You will have years ahead of you to explore Kabbalah as well as other wisdom traditions."

"Good." Lily sits back down in the bean bag with a crunch.

"This is how we heal the world, one heart at a time. For one heart holds the truth of all hearts."

– Astara

Tiny Space

I sit down again and cross my legs. I lean in and whisper, "And now for the million-dollar question of the evening. Where is the black hole, white hole center of the double torus of your own personal universe?"

Lily smiles and says knowingly, "My heart!"

I say with a playful Yoda voice, "The force is strong in you."

Lily laughs at the Star Wars Jedi reference.

I continue, "There's a place in your heart that shamans and yogis throughout history call the *tiny space of the heart.*[88] The tiny space of your heart is an infinity point in the center of your personal double torus electromagnetic field. The tiny space is also an actual physical space in your heart, and there is debate to its actual location. When I travel there in meditation, I trust my inner knowing takes me there."

"Ohhhh. Infinity point."

"It's about to get juicier. An infinity point means this where you flicker in and out of the vacuum like we spoke about. Your tiny space is the same as mom's, dad's, your siblings', and every being on the planet. Although your heart is your personal guidance system, it connects you with all hearts, with a universal guidance system. This is what some refer to as oneness."

"No wonder it's a time travel machine."

I emphasize, "Exactly. When you drop into your heart you can discover this special point. Imagine, you can see the past, present, and future all at once. Some call it the Janus Point. Janus is the dual-faced Roman god of the gates.[89] In my multidimensional view, the gate would have an infinite number of faces to see all timelines."

"Heart time is all time." She gently points her finger to her heart.

I nod. "And no time. It is beyond time." I lean in and say, "Let's connect sensitivity to intimacy. You live in a world that trains us away from heart intelligence including feelings and intuition. Our world view emphasizes the mind as the center of reality. Our head brain gets good at squashing our sensitivity flat with cultural messages of 'prove it', 'you're too sensitive,' 'stop feeling so much,' 'get over it,' 'be reasonable,' or 'can't you take a joke?' Diminishing emotional intelligence, intuition, and a human's natural sensitive gifts.

"Ugh."

"This creates a world where people stop listening to themselves or will do anything to avoid difficult feelings. That's at the root of addiction, of isolation, of loneliness, and disempowerment. We turn to outside methods to self soothe. We make poor choices."

"Totally. That would explain why I'm scared to have feeling be my superpower."

"I hear you. In your timeline, research is about to begin to change all that. I mentioned the HeartMath Institute earlier. It doesn't exist yet, but it will in a few years. They'll study the power of the heart, scientifically demonstrating the heart generates up to 100 times greater electromagnetic activity than the mind. They'll discover the heart knows what will happen seconds, minutes, hours, or even years before the mind. The heart is the seat of your intuition and your soul. The brain picks up the heart signal like a radio tower, and then sends it to the body."[90]

"Amazing." Lily is slightly bouncing in the bean bag emitting a rhythmic crunch sound like a heartbeat.

"It's my favorite topic on the planet." It's contagious; I bounce a little too, cross-legged on the floor. I'm now aware of my tight hips and spread my legs out. "Did you know that when you were conceived, your heart was the first organ to form?"

"No way."

"Yes way. And then your tongue. They are connected. Now you know why you like singing so much. You are expressing your heart. It's like you wrote in your journal entry today: '*My body is a sanctuary for my soul, and my heart is the guide to lead me down a path to many wonders of the world.*'"

I bow to her from the floor. Using a silly lounge voice I say, "Thank *you very* much!" An inside joke from our love of Steve Martin stand-up comedy.

Lily laughs the rest of Steve's line, "It's really great to be here!"[91] Lily leaps out of the bean bag.

I un-pretzel myself from the floor, stand and stretch. Appreciating my 47-year-old body, I move slowly forward finding my feet have pins and needles as I walk. I give her a big hug.

I can feel our hearts beating in unison. I whisper into her ear, "It's a joy to share this with you. You fill my heart."

I step back and feel the air shift again with my heart's sweet song. There's a pressure differential between dimensions and my ears pop. Lily's smile fades from view yet her warmth lingers in my field.

I'm back home sitting at my wood desk. I reread her entry. I read more passages. Hours later I can feel the weight of my eyelids. I turn off the lights and start the climb upstairs to bed. It's been a long heart-full day flickering in and out of the quantum field.

"There's a certain spirit that has returned to me."

– Lily Marie Livingston, Age 19

The Return

It is Thursday October 19, 2017. When I wake, I feel my journals two floors down. Their energy tugs at me in bed. With each visit and leap in time, pieces of me return. The world looks different; my energy is higher. My senses more heightened; colors are sharper. Food is more delicious. Orion kitty's shenanigans are more entertaining. I smell deeper. The breeze is breezier over my face and arms.

I lay in bed as daylight streaks through the closed blinds. A silent *"thank you"* ripples out to all the ages of myself across time. Ages I have reunited with, and ages I have yet to meet.

I move downstairs, ready for the day. I look at the clock. 10 am! I am sleeping in like a... Like a...I wait, look around and it slowly dawns on me. "Haha!" I laugh out loud in memory of my recent time-bending conversation. I'm sleeping in like a 19-year-old! I haven't slept in like this in years.

My inner child — of all ages — is having a play day within my psyche. A few nights ago, I dreamt I was in a room filled with balls of different sizes and colors bouncing all over the place. In last night's dream, Ryan and I were working on our company website and there was an on-screen menu of round spheres we could code. As I moved my mouse over across the screen, they bounced up and down. Even bouncy balls on the web! My inner five-year-old is connecting with me in my dream world. I loved bouncy balls as a kid.

I go down to the basement, pull out my chair, and sit down. Hot tea in hand, I'm ready to go. I open the floral journal. In the early morning hours of her timeline, 19-year-old Lily writes,

> *It's now about 1:32 am, and I just got home from a road trip down to LA. It was the best thing I could have done for myself. I'm in touch with my goals and I can't wait to keep remembering all the wonderful things I want to strive for and attain.*
>
> *I say 'remember' because this weekend I've realized something quite interesting. Ever since I can remember, I've had a pretty good idea of what I wanted to be, as far as a "good person who has a lot going for them," etc.*
>
> *And I see now that this knowledge of all the things in life that are important to me, are stored in my head somehow, my soul in some way, and all it takes is some sort of external or internal stimuli to help me revive or retrieve that vital information!*
>
> *This weekend I've done just that. Looking through all my photos at home, from when I was a kid to now, I see all the changes I've gone through. Not just physically, but mentally as well. It was a wonderful experience looking at my mom and dad at youth and seeing them now. It stresses to me how we must keep alive our intense souls, keep the flame alive and burning. It seems that we metamorphosize and change constantly, but it is that inner glow that counts. I must remember that...*
>
> *I discovered a whole new me lurking within the confines of my heart. Well, once I am out, I can't go back into hiding! Hello whole me, it is good to be back again! Monday October 16, 1989.*

I am impressed by how early my understanding of soul alignment begins. It takes me decades to embody that passion in the world and find a language for it, yet it's always been there. In her words, I see the results of our conversations as well:

> *And I see now that this knowledge of all the things in life that are important to me, are stored in my head somehow, my soul in some*

way, and all it takes is some sort of external or internal stimuli to help me revive or retrieve that vital information!

Her words are a time bridge I send my loving feelings and thoughts across. I think the word *soul* to her. Slowly my body vibrates with a new warmth, a sweet sound, and she's standing to my left. She sees her journal in front of me. She bends over to see the passage I have open.

"Hi." Lily says.

"Isn't it early for you?" I ask.

"I couldn't sleep."

"Why don't you get comfy on the gold couch and rest."

Lily goes to lie down on the gold couch and watches me as I buzz about my desk tidying up and humming. For Lily, it's been three months since we talked about black holes and hearts. For me it's been one night.

The old couch creaks as I sit at her feet. I ask, "What brought you here this morning?"

She answers, "I was wired from the road, then I heard the faintest whisper of the word *soul*. I swear it was your voice, like you were there! I got goosebumps, heard a high tone, and felt my ears pop like I was climbing a mountain or diving into water. Here I am."

"Amazing. That's what I feel right before I'm drawn to you."

"I want to ask you so much. I don't know where to start."

"I'd love to start with your amazing journal passage. You wrote about '*keeping the flame of the soul burning and retrieving soul knowledge*.' I think you're here because of all we've been doing together. I believe we have more soul loss to heal together."

"Soul loss?"

"In some cultures, they believe that when a major life event happens in a person's life — it can be either positive or traumatic — if we go in shock or feel overwhelm, a part of us temporarily splits away or disassociates. That's soul loss. It's natural for humans to have soul loss; we experience overwhelm in the course of life. If we don't call that part back though, it can hurt us in time."

"Like, that's totally our life."

"It's really common in all humans. But yes, that is totally our life. That's why soul loss is a passion of yours as you grow up."

"I'm so relieved."

I motion her feet to rest on my lap and scoot closer. I continue, "What overwhelms one person, may not overwhelm another. Soul loss does not discriminate, overwhelm could come from positive or negative events. It could come from a natural disaster, a surgery, a car accident. It could come from a wedding, a move, a promotion, or a birth. It could come from a death of a loved one, an emotionally charged incident, or even a chronic pattern that culminates into a tremendous tipping point of harm. Anything, really."

"Gosh, we must have a lot of soul loss! Like, look at our childhood." Lily looks tired. She rubs the palm of her hand up her forehead over the top of her head and sighs. She doesn't know yet that's a simple yet effective method to reset her electric body.

I smile inwardly watching her innate knowing in action and say, "Yes. Soul loss is an instinctual survival strategy in the face of deep pain. Our psyche self-protects by sending a part of us away if something is too intense for us to experience. The ideal is that when we are in a better place, that part comes back organically. But in our busy world that doesn't know better, that often doesn't occur."

"Everyone seems so busy. I get swept up in it too."

"Me too." I continue, "Soul loss is not taught in schools. Psychology uses the terms disassociation or splitting. Psychology doesn't understand where the part goes when it splits or leaves. Talk therapy alone often doesn't retrieve the lost part of our soul."

"I've not been in therapy yet, but I'm curious about it."

"You'll get your chance to explore therapy, and it has great benefits. Where therapy falls short, wisdom traditions can help. Shamanism is the oldest spiritual practice known to humankind. Some say it's over 40,000 years old, others say 100,000 years old! The term shaman translates as 'one who sees in the dark.' A shaman generates an altered state to journey into non-ordinary reality where the soul part resides to bring it back. They then blow it into the heart of the fragmented person. This is called soul retrieval. There are as many approaches to soul retrieval as there are tribes around the world. In certain cultures, where soul loss is understood, they intentionally retrieve a soul part just three days after an event.[92]

Lily chimes in, "I wish we taught this in schools!"

I affirm, "Me too. In modern times, we're so ignorant of soul loss that when current shamans go to help bring a soul part back, in some cases they travel decades back to find it. Three days vs. decades! Our world is filled to the brim with soul loss. Symptoms include blocked memory, apathy, chronic depression, anxiety, addictions to self soothe, post-traumatic stress, immune deficiency, chronic grief, and at worst, suicide."

Lily gasps in recognition, "In our time travel to each other, are we retrieving lost soul parts?"

"That is exactly what we're doing." I smile big and rest my hands over her legs. "We're positively affecting the future, the past, and the present in important ways. These subtle effects also radiate out to even our ancestors and descendants across all dimensions of space and time. Together we're inviting more energy and vitality back to us each time we invite more parts "home" to our soul throughout time. This is possible because time from a physics vantage point doesn't exist, and from another vantage point is occurring all at once."

"Mind blown again. I thought the black hole inside everything was amazing, but wow."

"When we know about soul loss, it helps reveal the truth of our world. In your journal you wrote about it. You wrote the *'inner glow'* and *'a whole new me lurking within the confines of my heart'*. The wholeness that lurks in our hearts is available to all of us, anytime. Some don't realize or know it. Sandra Ingerman, a Western shaman, who writes about soul fragmentation, says that when a soul part returns, it's light returning. [93] If we learn to absorb that light into every cell, we get healthier. I think you had some soul essence return to you on your road trip after looking at all those old pictures. I think that you allowed the *inner glow* or light back in. You may be integrating soul fragments which is why you had trouble sleeping."

"Totally. That makes sense. Oh my God." Lily's energy is starting to perk up. I guess she may even be getting some soul parts back as she talks with me and is being validated.

"So, here is what I propose. Let's go to a part of ourselves in time that needs to be invited home."

"I would love to. How?"

"In addition to dropping into our hearts, listening to the sound of our heart, and feeling each other, I think it has to do with our electric bodies which is our skin, hands, and feet. Earlier, you absentmindedly rubbed your hand up the center of your forehead and over the top of your head. That resets your electric body! Look at your amazing instincts." I wink at her and demonstrate, "You can also use the tip of your thumb or just a few fingers."

"I do that a lot. I will do it on purpose now." Lily takes her fingers and rubs up the center of her forehead.

When she's done, I suggest, "Let's hold hands to connect our electric bodies."

I reach out for her hand. Our fingers softly entwine. My hand's getting warmer, and my body slightly buzzes from our electric connection.

I tell her, "Close your eyes, breathe, feel me, and listen to the song of your heart."

Lily closes her eyes. I close mine.

I invite her with my words, "Create intention with me, hold my words in your heart as I speak. Higher Self, soul guides, please let us know where we are needed across time right now for the highest good of bringing wholeness to our soul."

The electricity of our bodies tingles my palm against hers. I hear the high tone of our heart in rhythm together.

> *"The truer I am to myself, the more connection I have*
> *with the whole world."*
>
> *– Lily Marie Livingston, Age 20*

Hand in Hand

We hold hands standing inside a small room painted deep blue. In front of us, in bed, is a younger teenage version of us with a young man. I begin to recognize my high school boyfriend, Duston. We're in his room. Lily and Duston are kissing in bed. There's heavy breathing and a lot of rolling around.

Nineteen-year-old Lily and I look awkwardly at each other. She lets go of my hands and silently signals to me with her shoulders raised in a shrug and her hands in front of her palms up.

I start to connect the dots of memory and realize this is the night I lose my virginity! As a 17-year-old, I'm just now emerging more fully into my sexuality. I'm filled with hormones and desire. Yet, I ache to be loved in a way that no one can fulfill; I'm looking for nourishing tender mother-love and supportive attentive father-love in all the wrong places. I would for years.

My wound exists all the way back to infancy with my first sense of rejection — it's pre-verbal and I'm not aware of it yet. When I was born, my mom was 39, about to turn 40. I was the last child she would have. After my birth, she struggled with postpartum depression.

My sister Maribel was 16 years old when I was born, so she was able to witness what I couldn't. Her memory is that mom would stay in her room all day some days. My exploration of this first year of life is that mom's depression made it difficult for her to bond with me, and as a result, I had a core wound of longing for the touch I rarely got.

Because 19-year-old me is even closer to this memory before us, she's grasping where we are. At 17, I was in a strange confusion about sex. I remember the thoughts going through my head that night. They weren't thoughts of the joy of expressing deep love through physical intimacy. Rather, they were anxious thoughts and trepidation.

I can almost hear Lily silently thinking on the bed, *"Please help me get this over with. If I have sex now, maybe I'll get to the other side of this gnawing fear and anxiety. He's doing all the right things, why do I feel so uncomfortable?"*

She's uncomfortable because she's pushing herself and not listening to her heart. She's having sex for the wrong reasons — instead of a sacred act of connection, for her it's a desperate act to conquer her fears and to fill that ache for core bonding. A goal that no one outside of her can fill. She has a twisted notion that on the other side of sex is empowerment and liberation. Unfortunately, rushing to get this moment out of the way doesn't help her face her fears, it perpetuates them. It doesn't empower her; it creates power loss.

This lost part of our soul is ready to come home. I let my awareness drop to my heart and to 19-year-old Lily standing by my side. I squeeze her fingers. She looks at me. I beckon her with my free hand and mouth silently, *come with me.* I lead her, hand in hand, to the side of the bed where 17-year-old Lily lies.

Lily and Duston don't see us as we walk closer. Their intimate dance has already begun and the look on Lily's face breaks my heart. Duston doesn't notice for he's in his own world, but her eyes are closed, braced against the pain. We see a part of her floating up away from her body. Nineteen-year-old Lily holding my hand sees it too; she is tilting her head up watching.

Still holding Lily's hand, I reach for the rising glow of light that's almost invisible. A transparent luminous 17-year-old Lily looks down from her place tucked just under the ceiling. My fingers extend all the way, as Lily floats down a little to reach my hand. Now the three of us are connected, hand to hand to hand, a reunion of soul ages.

I am washed with a feeling of love like I have never known. The air changes. My usual cool hands and skin hold a gentle heat, lights shift and move in my vision. I have goosebumps everywhere. We disappear from the room and reappear back to my basement timeline. Instead of just the two of us, there are three of us now. Ages 17, 19, and 47 gaze at each other.

In my timeline, it's night. The light above the desk is on, as well as one at the stairwell. High school Lily needs clothes. I dash to the side room to grab clothes from the laundry area. I pull out an old sweatshirt and jeans and hand them to her.

Seventeen-year-old Lily takes the clothes I offer her and begins putting them on. She steps forward to face us, looking around.

Nineteen-year-old Lily takes the cue and steps forward too.

We both look to 17-year-old Lily, silent. After many minutes of looking around, she asks, "Where am I?"

"You're in your future, exactly three decades from the world you remember. I am the 47-year-old version of you. And this is the basement of my home in my timeline in the year 2017," I answer. I point at the other Lily, "This is the 19-year-old future version of you." I smile. "She's just a few years ahead of you in college."

Seventeen-year-old me asks, "What happened?"

I take a moment and then reply, "Losing your virginity with Duston was overwhelming to you. You're the part of our soul that has been stuck in that timeline — you were lost inside of 1987. I call it a lesson and blessing combined: a 'blesson.' You learned something for your evolution — when you make decisions from a place of fear or pleasing another at the cost of yourself, you create soul loss. The lesson is you don't have to do anything you don't want to do. The blessing is you are reunited back to the fullness of your soul. Your *blesson* is complete. Welcome back."

Seventeen-year-old Lily says, "For me, no time passed at all." She asks, "Where was I exactly?"

"You were in what some call non-ordinary reality. Others call it Bardo. Let's call it another dimension. Inside another dimension outside of time, you were hovering in the room of your high school boyfriend Duston, frozen in the moment. You expected a bonding of love, pleasure, and joy. Instead, you experienced power loss. You were seeking to fill a very young wound of rejection and you abandoned yourself for someone else. In turn, you fragmented from yourself, from us."

"How did you find me?"

"We asked our Higher Self and inner guidance where to go to bring more wholeness to our soul. We were pulled by you across time to bring you home from this deeply impactful experience. It took the strength of both of us for you to see us, so you could come home. Now you are no longer stuck, lost, suspended in that dimension. You are back home with *you*. You will go back to your current timeline whenever you want, only now more whole."

"I barely remember what happened. One minute I'm thinking *'let's get this over with'* and the next minute I'm here."

"If we were to measure time for me, you've been lost for 30 years. For 19-year-old Lily, two years."

Seventeen-year-old Lily observes, "I felt surreal, like I was floating."

I extend my right hand to touch hers lightly and a tear falls down my cheek. "You were lost for a long time in my world. It's good to have you back."

Seventeen-year-old Lily takes my hand in hers. "Thank you for coming to get me." She's looking between me and 19-year-old Lily. "What do I do now?"

"You go home to your timeline in just a minute. Before you go, know that the love you are looking for in a boyfriend, cannot satisfy that ache for maternal love. The culture you live in has taught you a lie: that you must look for love outside you with sex and romantic love. Power is everywhere all at once; it is not outside you. Sex, romantic love, and intimacy can be a wonderful expression and remembering of that energy of love, but it's not *Source*. Look to yourself and the universe for the love you seek, then you will attract a more aligned mutual partner."

Nineteen-year-old Lily reaches out her hand to take 17-year-old Lily's other hand. With moist eyes and a big smile, she offers, "I'm so glad we found you. You helped me remember just how affected you, I, and we were by what we chose in that fateful bedroom just a few years ago. You're brave and amazing. You brought us to you, you know. You were ready somehow." She wipes her eyes and says, "I'm unable to find words to describe what this means to me. I'm so relieved to be with you both."

We stand hand in hand, a line of soul parts looking at each other, smiling. I ask, "As we stand together again, I feel something important happening across all our timelines. Do you feel it?"

"Yes!" Say my younger selves in unison.

"I love you both." I linger to absorb this moment. I look at all the parts of me gathered here. Although my mind cannot grasp what is occurring, my heart knows that I am getting stronger. With my hand holding theirs I add, "Can you see the light around you, around each of us? You may have to squint to see it, like looking at a painting."

They both look around them and at me. They begin to play with their eyes, opening them wide, closing them slightly, trying different approaches.

Nineteen-year-old Lily says, "If I look at you, there's like a subtle glow around you." She looks at the youngest of us gathered and smiles, pointing at her, "I can definitely now see it around *you*!"

Seventeen-year-old Lily looks around herself and at the other teenager version of her. "I can't tell if it's something I see, so much as something I *feel*."

"Whether you see it or feel it, it's there. Allow it in. When we talk about the soul, we're talking about light. The light hovering around us, that's our soul becoming whole again. All that you need to do is breathe it in. Or sponge it up. Whatever metaphor feels good. We are biophotonic — we are made of light — it's as natural as sitting and absorbing the sun's rays. This light will help you feel more alive, more vibrant again, more *you*."

There's a subtle presence in the room around us, and I can hear a deeper inhale and exhale coming from us all. There is light building and growing around and in us. Each breath seems to draw more into my body.

Seventeen-year-old Lily exclaims, "It's like lying at the beach in the sunshine!"

My hands delight in the heat we hold together. Like a circuit carrying electricity along a wire, we conduct our own power back to ourselves. A great *re-membering*. I gently squeeze both my hands to each of the parts of me.

"This feels incredible." I affirm, "I love you both. I'm always with you."

I'm in my basement again, alone. Which is to say, I am all-one. I'm cold from being tired and in the basement so long; I go upstairs to get warm by the fireplace. I feel integration of all these soul parts is already happening inside my bones.

I also know there is more of me to call home. Much, much more.

"What feels like a dangerous risk to our mind, | is a daring relief to our heart."[94]

— Astara

The Claim

It is Saturday, October 21, 2017. A few days have passed since I visit my journals and younger versions of self. My private sabbatical is over, and my devices are back on. My relationship with my partner Ryan has taken the front seat of my life, and it's in overdrive.

The impending threshold of marriage — our engagement — becomes a soul level invitation for us to claim our authentic selves. Instead of taking Ryan's given name, our upcoming wedding cues me to finally own the name Astara that has been residing in my heart for six years.

My name was revealed six years earlier in Oakland by my Soul Star or Higher Self, but I had only told a few close friends about it. The name Astara is as old as my soul. It was time to own it.

I finally step out of hiding and begin to declare my new name in the world. Yet, taking on a new name is the death of an identity. It creates a domino effect of both discomfort and support from my family, friends, and colleagues. Encouragement, anger, curiosity, grief, and humor radiates out in alternating waves. I have compassion for my friends and family. I know for some that asking them to call me Astara, after so many decades as Lily, is a stretch.

I didn't demand anyone use my new name. Yet, when someone calls me Lily, I can feel my entire body contract. That is the power of frequency. I have changed.

Throughout history, changing a name was a rite of passage in many traditions. The Bible mentions God delivering a name change in Isaiah 62:2, "And thou shalt be called by a new name, which the mouth of the Lord shall name." In Revelation 2:17, "He that hath an ear, let him hear what the Spirit saith unto the churches; To him that overcometh will I give to eat of the hidden manna, and will give him a white stone, and in the stone a new name written, which no man knoweth saving he that receiveth *it*." [95]

If my mom hadn't converted — if I were raised Jewish — as a girl I would have claimed a Jewish name at my Bat Mitzvah at age 12. This is the same year I kept my first journal. My Hebrew name would have been used at every Jewish life cycle event throughout my life. I did not have a Jewish name.

Since Lily was our mother's name, letting that name go brought up layers of unresolved heartache and grief alternating with awkward discomfort for me, my sisters, and brother. I don't like making others uncomfortable and one of my shadows is a heightened focus on how I am seen. That shadow lays long and low, so my new claim gave me a big soul classroom to learn and practice the paradox of caring for others while also staying in my own power. I was leaning into self-agency and sovereignty at a new level.

My new name revealed awkwardness to varying degrees for my siblings, yet they eventually found their way with accepting my new name Astara. From a bigger perspective, reshaping identity is not unusual in my family.

My mom left her Jewish identity behind to choose a better world.

My dad reimagined his identity in tandem with early retirement as he shifted his main role of breadwinner to become full time caretaker of my mother's journey through diabetes and multiple cancers.

When Sierra moved to Israel in her twenties, she found our grandmother Hannah's birth certificate to demonstrate her Jewish lineage and was able to obtain an Israeli passport. She reclaimed the Jewish heritage my mother left behind and breathed Judaism back to life for herself and her family.

My brother left the film industry in Los Angeles to forge a new life in the Pacific Northwest.

My sister Maribel divorced after 29 years of marriage and left the focused role of Navy wife, housewife, and mother. She earned her Master of Divinity degree and became a Reiki master and spiritual counselor in the second half of her life.

A star name can be remembered in the unlikeliest of places, just as a soul mate can be found when you stop looking. In our kitchen three years before, Ryan first had a hint of his new name. When our orange tabby Orion kitty ran by, he experienced the seeds of his star-name-yet-to-be when he heard his cosmic name.

Just a few months ago, our friend Atasiea gave us a remote Angelic Presence healing; during our video call, he referred to Ryan as Orion. Ryan and I both hear the star name subtly slip in. Ryan later reports he feels a lightning bolt go through his body when he hears his name again.

Just as when he first met my cat Orion, it is a similar burst of energy and emotion. The signs accumulate. Ryan takes the invitation of our engagement to claim his own star name as well.

Our new claim begins a new era in our intimacy. Orion and Astara. Star family. Soul mates. We agree to use our engagement to embody our star heritage and walk our true names out into the world.

"I am in a room of mirrors, spherical, world-like. I am reflected everywhere I relate, I connect, I touch. They may not realize it, yet ever more clearly, I see myself in them. In the passersby. In my sister, my mom, my lover."

– Lily Marie Livingston, Age 20

Mirrors

My relationship with Orion becomes the crucial laboratory to take new risks in intimacy. Ours is an audacious laboratory of vulnerability filled with raw, unpleasant, and gritty experiments. Together we are stepping into a new era, where growth, creativity, empowerment, and authenticity begin to hold more value than the cultural viruses of consumerism, avoidance, and codependency.

Thanks to the humbling mirror of my best friend and partner, I look at my shadows in a new way, learning to integrate the challenges and gifts of the dark and the light inside me. I am on my way to a felt sense of dignity I didn't know was possible. And Orion is doing the same.

In the early years of our relationship, I knew Orion struggled with addiction, what his therapist taught him to reframe as "problematic behaviors." That first day he moved in, Orion let me know that when he walked through our front door, he made an internal decision to stay this time, lean in, and change his life for good. Years later, I now start to fathom the heavy lifting required of both of us on the road to recovery.

Addiction is *familiar* to me, literally. That is how sobriety became a core value for my well-being. From my upbringing, I was aware of the myriad options of self-soothing I saw around me, primarily my mother's emotional coping through overeating, and my dad's workaholism.

Since our engagement in June, I became aware that to be intimacy ready at the level of our soul claim, we *both* have to get sober.

The first substance Orion set down was cigarettes. Just days after we got our first gong, he quit smoking of his own volition on September 12, 2015. Orion woke up that morning and said, "You want to join me for my last cigarette on the deck?" It was incredible to witness the power of the will when in alignment with the soul's knowing. With cigarettes now miraculously set down, he must form a new relationship with alcohol, sex, and food.

In the summer of 2016, I quit my high-intensity six-figure corporate job, which was my culturally accepted self-soothing technique. I was my father's daughter through and through. I constantly busied myself through projects, work travel, and volunteer organizations. This first step of softening my workaholism was sobering, yet it was just the beginning.

Both of our daring decisions contributed to birthing the restorative magic of our company Illuminating Hearts. Unfortunately, or fortunately, with our first-tier coping mechanisms gone, life just got real, real fast. We had only just begun.

Often, we can't see the disowned and rejected aspects of ourselves until a mirror shows us. That is the gift of relationship. For years now, our unresolved childhood triggers were being reflected through our partnership. We were already learning a lot about our past emotional fires through our present sparks.

During our tour out west, when Orion asks me to marry him, I begin to take the next steps to claim further sobriety in our relationship. I bravely ask Orion to stop drinking, and I begin to look at my workaholism in a more nuanced way.

Claims hold great power, and when we claimed our new star names, we accelerated our evolution.

Because we are now both healers who work together and live together, ours was not a typical love story. To be responsible healers in the world, we know we must heal ourselves at new depths. We peel the surface of our lives back and see the cultural virus of codependency we've swept underneath. We didn't realize how far down inside ourselves we had shoved our quirky survival strategies. All that gunk hiding out, waiting to be catalyzed. With neon signs and some painful airtime, tough love, and a sense of humor (when we can find it), ever so slowly we acknowledge and heal each trigger as they arise.

The illusion of a linear logical process falls away though. We are left with a complex spiraling biofeedback of our emotions, bodies, and relational cues. Simply put, things get messy. Our minds and protective personality resist enormously because it means the death of ego layers and old ways.

Thus begins a long arduous trek to unpack dark behaviors and unwind trauma together on purpose. The process started when we moved in together, yet now we wade through our egoic roadblocks at the next level. But, oh, the grace on the other side!

During the process, our sincere enjoyment of the other stays firm and remains our glitter glue. It's obvious that no matter how triggered we are, we still really like each other's company. The phrase "How good can you stand it?" becomes an inside phrase in our partnership.

And thus, when we returned back from our tour, Orion took my request to quit drinking to heart. He decided to face his alcoholism and get sober. He went back on the road to create his own healing sabbatical in Joshua Tree, California. He was there now, helping our good friend Artemis take care of her home in the desert while she and her partner James are away for three months. This includes caring for their dog Beowulf, our dog "Brown Dog," five fish and four goats: Rudy, Gabriel, Mimi, and Pipi.

He uses his time away to begin to shift his relationship to alcohol. He abstains for a month and his soul fragments start to come back for healing, release, and return.

His accumulated Post-Traumatic Stress Injuries[96] over the years have created compounded soul loss. Orion had been navigating a family legacy of mental toxicity along the male line, sexual abuse in his childhood from a grandfather, Survival School in the Air Force, and more. Such buried loss of power led to problematic behavior throughout all three of his previous marriages. Narcissism, or grandiosity, took hold inside him as adaptation to historic stress.

Orion married his first wife young, five days after his twentieth birthday. During their dozen years together, he remained unaware of the untended trauma inside him. He was living in self-noise so enlarged that he distracted himself through adultery, which led to a child born from another woman. A child he hasn't seen since his moment of birth.

After this event, even deeper shame took root. Years later, he and his first wife gave birth to a son, and he became a stay-at-home dad for four years.

During his first divorce, his self-shame leads him to abandon his son at age five. He saw signs of the harmful father legacy of mental negativity playing itself out in his role as a father. He didn't want to expose his son to his toxic criticism and judgment, but he didn't know how to stop it. So, he left. After being his son's caretaker for four years, he only saw his son rarely on holidays and birthdays throughout the year.

After leaving his first marriage he voluntarily checked himself into a psychiatric ward. His mental health was at its edge, and alcohol-fueled suicidal ideation took over. He quickly realized the psych ward wasn't the place for him and worked his way out. When he emerged, he began slow baby steps to the individuation his inner child had yet to know.

His second wife was a comfortable codependency. As friends and lovers, they lived together for years before they married, enabling each other through alcohol and sex to numb the ghosts of their respective unhealed past traumas. Orion experienced what it felt like to be on the receiving end of betrayal when his second wife had an affair. Nonetheless, he betrayed her through infidelity as well, and they divorced before their marriage lasted a year.

His power loss was now leading to debilitating anxiety. He began to have heart palpitations. There were times when his soul was communicating so strongly to him through his heart, he feared he was going to die. He didn't understand the heart's messages. Yet.

In this third marriage, he married a woman with two young kids, trying to be the dad he hoped he could be. He couldn't hold space for his third wife's emotional needs while he was still in his own unactualized depths. It was his third wife who helped Orion see he was a narcissist. He wasn't ready to set down his behavior or compulsive use of substances, and he left her and her two kids abruptly without a word.

In psychology, this is referred to as narcissistic discard. In shamanism, it indicates power loss so deep that Orion had to hide from himself to survive the consequences waiting below the surface. Just as a relationship would bring him to a place of potential, he would leave so as not to face the agony looming large. From an energetic perspective, he didn't have the circuitry or capacity to handle leaning in. Yet.

During all three marriages he was battling his post-traumatic stresses. His self-noise didn't just stop at volume level 10, it went one higher. He was struggling with mental toxicity that went all the way on the knob to 11. Mental toxicity that Orion and I now call the "boogeyman." The boogeyman is the inner judge archetype who has gone haywire. Instead of expressing the healthy discernment intrinsic to the archetype, the boogeyman is the judge aimed inward at self. The boogeyman is trying to desperately protect, but through a lens of toxic negativity, ends up catastrophizing everything.

Even after his third marriage ended, he gained the attention of women by using his looks as a weapon and finding relief through sex. Alcohol continued to numb his pain. Unfortunately, alcohol also turned off the moral compass of his soul trying to tell him *no, not a good idea.* The consequences of his negative behaviors were finally catching up to him. The worst of them was estrangement from his smart, beautiful, and talented son that he helped raise in the early years.

Even with his generous heart and kind soul, Orion unconsciously lived his energy sideways in the decades before he met me. I knew his unchecked grandiosity was a desperate attempt to mend his power loss. Each attempt wouldn't succeed because he was looking outside for the self that could only be met and known from the inside.

As soul mates, Orion and I are intrinsically connected. Before we even speak about it, I can feel the fear of his young selves and his past boiling up and out of him 1,500 miles away. I sense his egoic resistance to quitting alcohol and dying to his old behaviors. I have compassion for Orion. I know that as he sets down alcohol, he's meeting some ancient pain for the first time. Out of my own experience, I know the pain is immense.

In the first weeks of his sabbatical, our phone conversations are lovely and connective. Ever so slowly as the weeks unfold, our calls build in tension. I pick up on small signs over the last month apart — a new coolness in tone, disinterest in talking, dominating conversations, and expressing absolutes when talking about me and the world. That combined with his new friendships in Joshua Tree, including women neighbors, and I begin to also feel dissonant. With such an unspoken undercurrent of fear, thoughts bubble up. *What's happening to him? To us?*

I feel him pulling away, and it rocks me to my core.

What I know about relationship and the art of projection tells me he's mirroring a lesson for me. After living through days of difficult conversations and uncomfortable silences, I wasn't yet connecting the dots between my experience and his. It takes me weeks to learn my partner, as usual, is paralleling my expedition to recover parts of me. He was gathering soul fragments as well. No matter how many miles are between us, Orion is in his own version of awakening to soul loss.

Ultimately, I learn that with lost parts, they can sometimes create resistance to the return. And this struggle plays out within him, within me, within us. For weeks, all I can do is sit inside the tension with him. In moments, I fear we're falling apart, vibrating away from each other after so much time physically apart.

Little did I know; the opposite was happening; we were preparing to come together in a whole new way. Inside all of this, the glitter glue of our love is there. With some distance, my head runs through the litany of the issues I understand more each day, while my heart reminds me to have faith and see the good of what is unfolding.

In a session recently my therapist asked me, "Do you want to marry him given that there is so much work yet to do?"

As I answer her, I feel my response is to my logical mind as well. I say, "Orion is the most 'changing-ist' human I've ever met. I know there's a lot of work ahead, but I've seen firsthand how powerful he is once he decides something. He's grown leaps and bounds since he walked through our door, and I know change at that level is very rare for anyone. So, I'm all in."

Later, I would come to understand that we were in a necessary period of deconstruction and rebirth. In order to let old identity stories die within ourselves and in our relationship, we had to do a life review of past behaviors, heal, and make amends. If we were to step forward and truly create a new paradigm together there was a ton of inner work to do, with relational work as a catalyst. And there would be practice, lots and lots of practice.

His future was calling to him, just as mine was calling me, and we were answering.

...

It is Monday, October 23, 2017. The time arrives for me to fly to Joshua Tree, California to help Orion drive home from his three-month sabbatical. We've been in regular conflict over the phone. I'm weary as I take a cab to the Omaha airport and walk to my gate.

After I board, my plane is grounded at the Omaha tarmac for enough time I realize I'm going to miss my connecting flight in Denver. I don't want to be stranded overnight in an airport this disenchanted, so I get off the plane in Omaha, rebook my flight for the next day to go out first thing in the morning. I catch a cab home.

My protective personality fears the worst. *Is this a sign from the universe that Orion is not returning home? Am I not supposed to go to him?*

When I get quiet, and tune into the truth in my heart, I can feel my Higher Self and inner guidance gently responding to my fears, saying, *Trust. There is a good reason. Wait, not quite yet. Soon. Rest, sleep, and ground yourself. Everything is going to be okay.*

These words go in somewhere, deep down beneath the anxiety simmering inside me. I imagine that there is more than meets the eye. There always is. I breathe deep. I am feeling far from the creator consciousness I know I'm capable of. My fear lowers me back to victim mentality, and I spend most of the night trying to remember the truth of what my High Self said. *Everything is going to be okay.*

I know that I am inside power loss through fear. Only I can pull myself out of this energy leak and empower myself again. This should have been my first indicator that it wasn't our adult selves doing most of the talking these past months. Like challenging children, our inner teenagers and young twentysomethings were vying for their return.

*"The universe romances you every day and the darkest
night allows you to see the stars."*

– Astara

Change the Channel

The next day, I fly smoothly to California. Orion picks me up at
the Palm Springs airport. When I land, we hug deep and long, as if
we haven't seen each other in a year. He feels completely different,
and so do I, closer somehow through the vulnerability of leaning
into the distressing friction. Orion drives me to Joshua Tree. We
pull up to our friends' homestead out in the desert. We are greeted
by Beowulf, our friends' large black desert dog with golden eyes.

Our beloved Brown Dog runs to welcome me. Brown Dog is a
medium sized mutt, with a hound face, pit bull muscles, and short
legs inherited from his dachshund ancestors. Brown Dog is more
used to the landscape of the plains, back at home. He followed his
human, my partner, into this foreign land of cactus, coyotes, heat,
sand, and Joshua trees. He just had a run in with a beavertail prickly
pear cactus for his second time, trying to dive for a small desert
rodent, so he looked as wiped-out as Orion and I felt.

With both of us already feeling raw, we enter a week of high desert
intimacy storms: dialogue, argument, negotiation, and surrender.
Walk the goats. Walk the dogs. Sleep. Eat. Rinse. Wash. Repeat. Over
and over for three days with our unhealthy egos getting louder. Even
with all the knowledge we have accumulated over the years, it is
difficult for either one of us to practice our wisdom this week. We
are caught in the "win-lose" metrics and can't seem to rise above the
pull of what Martha Beck calls the furies or the stabbies.[97]

Those parts of us that feast with a fury on our debilitating insecurities, stabbing at us with our worst fears—out and out lies to ourselves—to keep the status quo. The furies and stabbies have one main mission: prevent success, growth, and love at any cost. Peace and presence would mean an end to their reign.

Anne Lamott, in her book *Bird by Bird*, describes it as tuning into the radio station K-Fucked or KFKD. [98] If you are not careful, station KFKD will play in your head 24 hours a day, nonstop, in stereo.

Out of the right speaker in your inner ear will come the endless stream of self-aggrandizement, the recitation of one's specialness, of how much more open and gifted and brilliant and knowing and misunderstood and humble one is.

Out of the left speaker will be the rap songs of self-loathing, the lists of all the things one doesn't do well, all the mistakes one has made today and over an entire lifetime, the doubt, the assertion that everything one touches turns to shit, that one doesn't do relationships well, that one is in every way a fraud, incapable of selfless love, that one has no talent or insight, and so on.

Years ago, I took an improv class and my teacher shared about two similar opposing messages from within. She described one as a sweet little imp that sits just over our right shoulder, dosing out kind, supportive love into our ears. She described the other as the nasty little imp that sits just over our left shoulder, dosing out poisonous criticism and attack into our ears.

She puppeteered her right hand opening and shutting like a mouth, talking over her shoulder telling her how wonderful she was. She shoved this generous hand down, again and again. Each time her hand "spoke" lovingly she disregarded the voice.

Then she mimicked the voice over the left shoulder. Her hand opened and snapped closed whispering in a hiss about her lack of talent, unworthiness, and highlighting failures. She fed that hand an invisible cracker. We all laughed. It was nervous laughter for we knew what that felt like.

She stopped and silence set in. Looking at each of us, she recommended we feed the self-love on the right more, instead of feeding the attack on the left. This was the only way to sustain the demands of improv—what I now see as building resilience and adaptability muscle for the unknowns of life.

And now in the ego chaos with Orion, I realize I am feeding the demon imp on my left shoulder. So is Orion. We are both solidly tuned into KFKD where our ego vacillates between grandiosity and the tear down. The station is coming in clear as a bell. Our small selves are beating us up internally through our triggers, with our turmoil spilling onto each other. Days of this. The cycle of energetic heaviness and discomfort spin out and out and out. I fear our relationship won't be able to take another argument.

Suddenly, a small light shines through the cracks.

Friends that own the desert house Orion has been care-taking return home. James and Artemis arrive tired and weary after being away for months. Their exhaustion and ours is outweighed by the grace of togetherness. They offer safe harbor from our relationship storms. It takes an influx of different energies to help us move ever so slowly towards a new vibration.

And the next morning another small miracle arrives.

When I wake, I go off walking alone in the Yucca Valley mesa just outside our friends' home. I feel my inner 12-year-old, my 17-year-old, and my 19-year-old. And now, for the first time, I get the idea to call on my future self. If I can help my younger parts, I am sure there is an older me that has some solid support they could send my way.

They all whisper loving ideas to me as I walk, so I listen to them instead of my fears. I refuse the furies, the stabbies, and turn the dial from KFKD. I claim my truth. I chant. I breathe. I claim a new vibration with words of love. I breathe deeply again. I imagine myself whole. I connect with my heart as my time travel machine and the center of my knowing. I ask for a miracle from my Highest Self. I ask the universe for guidance. I audaciously ask for the world.

The asking feels so big, yet in my center I know it is right. I breathe deeply all the while, creating spaciousness so I can hear any guidance when it comes. I wander like this for about an hour, a walking meditation, a conference call to the cosmos, focused on the beauty within yet deeply attentive to the stark beauty around me.

When I return, Orion is smiling. His voice is soft. Something has shifted.

Orion has just experienced DMT (Dimethyltryptamine) for the first time and his consciousness and his heart are blown wide open. DMT is a tryptamine compound not only found in the human body, but also in over 60 species of plants worldwide.[99]

One of the plants that holds this psychoactive chemical is Ayahuasca, an entheogenic brew made from a South American vine that is becoming more commonly known in Western society despite its illegality.[100]

An *entheogen* is a psychoactive substance used in a religious or shamanic context. It stems from the Greek and literally means "generating God within," or "generating the Divine within."[101]

I am physically sensitive and intuitive. I easily access altered or expanded states of being without the use of plant medicines. In fact, these plant-based psychoactive substances, which have become more widely known since the 1960s, are already in our brains. The chemicals through sacred plants help us access our innate chemistry. I eat clean, drink clean, and typically shy away from such medicines. I prefer my medicine to be meditation, shamanic drumming, physical activity, working with my energy and Merkaba, and sleep induced dreams to access the spiritual information I desire.

Even so, my heart whispers, *be open to this experience*. My heart knows this is a rare moment that will not come again. My heart says, *this is the manifestation of my walking meditation*. I can't ignore or turn away the clarity I asked for. My calling in a miracle during my walk delivers this unusual and rare offering of DMT for us both.

Orion completes his DMT experience ten minutes prior to my return from the mesa. He's leaning close. He looks straight at me without wavering. As he shares his experience, his body language, eyes, and warm tone tell me everything I need to know. He is smack dab in the center of his heart. This turn of events turns up my faith knob, even with my beginner's mind.

Orion says, "Will you try this? It has helped me, and I sense it will help you."

My heart whispers *yes*. My future self says *yes*. Out loud I answer, "Yes."

I walk into the living room and sit on our friends' purple velour couch. Orion sits in the orange leather love seat catty-corner to me. His intention is to be support. Our friend James facilitates the experience with sacred reverence. One moment, I am aware of Orion observing my DMT experience, the next moment everything solid disappears, including my body. My ego is on the sidelines trying to talk to me, but I can't hear it. While inside the experience, my ego is separate yet there; it cannot get back in.

The veil between the seen and unseen worlds is lifted in seconds. I am aware that I am in my body, but not my body. I see a brilliant-colored grid, almost neon-like in brightness, that connects everything. The walls disappear, but I can still sense where they are. I see the desert beyond through what just minutes ago I thought were solid walls. I see into and through everything. Only love exists. Compassion and trust flow in my veins. I keep hearing voices say, *you are here*. I sense they are my soul guides. I hear that phrase repeat the rest of the time.

What seemed like eternity, was only ten minutes. Those ten minutes will always be with me. As a highly visual person, it felt like a grand reveal from the Earth, to gift me visuals of the quantum field I have been studying for years. I feel held by the universe in a way I didn't know was possible.

Witnessing each other in the deep meditative state induced by DMT, blasts our relational consciousness straight from the KFKD channel to the higher octave channel of love. I had begun connecting to the channel of love on my walk. Now we're holding it in partnership. We've taken one long escalator instead of taking ten physically demanding flights of stairs.

As Ram Dass has said, your suffering becomes functional for your awakening. Your suffering literally becomes grace.[102] Grace was pouring in, as, and through both of us now. We would later have days to unpack the "blessons" from our friction on our road trip home to the heartland.

Since I was a young adult, I knew that everyone and everything was my mirror. As my 20-year-old wisely wrote in my journal in 1990,

> *I am in a room of mirrors, spherical, world-like. I am reflected everywhere I relate, I connect, I touch. They may not realize it, yet ever more clearly, I see myself in them.*

Two decades later, I practice this knowledge inside the longest intimacy and relatedness I have allowed to date. Although Orion has been married three times, I have not been married once. Because of the time we spend together as business partners, best friends, and lovers, Orion and I have seen the bulk of each other's shadows. He is my greatest mirror, and I am his.

Our "intimacy readiness" depends upon our ability to reflect consciously what is below the surface of our lives: the parts of us we may suppress or dislike — as well as the parts we love but are afraid to express. There are many opportunities to dive below the conscious into the ocean of the soul, but none are more powerful than the practice of deep intimacy.

I surface from the depth of the DMT's influence, yet I can still feel that feeling for days after. Weeks and months later, I can access that expanded consciousness at will. Something has clicked into place.

The unexpected gift of DMT helped me drop my fear-based victim identity long enough to know the aim of my protective personality better and see a bigger truth. The parts of me convinced something is happening "to" me in life, rather than "for" me are starting to fade into the backseat of my life. The parts that resist big change, know that such change might lead to my annihilation. They are right, they are facing a death of identity. I turn to them and let them about know the expansion I glimpsed inside my journey. I let those scared parts know that my new identity was truer than the one I was clinging to before.

My time travel to meet myself deeply, my soul retrievals, my learning, the past three years spent with Orion, all laid the foundation for the deep shadow exploration with my beloved in the desert. We knew it was a brutal and beautiful gift to be such a mirror for each other. To use the brilliance of author Glennon Doyle's words, it was "brutiful."

> *"Life is brutal. But it's also beautiful. Brutiful, I call it. Life's brutal and beautiful are woven together so tightly that they can't be separated. Reject the brutal, reject the beauty. So now I embrace both, and I live well and hard and real."* [103]

We emerged triumphant because we lived hard and real and excavated the beauty inside the brutality of our past. We knew there was more practice ahead. More stories to be revisited, respected, and renovated.

More hard. More real. More beauty.

And we would have the rest of our lives to practice together.

> *"Something beautiful is growing, blossoming behind the*
> *visible, behind closed eyelids, between seen and unseen."*
>
> – *Astara*[104]

Other Lives, Genetics, Culture & Me

Back home in Omaha, I start to integrate my new choice, my new world. Since we drove home from our breakdown to breakthrough experience in California, my partner Orion begins decompressing from his life-changing Joshua Tree experience, re-emerging into our Omaha world and our work together.

After the last three months of solitude, it is a perplexing puzzle to carve out me-time again while supporting Orion's re-entry and the ongoing energy of running a new business. How do I enter the quantum wilderness when I am perpetually busy?

Since my mission is to learn about intimacy, one of my soul classrooms is clear: learn how to claim space for me in the midst of merging with another.

It is historically and culturally uncomfortable to permit myself to put me first. There are many, many old stories about self, service, and purpose creating a glitch in my forward movement.

Weeks pass, months pass, and despite all my best efforts to try for self-care during the holy-days of the last few months of the year, I begin to melt…down. The new year approaches, and I feel like a woman-child; it seems I have energetic tantrums every other day. Somewhere in my highest knowing, I am aware that the time travel and soul defragmenting I have done to date is paving the way to embody a particularly nasty melt down. Melt down becomes a literal melting of self. When self meets self like this, honoring what is and feeling through it is crucial.

As with the classic childhood song and book of *Going on a Bear Hunt*, one of the verses echoes in my head.

> *Uh-uh!*
> *A forest!*
> *A big dark forest.*
> *We can't go over it.*
> *We can't go under it.*
> *Oh no!*
> *We've got to go through it!*
> *Stumble trip! Stumble trip! Stumble trip!* [105]

Going through it is the power. I am deep inside it. I am not neutrally observing my own despair, I am not rising above it, or journaling about it. Fully inside the shadow work of my doubt. *I am going through it.* Big time.

In this instance, I can't "see my own nose." The mirror to help me "see my one nose," is my partner. Orion helps me see me through the reflection of our interactions. My internalized toxic doubt is debilitating me.

I am caught in ancient self-deprecation sludge I used as a coping strategy over years and lifetimes. Only one simple act is needed: I must ask for what I want. To learn what that is, I must turn within and ask myself. Way before Orion, way before this life, this fear has been there. In all my relationships, from romance to friendship, the "what do I want" lesson has been as scary to me as the fear of death.

Ironically, as I unwind these layers, an outworn identity of how I show up to all my relationships *will die.*

What I have learned in my soul investigations is that when a fear is this pronounced and perpetuates itself, it has roots inside me in more than one dimension. Deep inside the well of my subconscious are **four layers** that contribute to such a colossal fear.

The first layer is rooted in my soul memory. It is an ancient part of my soul that remembers when asking such a question did indeed kill me. We often call this a past life. Since time is not linear, and everything is happening all at once, a better descriptor is "other life."

The second layer resides in my blood and DNA; genetically our bodies are data storage devices. I inherited my ancestor's fear of death when they asked for what they wanted in other decades and centuries, and it didn't go so well.

The third layer is a cultural agreement. I use the term *cultural virus*. I live in a culture where the silent and not so silent message is, "to belong or be loved you must give up your wants in service of others." We are hard wired biologically to belong; therefore, that cultural virus has immense influence. It dovetails with our genetic memory, that we emerged from tribes where to stay alive we had to align with the group.

The fourth layer emerges from this life and upbringing. Young me was raised to suppress her wants in an ongoing pattern that created a subconscious habit. In a literal way, death was a potential to young me. If I hadn't suppressed my wants as a child with a narcissistic mother with undiagnosed bipolar symptoms and borderline personality traits, I could have been hurt or worse.

Because of the work I do as an intuitive healer, I knew tending to just one of these layers will not fully unwind and release it. I have to unwind them all.

I bravely find a nearby state park to spend the week at a small cabin in the woods. Right before I go, wham! Orion and I are smack in the middle of another dark forest on my bear hunt.

> *Uh-uh!*
> *A forest!*
> *A big dark forest.*
> *We can't go over it.*
> *We can't go under it.*
> *Oh no!*
> *We've got to go through it!*
> *Stumble trip! Stumble trip! Stumble trip!*

A day before I leave, we both have old parts emerge, fiercer than ever. For Orion, it is the need for space to process, and not feeling he has it. For me, it is the self-deprecation that emerges when he needs space, and I feel abandoned. I drop into my wound like it is my highest calling to go the furthest into it I can. I do it like a champ

"Love yourself like your life depends on it. Because it does."

– *Anita Moorjani*

Dragons

It is Monday, January 29, 2018. Here I am, recovering from the mess of my shadows some more. I am one part embarrassed, one part learning to be present, and one part trying to accept all of me. The sound of geese at the edge of the Platte River in the distance, the fire roaring in the fireplace behind me. Five days of this bliss ahead.

I toss myself with great passion back into my journals. It feels like a reunion. I am reading through my entries when I was 20, in the fall of 1990. I can't wait to meet my 20-year-old self. Her wisdom astounds me.

Twenty-year-old Lily doesn't know how wise she is yet. She is ripe for the world, dreaming, hopeful. She's creating beautifully. She has no idea at the time. She is taunted by that self-deprecation demon, filled with fear and doubt. I still know that awful feeling intimately 27 years later.

I flip through the back of a journal and Lily's dream entry catches my eye.

My thoughts return to a dream I had a couple of days ago that haunts me even now.

...

In my dream, I was in Los Angeles and a tornado was coming to the city. My parents and Jaden were there. The air was heavy, it was raining and windy, and I was stuck outside trying to get into the shelter of my parents' house. I couldn't get inside and panicked. What if I was sucked up into the tornado? What if I was killed? Thrown thousands of miles away? As I sat there worrying, I finally found a window open and crawled in, meanwhile listening to the sounds of destruction all around me. I ran to my parents' bedroom and stared out of their windows to the city below where sounds of crushing houses, alarms going off, fire engines, and earth-shattering screams could be heard.

…

This is where my dream ends, waiting, just waiting for it to reach me. The dream conveyed to me the feelings of stress and anxiety plaguing my being these days. This tornado is a metaphor for the hectic life I create. I want to get rid of this storm, I want to find the center, the eye, and dwell there for a while. Then maybe I can build the proper bracing and underground shelter for the tornado about to strike. I need peace of heart and mind. Show me the way whoever you are! Saturday, September 15, 1990.

What divine timing this dream. The symbols fit the current 20-year-old fears I was facing as much as the 47-year-old fears I am facing.

I am excited to be her *whoever* across time.

As I acknowledge the gloomy weight of self-deprecation I have been so recently plagued with, I can feel her getting closer through our shared experience. All my senses expand into her dimension. I hear the hum of my heart. I feel my ears pop from the pressure change.

I am in a large room with a nicer fireplace than my small cabin. I quickly recognize the front apartment of the large old Arts and Crafts house I rent out with my friend Kylie in North Berkeley. Because of time travel being what it is, the visits feel recent to me in month time frames, but for her, they are years apart.

Lily is sitting on the couch, in sweats and jeans with her journal open on the couch next to her. A pen lies in its crease. She is silent, looking at the fire. I walk around the couch, so she can see me.

"Hello again."

"Oh. Hey." Lily looks at me as if she can't quite place me. She's used to students dropping casually by. When she sees I am not a student, her voice rises in pleasant surprise, "Hi!"

I want to say so much. I start slow, "Hi! Do you remember our last visit?"

"At first, I wrote them off as my vivid imagination. I guess that was how I could process it." She looks back at the fire, crackling along. She adds, "I do remember you."

I offer, "There's wisdom there. Funny thing about imagination is that is where everything begins. Your journal design first started in someone's imagination. The pen you are writing with. That fireplace. Everything."

"Maybe that's why I want to study design. It's all imagination!"

"Truth!" I stand looking around the room. I turn to Lily and announce, "I read the dream you just wrote. The scary one about the tornado in Los Angeles with Jaden and our parents. You wrote, *I need peace of heart and mind. Show me the way whoever you are.* Drumroll…I am your whoever!" I smile and walk to the couch.

"Thanks for being my whoever. Come sit here." Lily moves some books to make room.

I ask, "By the way, where is Kylie?"

"Kylie is out to dinner with her sister. She'll be gone a while."

"Good to know. So far, my visits have been just you and me each time, or other ages of us, joining us. I am curious yet relieved."

"I am curious as well. Maybe there's a quality or energy that creates a boundary to the outside world."

"I like that. Has anyone told you lately how smart you are?" I sit down, and the fire feels good. I perch my right leg on the couch to face Lily with my grin and lean back.

"Not today at least." Lily smiles.

"Well, you are. And as you get older, you just get smarter." I wink at her knowingly. I continue, "Let's dive into your dream. What is the tornado for you?"

"It is pure fear, I guess."

"What is your worst fear right now?" I ask.

"My worst? Hah! Where do I start?" Lily laughs and looks around the room.

I laugh with her. I'm also aware of sadness weighing on her. She looks down at her hands. She is now folding and unfolding them nervously.

"Start in the beginning, middle, or end. For me time doesn't matter," I say.

Lily slowly gets it and her mouth scrunches into a small smile. She starts, "Okay. Well. Hmmm. I fear my relationship. Any relationship."

I nod, encouraging her to go on.

"I see the patterns." She begins speaking faster, "I get close to someone and expect the worst. I feel so insecure. I'm scared of making the wrong choice for where I transfer to architecture school. I thought Berkeley was the obvious choice, with Sierra being here, and the classes I have been taking streamline me into their program. But Jaden is at Cal Poly San Luis Obispo, and I want to be nearer to him. I don't enjoy our long-distance connection. Also, the school there is cheaper than Berkeley, and there is a better, smaller professor to student ratio."

"What do you think the pattern is?"

Lily ponders in silence. Finally, "I guess the pattern is that part of me that expects the worse."

"Ah, the tornado."

"Yes. The tornado. There are all these doubts that whir in my head about moving there. Is it for him? For me? I make lists. I weigh pros and cons. I spin and spin and spin."

She stops abruptly. She smacks her hand over her mouth and her eyes go wide. I love such ah ha moments. It is super fun to watch me have one!

"Oh my gosh. The Tornado! I spin and spin and spin!" She jumps up from the couch and spins on cue. And then she stops. The fear creeps back. She sits back down in with a sigh. "But underneath it all, I'm like, just super scared and doubting."

I offer gently, "Okay. Listen. I know that feeling. We share it. I'm here to tell you the silliest simple thing. It will probably annoy you. And then I am going to tell you some other things that will hopefully lift your spirit. Or what I call in the future, lifting your vibration."

"What is the silliest simple thing?"

"It's going to be okay." I say the words slowly and smile.

Lily sighs and shakes her head, but she can't resist smiling. It's not exactly what she wants to hear, yet it is. A part of her wants validation through data, direction, evidence, and proof. Another part of her just wants to know it is going to be okay. I speak to that part. She finally asks from the strategic brain, "Seriously? This is your great wisdom?"

I offer, "Yup. I need to say it because we both need to hear it. There is a reason my partner says this to me all the time. It turns out we need to hear it a lot, even 27 years into your future. I have gotten to enjoy the phrase and slowly, but surely, I'm learning to believe in it. In your future, I am still learning about doubt and our critical mind. I think the worse quite often and spin and spin and spin. I'm here to help us *both* with our tornado and with our need for evidence and strategy."

"So, you have more for me?"

"I do have more for you."

"Good."

"The fancy word I use in the future for what you are feeling is 'self-deprecation' and it is one of our nastiest, most persistent drag-ons. It's our number one demon. It's the tornado in your dream. The illusion it spins into your world is that no amount of striving will please others and that failure is imminent. We learned that growing up. Mom placed some hefty and sometimes unattainable expectations on you and our siblings. At the end of the day, you couldn't please mom. From report cards to chores, from talking to silence, you never knew when a situation would blow up — no matter what you did."

"That's it. Oh my God. You nailed it. That just makes me so sad."

"Me too. The tornado of self-deprecation is a coping strategy to all that, but it terrorizes you and me. It threatens with this lie: there's always something awful you must prepare for. This threat is going to rip and tear apart everything you care about. The paradox is it also believes you can't prepare for it. It is convincing. I have a few years on you learning about it. The doubt that emerges from the dragon of self-deprecation has an actual goal or purpose. It wants to fulfill its purpose. It wants to protect you, us, in a way."

"I kind of get it."

"So, here's the strangely complicated truth. You might think on the surface of things it wants to protect you from failure. It actually wants to protect you from succeeding. There's a part of you that is more afraid of succeeding than failing."

"Woah. Like, it's protecting me from failure and success? I hadn't thought of it that way at all."

"It's a paradox. If you succeed, all eyes of our family, and possibly the world, will be on you, and the worst outcome would be to succeed and then lose love. Mom may be jealous, siblings may be jealous, there may be passive aggression to deal with or worse. Any of those fears in their extreme trajectory in your mind, most likely lead to exile and then death. Fear has no volume control."

"It does feel like I'm going to die."

"Self-deprecation's fear is not only that 'I'm not good enough', its deepest fear is that 'I'm quite good.' That if you allow your essence to exist fully and unabashedly, the fear is: you will be annihilated. As odd as it may sound there's a pay-off to everything, a reason it exists in our life. The benefit of self-deprecation is to make self-smaller, so as not to be a threat to others or to be too much."

"Oh wow."

"Do you find yourself apologizing a lot? Or qualifying things before you speak?"

"Yes! All the time."

"It is *appeasement*. Appeasement is defined as 'making concessions to potential aggressors in order to make peace.' Do you feel you have any aggressors in your life?"

Lily is afraid to answer this one. She is silent and looks straight at me. I think it just hit her in this moment, how much I am truly her. I sense she is beginning to feel known by me.

After a while she answers softly, "Yes."

"Who?" I'm pushing, and she knows it.

She bends her head down a little and almost whispers, "Sierra."

I wait for a minute before I ask, "Anyone else?"

A long pause. She says quietly, "In the past." She pauses again. "Mom."

She looks at me and I stay neutral. I want her to find her own way.

"Well. Still sometimes mom, but less than before."

"Anyone else?"

"I can't think of anyone. Sometimes I think Pearl, Sierra's roommate in the upstairs apartment. She can get upset like she has her own volatile weather system. That kind of emotion scares me; it feels reckless. Yet, I see it in me too."

"Yeah, I have seen that kind of reckless behavior in me too."

Big sigh, "Yeah."

"Listen. You will meet many agitators, challengers, interrogators, provocateurs, and otherwise aggressive people in your life journey. You will aggress sometimes too. You must face those shadows in yourself. When you befriend that volatile reckless part of you and integrate it as an ally, you get your power back. Although it is reflecting outside of you, it is an invitation to accept yourself. It is imperative that you dare to be *you* — honestly and audaciously. By the time you are me, you are going to feel more you than you ever thought possible."

"I want to be me. But every cell in my body says to stay small or else."

"I know. I feel it often. It's in our blood and DNA. It's in our culture. It's in our upbringing. It's also from our past lives."

Lily lights up. She loves this subject. "That's a lot of layers you mention. I never thought about the scale of it before. I usually only think about my childhood. No wonder it's so big in me!"

"It runs deep. That's why I am still working on it at 47." I wink at her. I affirm, "Honor the scale of it, but keep working on creating new habits of empowerment. It's okay to have passion. When you own your own aggression and allow that part of you to become known, you will project less. It's an important and necessary part of life. You're building muscle to capacitate your shadows and their gifts. Up until now, and especially when we were younger, our survival depended on letting go of any passion and need that might conflict with another. For young you it was mom. And then Sierra. And then all intimate relationships. We naturally picked up that habit. And they struggle with the same pattern as well!"

Lily looks pale. I stop. She looks up at me when I stop.

I say gently, "I know this is a lot. Are you okay?"

She nods, "I am. It's so spot on that I guess I am a little in shock. It's hard to look at my shadow of aggression."

"It is. Yet, you're stronger than you know." I continue, "Even when you have no reason to doubt, you go to the habit of doubt and self-deprecation to protect yourself from potential aggression. Even when there's no aggression to trigger the habit. That's how a habit works. It self-perpetuates, and the brain is your habit factory. So now, you go to doubt and anxiety often with no provocation from the outside. Your boyfriend Jaden. Other big decisions."

"Like which school to go to."

"You name it. It is like you switched fields in your own game and moved from offense to defense. You are in a vigilant prevention strategy mode. By staying small, you think you might prevent this ghost of aggression in the future. But it doesn't work. The aggression still exists, but it goes underground as passive aggression and eventually depression. What you are left with is a tormenting habit, and you feeling very small."

Lily is quiet but listening intently. "Wow."

"There was never anything you could do to prevent the aggression in your past. There is still absolutely *nothing* you can do to prevent aggression of any kind in your future. You cannot make someone feel comfortable. It's not about you, it never was. Not for Sierra, not for mom, not for any other people that feel upset around you, near you, or seemingly because of you."

I glance at her before I continue, "Even when they say it's about you, it isn't. Of course, you're here on this planet to be in relationship, and to learn how to relate to others, and to learn about yourself and to evolve and grow. Yet, you're here to learn to stand in your power. Learn the difference between what your unhealthy ego tells you and what your heart says. When you stand in the truth of your heart, you can't help but light people up. Sometimes they will love you for it, and sometimes they will hate you for it. That is their free will. Think of it as the small tax you pay on your honest expression."

"The tax I pay!" Lily gets up from the couch again and stretches. "So true. Holy holy. Like, this is epic." She looks at me and away. "I need to walk or pace or something. I have so much energy in me."

"Pace away!" I smile, "Movement always has soothed us. And yes, this is big." I watch her walk back and forth. I walk to her, and she stops for a moment. My eyes lock into her eyes, "I am going to tell you straight. You will never be clever enough, wise enough, funny enough, pretty enough, kind enough, passive enough, or appeasing enough to change Sierra's, mom's, or someone else's trigger. It's theirs. You may have shown them the button, but only they can push it. And it works in both directions, no one can do something to you. None of us are victims. You create your life. Even when circumstances are beyond your control, you can choose how you respond."

"Wow. So, you're saying that my doubt is just a bad habit? And that it stems from my childhood, past lives, culture, *and* genetics?"

"Yes."

"And that there's nothing I can do to keep Sierra from being upset with me? Or mom? Or anyone else?"

"Yes."

"So, what do I do when they next get upset? How do I break this habit? It's so strong."

"First, acknowledge self-deprecation is your dragon, but you are not the self-deprecation. Acknowledgement is the cake. The rest is icing. Let that part of you know you see it and understand why it is scared and wants to protect you. Next, thank it for loving you so strong and big. And then tell it, that form of protection is a lie, even if that part of you screams otherwise. It is afraid of dying and not having a role anymore."

"Ugh. I would love to have it go away forever," Lily says with a big sigh.

"I know, me too. The thing is, it will never fully disappear, but it will no longer hang out unconsciously in the driver seat of your life. It will transform from being an unconscious habit, to a part you befriend and love to a new place."

"I definitely want it to stop driving me...crazy."

"You can do the driving with your heart at the steering wheel. It just takes practice. And be easy on yourself along the way. Tell the self-deprecation dragon breathing doubt-fire on you, that you don't believe the hype. Tell the dragon of doubt that you know that your acting small will not achieve anything helpful. Instead, it just makes you feel powerless and sad. And if you did need protecting, which you don't, self-deprecation doesn't work. Tell that part of you that you're not going to give away your power. That will remove fuel for its fire."

"That's it?"

"Next, build new habits. Be willing to be successful. Stop making apologies all the time. Expand yourself at every opportunity. Learn how to validate yourself. I know it feels like a lot. But I tell you what, you are me, and we are smart, adaptable, and strong. And don't be alarmed if after I leave, an opportunity immediately arises to practice handling your self-deprecation. It probably will for me too. It doesn't mean there is anything wrong with you or me, it just means we are delicately rearranging the universe to practice our empowerment."

"What fun. Practice. Learning." Lily sighs, "Ugh."

"It may be hard to believe, but you will strangely savor the practice in time. I live for this stuff! After you talk with that part of you as best you can, and feel all your feelings, a good next step is to lift your spirits. I call it raising your vibration. Do something you like. That will bring your power back, almost immediately. Write a poem. Swim. Dance. Watch a sunset. Read a book by an author you love. Walk to look at a view of the bay. Do art. Play piano. Sing. Stand with your arms outstretched in the air and say 'Yes!' Watch an inspiring movie. Write a gratitude list. Anything that helps you feel joy again. When doubt and fear takes hold, recognize it for what it is. Don't give fear more fuel. Instead fuel up on trust, love, and joy."

"That is exactly what I hope to do."

"Good. I am here if you need me. Time doesn't exist like we think, so just believe, and I will be there. As I practice, you practice. As you practice, I practice."

Lily sits back down next to me. She grabs my hand. We look at the fire together.

I lean over and whisper, "I love you. You've got this."

I close my eyes and feel the tingling of my electric body. My heart rushes with warmth. I hear my own high note and smile.

I am back in my small cabin in the Nebraska woods. The fire in my cabin is out, the dying embers turning to ash. There is a chill in the air. It's a whopping nine degrees outside, and I head to the bedroom to ramp up the heat. As I head to bed, I think about my own "tornado" dreams I have been having lately. I am buoyed by my talk with my 20-year-old self. I feel sorority with her amid the parallel of my own challenges in my timeline.

Tonight, I sleep. Off I go to befriend some dragons across time and space so I can fly with them to new lands.

"The truth of who you are is not outside you."

– Astara

Surprise

It is Friday, March 2, 2018. Orion and I take Brown Dog for a walk at the lake on the other side of town in the newer suburbs of Omaha.

Just last year, After his first attempt at sobriety in Joshua Tree, and our burst of evolution last fall before and after our DMT experience, Orion formally quit drinking December 2, 2017.

Orion wasn't drinking anymore, but with the numbing removed, the volcano of his past pain erupted. I was suddenly living with a "dry drunk." His energy moved from numb to intense moods, which made for one nasty, grumpy roommate. I shared with Orion the difference between abstinence and recovery. I told him he had to go into recovery or move out. I didn't see it as an ultimatum, but rather the honest-to-god truth that I couldn't live with his abusive moods like this.

Although my personality was scared, my heart knew it was the catalyst he needed. On February 8, 2018, Orion stepped in earnest into his recovery journey with alcohol. He thanked me later for setting such a strong boundary. It wasn't easy, but it was gorgeous.

Now, as we walk, I take inventory of the recent beauty since my brave stance and his resulting brave choice. Orion committed to mindfulness-based recovery meetings and started therapy to heal his sexual addiction. He made amends with all three ex-wives, his younger son, and me. He plans for more reckoning and repair work with his past. He continues to reach out to the women he knew briefly so many years ago, the one he cheated on his first wife with, and waits patiently for any word. He longs to meet the older son he has never met. He dreams to build a healthier father-son dynamic and form a deeper intimacy with his younger son through his first marriage.

I smile remembering what Orion has been saying inside this potent time, "I am grateful to make amends, I truly regret the pain I have caused others through my addictions and problematic behaviors. Yet, I don't regret my journey. How could I? It led me here, to you, to knowing myself more deeply." Repeating the wisdom of Ram Dass again, he says, "I see the grace of my suffering."

Later, he said something so profound, it echoes my own path of intimacy with myself as I heal the byproducts of historic shame and grief. "I get to be broken. I get to be broken in love. We all do. I get to be broken open through love until I learn how to love myself. And the funny thing is, once you love yourself, you realize you were never broken in the first place."

Orion's humble wisdom is my inspiration.

On my journey to love myself, I am making steps to face my over-work patterns as my main coping strategy. It is two years since I left corporate architecture, but I still have the busyness bug. It is there, just in a new disguise. I am doing what I love, yet I am exhausted as a small business owner. There had to be a healthier way.

Orion was asking for more intimacy emotionally and energetically. I decided he was right and leaned in to shift my schedule. I made more time for me, which helped me make more time for us. Because of his powerful choices and mine, we are walking with a renewed peace in our hearts. Our "intimacy readiness" is at an all-time high as we get cleaner and sober up our lives.

Lake Zorinsky is one of our favorite places to go because there are 11 miles of walking paths away from cars, giving us access to trees and the shimmer of water. Although it's a man-made lake, it recreates an oasis of nature inside our urban reality. Depending on the season, we can stumble across deer, turkey, blue heron, cranes, black squirrels, and other wonders. It is late winter, and snow has melted. Ice crowds the edge of the walkway. Where the ice is melting, patches of brown dormant grass is revealed.

Orion is walking quietly in stride with me. Brown Dog is in between us. The clack, clack, clack, rhythm of his paws on the concrete lulls me into a meditative state.

Moving meditations are my favorite way of going inward.

In my quiet state, I hear my heart hum. A ringing in my ears get stronger than the bird and wind sounds around me. Without my journals nearby and no specific emotion pulling me, I wonder what dimension is opening. A woman my height and build with short hair is coming into view next to me, walking to my right. Her hair is almost all grey. She turns and smiles, her feet in stride with me. I smile without thinking. I know this woman. She turns and smiles again and says, *"Hello beautiful."*

My heart expands and I feel taller in her presence. Future me is here.

> *"I see now that the knowledge of all the things in life*
> *that are important to me are stored in my body some-*
> *how, in my soul someway. All it takes is some sort of*
> *external or internal stimuli to help me retrieve that vital*
> *information."*
>
> *– Lily Marie Livingston, Age 19*

Remembering the Future

As I walk, I feel the edge of tears at the corners of my eyes. Future me. A sure sign of my heart truth unfolding. Her presence hangs on me like a beautiful scent. Future Astara exudes confidence. Her smile. Her eyes. They are mine, but there is a new light in them I cannot name. Yet.

In my timeline, as my thoughts stumble around business and financial concerns, in walks older me in a totally different state. I am hungry for her confidence.

"Hello." She pauses and looks around at the beauty of the lake, grasses, and trees. She turns to look at me, *"I know you're scared."*

I turn to her. She's smiling. Hearing her words soothe me, just knowing she knows.

She adds, *"You may not understand this for some time, but it is good to say. You're scared, but you needn't be."*

I keep walking, knowing that Orion can't hear this or see her. This is for me. I send her a silent thought, *"I am scared!"* A silent tear rolls down my cheek. I tend to my emotions. I admit to myself and her, *"All of the time."*

Future Astara sends me her thoughts. *"Of course, you are scared! And you will be. Again and again. I'm just here to remind you that your fear is not only okay, your fear is a sign of success. To pursue your dreams inside this dense world with a culture shaped by the 'win-lose' mentality can be tricky. As you say yes to your soul path, fear will arise inside this world because you are surrounded with internalized and externalized messages of why it won't work and how you are crazy. If it does work, you then think 'why should you succeed and not someone else?' The 'win-lose' metric is actually a 'lose-lose' metric. You know all about the double-bind of the fearful mind, where you are 'damned if you do and damned if you don't.' You are in an important part of your chosen soul journey — to feel fear in the midst of all this complex concentrated energy of the material plane and take action anyway."*

I wipe my cheek in the cold air as I continue to walk.

Future me shares, *"This moment was designed by us. It's no accident that I'm here with you at the potent age of 47, after you publicly claim our name to family, friends, and clients. All your time travel up to this point has been to our past selves; except of course that walk in the desert where you felt me."*

I smile at the memory. I think to her, *"I could feel you! I had forgot!"*

Future me giggles and says, *"It takes a lot of repetition to have your connection with me get solid."* She walks closer and continues, *"Do you know you have done the miraculous? Soul retrieval of our core parts has given us healing and unwinding across time. Your renewed strength is what allows you to see and hear me. My renewed strength allows my messages to become stronger so you can hear. Do you see? You and I exist at the same time; our healing is simultaneous."*

I feel so much peace taking in her words. I think, *"This is amazing."* Yet, I know she feels the grace of my expanding heart too.

"It is absolutely amazing. Because of the circuits you have built through all your journeys, you are able to see and hear your future self now, and soon so much more. I've been there with you silently watching and observing since you started. Now you are strong enough to see me and hear me reaching out to support you."

"I'm so happy you're here. Truly. I have so many questions!"

"And I have answers. At least the ones that are helpful for your now."

"Will Orion and I get married?"

"Yes. This year!"

My mind is blown. Right now, the speed bumps and resistance inside my relationship with Orion seem too huge to traverse. It also seems impossible to pull a wedding together so fast, but I trust her.

"Will I succeed at Illuminating Hearts? I mean, will I make a living in following my soul's calling?"

"Yes."

I breathe that in. I know it's true, yet I'm overwhelmed by the seeming gargantuan task ahead for Orion and me. Just knowing that those two big stressors of marriage and business do not have to deplete my energy is a relief.

"What year are you from?" I think.

"I am from 2030, I am 60-year-old you." Older me then offers, *"Those two questions you pose — Illuminating Hearts success and following your soul's calling — lead to outcomes beyond what you can imagine right now. I will be here to help you along the way, for the way is not smooth. Or easy. There will be days when you will want to give up. But you won't. We won't. Trust me."*

My eyes are forward on the path as we walk, and I am beyond excited. It doesn't last long. Joyful terror flows in and mutates into "brutiful" grief. More quiet tears come. Orion doesn't notice. I am grateful to have this intimate moment of solitude right next to him. It has always been a fantasy of mine to share deep self-intimacy quietly with someone else.

My future self is medicine to me. Just her presence. She energetically reaches her left hand to meet my right, and we walk hand in hand together. Further on the path, I see my younger selves standing there watching us walk toward them. Ages 5, 12, 14, 15, 17, 18, 19, and 20 begin to walk toward us through the trees. I can feel them merging with me now, gathering more of my soul into wholeness.

A wave of energy begins at the top of my scalp like gentle fingers tickling. I feel it wash over my head like invisible sparkling water flowing down. An electric current zips down my spine and back up again. The soles of my feet open like flowers to the pavement as I walk. I meet the path with a spring in my step.

Electric is the word. Every inch of me alive with awareness of this moment.

I turn to older me. She steps inside me — the gate of my heart — as her thought arrives, *"When you need me most, I will be here."*

My smile takes up real estate and I walk taller. She is here, inside me.

*"What are a few lifetimes, when standing in the dance of
eternity?"*

– Astara

Cosmic Conference Call

It is a Friday morning, March 27, 2020. I am 49. It has been a
little over two years since I started my time travel adventure in the
quantum wilderness. Traveling timelines through the prompt of my
journals has led me to a myriad of new timelines all with fresher
vantage points on self. I know in my bones, cells, and even the space
between my cells, these connections have transformed me. They
continue to shape my entire life in ways beyond what I can wrap
my head around.

Meeting myself across time in this way has altered everything.
Alchemy becomes my way of life.

In this now, I am aware of more dimensions of being, more soul
tools, and more ability to expand my senses. I am officially no
longer just an architect. I have been practicing intuitive guidance,
soul coaching, and sound healing for a while now. I am comfier as
a multidimensional traveler of worlds.

The last few months, humanity was shaken by a unification event
unfolding across the planet. A new virus spread worldwide, and the
powers-that-be named it COVID-19.[106] Just last week, the World
Health Organization officially announced a pandemic when COVID-
19 steamrolled through 114 countries in three months.

Orion and I watch the news online, our social media feeds, and
talk with friends. We keep our eyes and ears open to information
as it comes. For the first time in my life, or the lives of my parents,

we are in a quarantine across the globe. The last pandemic was in 1917 when my grandparents and great-grandparents were alive.

With quarantine underway globally, life has shifted overnight. We are concerned for friends, family, and all of humanity as we collectively try to sort out what is happening. We are unaware that everything is about to change in profound ways.

The quarantine has shut down our event-based business, and our bread-and-butter work has dissolved overnight. We cancel over a dozen Sound Alchemy events in a few days, all scheduled for this spring. Scary as it is, I sense that there is a deeper gift at hand.

From a shamanic vantage point, we call such a gift "an ally." It may seem a stretch to see a virus as an ally, yet it is. My willingness to bring neutrality to the messages a virus brings helps me live inside my cosmic love story. It also helps me use the information creatively as medicine or support along the way.

Some allies, like a virus, can be deadly if abused or misunderstood. If harnessed, it can be an awesome helper, and this requires having respect for it and meeting it with awareness. One must approach any ally with respect and treat it sacredly.[107]

We accumulate allies along the path of life. Allies help us see with fresh eyes the world before us. They offer support, help, and medicine of various forms along the way. Some allies are friends and acquaintances that support us in times of need. We also become allies for others.

Working with allies is a great way to transform the "win-lose" metric in my life; when I acknowledge the myriad ways allies show up, I steadfastly reside in the "both-and" universe of our shared cosmic love story.

Some allies are strangers that cross our path, never to be seen again. In the winter of 1996, at age 25, I flew to France on a pilgrimage to see some architecture treasures. After, I was on my way to meet up with my sister Sierra in Rome. From there, we would journey to Israel together, where she was living at the time.

On arrival, the Paris airport loomed large before me. Multiple languages. Signs I didn't know how to read. My French was non-existent.

It was a whole foreign wilderness waiting for me with few tools. I had to find my train to Le Mans where I had booked a room for the night. I looked at my train ticket. I had a very short window to get there. I was tired, lost, and afraid to be stranded overnight in the airport alone.

A French woman approached me picking up on my distress. She had straight light brown hair that fell past her shoulders. Her smile was warm and kind. She softly asked in a delicious French accent, "Can I help you?"

"Yes!" I blurted out. Relief and embarrassment washed over me at the same time. I explained to her my situation and lifted my ticket for her to see. I was beyond grateful she spoke English!

She looked down, saw my timeline, and said, "It is going to be tight, but I think I can get you where you need to go." She looked me in the eye and directed, "Follow me. Do everything I do."

I did. Every move she made, I mimicked. Through tunnels, past ticket machines, and along platforms. When I got stuck at a turnstile, she circled back to help me, and off we went again. As I got used to the rhythm, we picked up speed. Minutes later, we arrived at my train platform, both of us out of breath.

She turned around and lifted her arms to direct me to the train doors and said, "Voila!"

I jumped on and turned around to thank her. The sound of the conductors announced in French we were departing. Every fiber of my being was alive with gratitude. I looked at her from above.

"How can I ever thank you?" I asked.

She smiled again and said, "It was my pleasure." Her kindness, her soft smile, and her wondrous accent. Oh, how I loved her. I didn't know her at all, but I loved her.

The doors of the train closed shut. She was smiling and waving through the small window. I waved back fiercely with a few tears finding their way down my face.

An ally.

To this day I still remember the gift of such loving support from a random stranger. My very own Earth angel. I would never see her again, yet I would remember her always.

Some allies show up in our lives for a longer duration. Healers or therapists that you go to repeatedly to help you overcome a chronic spiritual, emotional, mental, or physical issue. It takes a village to raise each one of us.

There are plant, animal, and mineral allies. The creatures that show up to support, protect, and heal us when we are in need — both seen and unseen. My passion for shamanism combined with my love of nature as a sustainability leader brought these allies into focus for me time and again.

Sometimes nature even becomes an ambassador on behalf of a deceased loved one.

At age 39, just after my father died, my siblings and I, fresh with grief, huddled in a quick meeting in his kitchen to discuss my father's memorial. My two sisters stood facing each other in a heated debate about a financial detail. My brother and I stood near them, not sure what to do. We knew it wasn't about the money. We had so much compassion for their pain, we stayed silent.

A few minutes in, we became aware of a black bumble bee over our sisters' head buzzing around. It was an unlikely place to find a bumble bee.

They didn't seem to see the small noisy ally as their raised voices continued to move their grief energy. The bumble bee then generated a louder sound by flying against the ceiling again and again with a persistent pulse.

Buzz, buzz, buzz, buzz, buzz! The bumble bee bounced against the ceiling again and again.

It worked. The bumble bee got their attention. They stopped arguing, and the bumble bee stopped its persistent ceiling bounce. In the new silence, we all looked up to watch it fly to the dishwasher. The bee landed on the top rack edge where my father liked to keep *buzzzzzy* at night cleaning after dinner.

My brother swooped in to capture the bee. I moved to get there before him as I exclaimed, "I got it!"

I scooped the bumble bee easily into my hands, walked outside, and set it on top of the glass patio table under the stars my father taught me. The small black creature turned towards me. My chest was tight with grief and love as I said, "Thanks dad." It flew away. I walked back inside processing the connection with my ally.

Some nature allies are related to power places like springs, mountains, forests, or a river that we have a special relationship with. *Some allies are related to the elements* like lightening, thunder, wind, water, earth, and fire. *Some allies are related to weather.* An ally could be the spirit of a storm or any big weather event.

Animals in the world might be the easiest ally for many of us to grasp. From my intimate relationships with pets to animals that cross my path, animals have taught me lessons about unconditional love, patience, empathy, and compassion. They have even slowed me down to help me avoid injury or helped me heal after one.

When I was 23, I had just flown back to the states from Prague, Czech Republic. I was returning after a summer abroad for a design course. I had just landed and was hanging out with friends on the Cal Poly San Luis Obispo campus — where I went to architecture school — when my jetlag hit me like an anvil. I said my goodbyes and walked home. I could barely keep my eyes open. I felt drunk but had not had any alcohol that night; I had never been tired like this before. I almost fell asleep walking. It was scary.

I looked up at that moment and a deer, buck, and two doe stood before me in the middle of my quiet neighborhood road. Maybe I was dreaming. I rubbed my eyes. My unexpected, graceful escorts were still there. I heard their hoofs on the asphalt road and their breath in the night air. I followed this four-legged family slowly. My curiosity in them gave me enough adrenaline to keep me awake. They stopped. I looked around. There was my house, right in front of me. I went inside in a reverie.

When I woke up, I was fully clothed on top of the covers. I rolled over and remembered the whole thing. I felt cared for. *My deer allies walked me home!*

At age 34, I was driving at night along Sir Francis Drake Boulevard in Marin, California. I was visiting some friends. A deer jumped in front of my car. I slammed on my brakes and was able to miss the deer. Less than a minute later, I heard a crashing sound ahead of me. I looked ahead to the intersection a few hundred yards in front of me. Two cars had just collided. I was slowed down just then by my perfectly timed ally. I was relieved I had not hit the deer. I was quite aware I would have been involved in that crash had the deer not stopped me.

Some allies are soul guides, loving ancestors, and spirit helpers. They support us from the other side by nudging us to act from love or send us warning signs to avoid danger. These allies may be old friends or relatives that have passed on who watch over us. Some may be powerful teachers, avatars, or soul guides who have looked after us for lifetimes.

At this critical time in our evolution, I believe COVID-19 is a powerful ally for humans. Just as we experienced the disruption of business as usual in our company Illuminating Hearts, this coronavirus arrives as a disrupter on a global scale, stopping many of us in our tracks. In the quarantine, and its aftermath, we get to reconsider our habits, our patterns, our beliefs, and even our focus as humans. This virus is helping us take a fresh look. Inconvenient? Yes. It is impacting many and I do not make light of this. Many are dying. It has upset our family's security and billions more.

Yet, we have a choice in how we respond to any crisis. It takes a creative open-mind and heart to see COVID-19 as a powerful ally. In a very short time, it has gotten millions of us to reevaluate our lives, our goals, government, our way of doing business, economies, health care system, educational system, military, our relationships to each other and the planet, climate change, our use of resources, and on and on.

I sense we are just barely getting started with the disruption, and my knowing tells me there is a long road ahead. Although there is a tight grip in my gut as the unknown looms, I take a deep breath to calm myself. I want to connect with the spirit of COVID-19 as an ally, to find out what I can.

The Earth and cosmos are singing to each of us, yet we must slow down enough to listen. I sit cross-legged on my meditation pillow, with my zafu and zabuton— a firm round cushion on top of a larger meditation sitting mat — propped up under my hips and legs for comfort. I close my eyes to begin to work my own energy, my Merkaba.

Eight years earlier, I was trained in activating the Merkaba.[108] The term Merkaba originates from Hebrew. It means "throne-chariot of God" in ancient Jewish mysticism. In ancient Egyptian hieroglyphics, *Mer* translates as rotating light or pyramid, *Ka* as spirit or life force, and *Ba* is body or physical reality. *Mer-Ka-Ba* means the spirit/body inside of counter-rotating fields of light. Picture wheels within wheels — or spirals of energy — as found in DNA, galaxies, and water flow. The Merkaba technology that we are all born with, but not all of us activate or work with consciously, transports our spirit/body from one dimension to another.

A beautiful compliment to my Merkaba activation is my understanding of the advanced Energy Codes© by Dr. Sue Morter[109] as well as various shamanic healing practices. My inner knowing as a soul has translated all these practices for me over the years, so I could synthesize the ways each tradition has informed the other. From there, I have created my own approach I call the "Cosmic Conference Call."[110]

Using breath, energetic awareness, and somatic movement, I connect with the energy field inside and outside my body. This includes my electromagnetic toroidal field that recycles Source energy without any effort on my part, as well as my energy centers or chakras.

After I am fully connected to the energy I am, my call with the cosmos starts. It is then that I stumble upon my first clear conversations with my guides.

I hear the words *we are here.*

Although I have had a strong intuition my whole life, I was surprised to hear these words. At the middle of my life, I have strengthened my intuition muscle to such a degree that I easily connect with the quantum field. I converse with parts of myself at different ages to evolve my story. I have conversations with my Higher Self for guidance. I have heard the words of clients' deceased loved ones and translated their Higher Self to support my healing sessions.

This was different.

I hear these words clearly in a way I have not experienced before. Allies that have been working with me for lifetimes were speaking to me. I could hear them. I was hearing my soul guides. Until this moment, I always knew they were there, but their messages came in more nuanced forms.

We are here.

We are here is shorthand for we are here for you now. Thank you for being the oracle you are. We have much to say, and through you. You bring a humor, wisdom, and sincerity that is needed to receive our messages at this time. You have resisted us in the past because you have been afraid of what would come through. You were born with the golden key, and now you have used it.

Your inherent energetic architecture helps you communicate with us. You will teach many to remember and activate their own cosmic phone line to their wisdom. This is how you give birth to stars.

The golden keys are in your body. As you squeeze the muscles at the base of the spine and breathe in the belly, this piezoelectric pulse ignites the vagus nerve and the spiral of the cerebrospinal fluid. The electricity generated sends a signal to your pineal gland. As you feel into the location of the pineal gland, you simultaneously engage the gate of the heart. This turns your channel to "on."

You have been building the circuitry for years, you have turned the key before. Yet in the crescendo of the last few weeks and months, you have built the last circuit you needed to truly hear our vibration which come through as words in your mind. This process combines all the golden keys into a larger key, unlocking the gate of your heart so that you can hear us.

Your angst, your old stories, had to come up for release so you could find the opening in your own right time. Insecurities. Self-imposed limits. Sensitivities enhanced. What you call shadow work is a revealing of the hidden gifts and wisdom waiting for you behind every suppression.

Therefore, it is important you are kind with yourself for your shadows; be kind to your shadows. All of these coping strategies were serving a purpose throughout your life, a purpose that no longer exists. Release your old construct, based on old conditioning, so you can make space for your deeper knowing that has been there all along.

Just look at all your journals. Your poetry is a knowing that translates love into words. What you call making love is merging with the divine in all things. Your poetry serves that essential quality of aliveness, which serves your alchemy.

You are trust. So, when you trust, you allow you. It is time to share your open knowing with the world. You will know when and how. There is no urgency. Ever. Yet the time is now. Always and in all ways.

Embrace all the aspects of you: those that you are uncomfortable with, those that please you, and those you do not even know you have lost. The return brings more vitality to you. As you open again to these aspects of self that you have once shunned, you become available to love within and without. Turn your eyes towards the stars. Remember your wholeness. Remember your holiness. Merge again with Source.

I sit there astonished, processing. My heart beats faster. I shift my sitting position. I feel questions arising inside me but don't have to form them. The guides continue:

When it comes to the virus, it is one thing to dialogue with the fear, it is another thing to entertain it. This virus is ushering a global unity event. It is a grand revealer that will change the narrative of the human story, but it will take some time.

Empower your psychological self. Lean into your shadows and discover new ways to inner parent yourself.

Empower your evolutionary self. After you reframe your shadows, then move on to the vision of possibility, that which is opening. The shadow and the vision can happen simultaneously. Your mind will not understand, only your core will grasp that the psychological and evolutionary co-exist.

Empower your mystical self. The visions you see are being realized. Do not worry or concern yourself with how. Real and miracle. Pragmatic and possible. You are all at the same time.

This is your multi-dimensional nature: psychological, mystical, evolutionary. You are learning how to hold multiple dimensions and perspectives: past, present, and future. One step at a time is all you need. You know enough now to access your alchemical wisdom.

The future of humanity is relational. In terms of relationships, you are all here to sing the song "Let it Be."[111] Each human on this planet is learning to practice paradox. Some will get it faster than others. Give space for self and other to be inside their respective personal adventure. Be honest. Be kind. Both are possible. The variety is a joy waiting to be opened each day.

I sit and breathe. It is as if each word is a crystal with multi-facets. I feel the power of their message like a cool drink of water hydrating me. I say, "Thank you. Hearing you is all so new and so beautiful." I add, "A part of me is slightly overwhelmed and afraid. What will people think if I channel? How do I share this?"

The guides respond.

We sense your fear and separation. As you claim who you are in truth, you dissolve that illusion. You are with us now. Do not fear us. Do not fear our messages, nor our use of you, for you are a part of us. Not at the level of what your personality knows — that part of you is habituated in competition and calculation to survive the world. That part of you was born of years of thought and practice. She learned how to be in the world by the agreements of your mother and father, your siblings, teachers, and friends.

You are a part of us. The part of your soul that exists beyond the limits of your material plane or dimension, that aspect of you that is not bound by the body. Your Higher Self translates our messages to you. What is learned may be unlearned. This is the good news. You can learn anew, and it won't take you years this time. You have tasted the upper room, the higher octave, the claim of your divine knowing. [112] You have sampled the frequency there.

When you slow down your reaction to a response, you have stepped out of the known and into the now. The now is never known. It is always the unknown. No matter the desire and longing for the known, that is not what you came for. When you slow down, you open space for the truth. The truth may arrive as a feeling, which may be uncomfortable. That discomfort is essential to your next step. Put the device down often. Create quiet. Sit. Listen. Be. Nap. Do nothing, as often as you can. Take breaks in your writing and channeling. Be intimate with yourself. This is what meditation means: self-intimacy.

When you next sit down to channel, trust what is coming forth. This way, you let YOU come through.

The future is indeed relational. Your journey of intimacy with Orion is not only life-changing for you both, but also life-changing for others. As you learn, you lift others. Your identity cannot see this now, yet a part of you remembers, and that is the part that guides you along, that reaches out to us.

When it comes to Orion and other relationships, do not suppress your needs. Your suppression of needs is older than this lifetime, and a misunderstanding of what service is. Honor your needs, express, and ask. At the same time, you are learning to let the need lift to the upper room. A need cannot exist there in fear and separation. The need becomes distilled down to its purest form which is love. Love does not strive. Yet, love expresses. You are not here to live and learn alone. Needs are beautiful and you are complete as you are. Both hold hands in the dance of life.

My electric body, my skin, feels alive. My heart hum is strong and clear. Presence vibrates through every cell.

Since my guides came into my life more clearly, I now stand in a kind of permanent cosmic conference call. I take this down-time through the pandemic to channel as an everyday practice. I embrace the magnificence of my body, while saying yes to my soul's instructions. As I live into my name Astara, the stars speak to me. The narrowness of my upbringing tugs at me as I expand into a multidimensional perspective. I respect the tension. Compassion and honesty unite, leaving room to hold the brutal and the beautiful. The sacred and profane are both welcome as I activate this new permission slip.

The stars whisper, *You are a channel to the stars. You teach others. This is how you give birth to stars.*

"You are never alone or helpless. The force that guides the stars guides you too."

– Shri Shri Anandamurti

Planetary, Intergalactic

It is Sunday morning, March 20, 2022. It is the first day of spring. About this time of year, I get impatient for new signs of growth, desperate to feast my eyes on anything green. As a California native, my muscle memory is still oriented to the warm temperatures and irrigation that allow greenery and colorful blooms all year long. When I moved to Nebraska, I enjoyed being reacquainted with winter. The full force of the four seasons had been absent from my life since my early Ohio days. I love watching crisp fall become snowy winter, but by mid-February or early March, the brown of winter takes its toll on me.

I get out of bed and hear Orion moving around downstairs. The smell of omelets, butter, and coffee wafts up through the stairwell. I walk to the bathroom window, pull up the blinds and look out. Darn, still no green in sight.

As I walk to the closet to change, my heart brings my "Vernal Equinox" poem to mind. I often think of this poem each first spring day. I recall the last stanza with a fresher perspective:

Like the Cereus that only blooms | once a year in the middle of the night. | When no one is looking, | something starts, | shifts, | gains new physics.[113]

As I start to get dressed, a new gestalt offers itself to me. In my words I see my "psychological-self" that hopes for past resolution. I see my "mystical self" that seeks the eternal now. I see my "evolutionary self" that desires new visions of the future. All these archetypes coalesce beautifully and unexpectedly in the poem of 31-year-old me.

I think, *How did I know this?*

Starting in my late teens, I've been hungry to understand the past and heal. Since the earliest I can remember, I've been mystically oriented towards the eternal present moment inside the heart, nature, and the stars. Starting at age five or possibly younger, I've been evolutionary, remembering the future all along. I have become the *new physics.*

Outside of time, *when no one is looking,* all of my extraordinary events have already happened and are always happening. When I wrote the poem at age 31, I was beginning to translate my future, I just didn't know it then. Inside my heart, every dream, every poem, every channeled message, every life choice has been a soul re-membering. I have been saying *"Yes!"* to my soul longer than I realized. I already had intimacy with myself across time; all of it was happening at once. I just had to remember it.

I think, *My whole life I've been practicing this? Wow!*

My heart answers, *Yes.*

Smiling, I remember the bold alchemy statement and say out loud to my empty bedroom, "Behold, I make all things new."

I roll out my purple yoga mat on the amber and brick red Persian rug by my bed. I begin to stretch and ease into my body. I take further inventory.

Today, just three months from turning 52, I am approaching nine years since my epic move to Omaha and eight years since the pivotal day I first met Orion. I inhale and stretch into downward dog. I exhale.

I realize it's been seven years since we boldly started Illuminating Hearts together, choosing energy healing combined with sound healing as our full-time gig.

I inhale and feel my spine go longer. I exhale and spread my toes.

Almost six years have whizzed by since I leapt beyond the known of my corporate architecture world.

I inhale and fold into child's pose on the mat, curved in and letting my spine rest with my head touching my arms folded beneath me. I started channeling the stars in earnest two years ago when the pandemic began, allowing more intimacy with the cosmos. I eventually named my collection of soul guides — the non-physical beings communicating immense soul concepts with me — the Galactic Council. Although we had to rearrange our event-based world then, our private work has been taking off since I started channeling my guides.

After some further breath and stretching, I roll up my yoga mat, lean it against the wall, and walk to my tall narrow nightstand. I pick up my phone to check my email and texts. I read a client text of beautiful gratitude from their session yesterday.

After seven years of formally sharing my intuitive soul healing gifts as my new profession,[114] I now have hundreds of clients that I have helped build bridges to their young self and future self across time, revealing healing and building confidence for full-permission living.

I call their testimonials "love letters." I savor every single one. Reading a client "love letter" first thing in my day feels like gold because helping my clients is my "why."

Standing in my bedroom I feel solid, yet I know I'm 99 percent space arranged just so, flying through the Milky Way on a planet with so many humans evolving, and all of us trying to live together. When I get word that I've been helpful on another human's path, my heart sings. I'm aware that my persistent hunger to help others stems from a feeling of not being able to help my mom heal so many years ago. Her adult struggles with her difficult childhood unknowingly instilled in me a drive to be a healer, and although it had its challenges, I am left with the grace she gave me.

Each reflection a client gives me feels like a revelation. It's difficult to describe the feeling of fulfillment when I experience the impact that living into my soul calling has made in others life.

I had known contentment at a soul level was possible by living into my dreams, but I never knew it could feel like this. There's a joy that surges through me in moments when I find good news and want to shout it from the mountain top. This is bigger than that. It's immeasurable, priceless, and warms my whole body from the heart outward.

I text loving gratitude to my client and set my phone down. Brown Dog is stretched out happily on our bed. I make a casual attempt at straightening the comforter and pillows around him. I curl up next to him to give him scratches behind his ears and rub his belly to share in the love I feel.

I have been visiting the tiny space of my heart so often — where I step into eternity, into the unknown, free of time — that I now practice timeless creatorship easily from the gate of my heart. I inhale the unwritten and exhale out the unanswered.

I think about what the equinox is. I inwardly smile as, *"my heart as the equator,"* comes back to me from my conversation with my 19-year-old self. The equinoxes are the only times a year when the sun shines directly on, or perpendicular to, our equator.[115] So, I turn my attention to our star, the sun, shining on the vista of brown outside. Young me reminded me that my body's like the Earth's body. My heart equator is where the new physics begins.

I keep discovering ingredients to live my creative soul-aligned life. In addition to synthesizing the psychological, mystical, and evolutionary, "on purpose-ness" is an important ingredient. The wisdom of Dolly Parton whispers in my head with her smile, wink, and honeyed Southern voice, "Find what you love and do it on purpose."[116] Dolly, I'll see your insight and raise you one. Creating intimacy with self and others on purpose is the game changer.

Everything — *and I mean everything* — each of us does affects the world around us. That is why it's best to wake up to our shadows, our desires, and learn what makes us tick. It's important we activate what we are here to do and be, so that we can switch timelines and step into the cosmic love story together. This is how we collectively *re-member* our global future.

I can choose an "either-or" or "win-lose" or "lose-lose" story, where I worry there isn't enough to go around, my life isn't as good as my neighbor's, and that my world will be taken from me. Or I can live into the "both-and" or "win-win" story, where I understand that there is enough to go around, my life is uniquely designed for me, and I have plenty of love to share.

I picked the "both-and" version years ago. I've been writing new worlds into being with firm hands for decades now. When I first sat in my basement to open those journals, I knew it would be influential, but I didn't realize it would become alchemy. Lily of all ages has returned wonder and power home to me. Future me has given clues to my magnificent future that awaits. The self I have known has been transposed to the higher music of my souls true calling.[117]

My recent time travel has built incredible circuitry in my body and field, reflecting upgrades in my world. I am no longer writing in the basement where my time travel started. In this now, I write upstairs in a newly designed workspace. I have moved into the literal metaphor of the "upper room" my guides refer to.

The news, the banks, and the shifting global climate inside and around me still upend me some days, but with my inner guidance intact and my guides by my side, I feel ready for what comes. My soul syllabus has a particular focus now, teaching me about accountability and acceptance. The oppression out there can only exist if it is also inside me. Dang. That darn hologram.

I get up from the bed and go to the window again. Although the lawns, trees, and foliage are all brown, I get that I'm the green new growth I'm hungry for.

I am paving new ways of being that are self-organizing, generous, and collaborative. I practice every day, multiple times a day. Some days are better than others. I practice getting my head brain, heart brain, gut brain, and entire body to work with each other more fluidly and lovingly. Building coherence is how I hold the tension of paradox — the tension of Knowing (with a capital K) and not knowing, *at the same time.*

I see the opposing forces of right and wrong, alike and different, revealed for what they are: teachers. Even "tor-mentors" are mentors of some kind. The great disorder of intimacy in society is a distant drone note pressing me inward. I embrace myself. A new era of intimacy beckons. A yes to me is a yes to life, and a yes to the world.

I hear the Beastie Boys in my head as I feel the hip-hop pulse of the cosmos asking me to step up my dance of intimacy, this time in intimacy with the stars. "Gonna shine like a sunbeam | Another dimension, new galaxy | Intergalactic, planetary."[118]

It is then I hear the familiar hum of my heart and feel the whoosh of electricity flow through me. Next to me, a woman appears with all grey hair and a big smile on her face. It is me. She leans in and whispers, "You are going to love what I have to tell you."

I smile and say, "I'm ready."

How the Stars Tell Time[119]

By Astara

The telescope of my mind
explores elliptical orbits
spiraling their dance around the sun, our star.

Somewhere, beyond my eyeline,
or even my imagination,
different planets orbit another star.

Far far away the stars wink.
My senses try to measure just how far,
far far away is.

The speed of their light,
lit billions of years
before my gaze locks in.

Yet the magnet of my heart
that surfs electric currents,
crosses the distance in a flash.

Within my earthly senses,
and the limited logic of mathematical equations
trying to grasp the breath of existence,

lie the rods, cones, light receptor cells,
telescopes, planetariums, wires, satellites,
codes, and insatiable algorithms.

Beyond all our inadequate constructions,

as well as within them,
lies an electric truth:

field-aligned currents
carry love instantly
between me, any star, or planet.

Electromagnetic space currents send messages
between me and me
dancing in different timelines.

The stars wink enthusiastically.
Their Morse-code twinkle
confirming my limited sight.

I wink back at the sky knowingly,
sending the spark of my
response in an instant.

What is time? I whisper.
The stars answer,

Time is a gate.

Past and future,
abrupt and fluid,
slow and swift,
linear and non-linear,
binary and non-binary,
exist all at once.

Constrained and limitless,
one-dimensional and multidimensional,
time is shaped from where you stand.

Where is the gate? I whisper.
The stars shimmer and whisper back,

The gate is your heart.

Acknowledgements

Although I put the words to page, I did not write alone. This book was written in collaboration with an entire team of earth angels, loving ancestors, and spirit guides.

A cosmic sized thank you to my husband Orion. Your fierce encouragement and abiding love gave me the support and fertile space to blossom my story. Your audacious honesty fueled my willingness and perseverance to dive into the shadows to bring this personal opus to the world.

A bow of eternal thanks to my mother, Lily, who fueled my bravery, my joy of learning, my art, my poetry, and my most valuable lessons. A wave of deep appreciation to my father, Carlyle, who gifted me the stars, my independence, my work ethos, and my love of books. You both not only handed me the keys to freedom, you helped me open the door. May your memory and legacy live on through these pages.

I am thankful for my siblings Sierra, Tim, and Maribel who in so many ways have made my stories possible. Thank you all for a lifetime of great conversations individually and together. You have brought me steady presence, giving me buoyancy inside the rough waters of life. Even across the miles, your presence is the wind that carries my sail forward.

Sierra, thank you for being the first to tutor me in writing composition and readability. Thank you for reclaiming our Jewish heritage. You've been a generous resource revealing to me the beauty within Judaism. Thank you for diving into our great Aunt Eva's manuscript, offering me new dimensions of thought about a relative we never met. I am grateful for all that you bring to our family!

Tim, thank you for loaning me your sci-fi books all those years ago. Thank for your support and encouragement, especially your prompt response as I persistently texted you family history questions.

Maribel, thank you for being my book cheerleader. I am grateful to you for showing me what intentional evolution can look like, modeled inside the long game of life. I am specifically grateful to you for sharing your Master of Divinity expertise, helping me find just the right bible references.

I place my hand over my heart with a deep bow to my soul friend Andrea Howard. Your kindness, active support, and cheer along my writing journey has been crucial to this book. Your willing reading and feedback helped me smooth out so many wrinkles, even up to the final hours! Words do not adequately reflect the depth of gratitude for your active friendship in my life.

A big thank you to my soul sister Jessie Maran. Your heartstorming and thoughtful co-dreaming were in fact the initial germination of this book. I literally couldn't have written this book without you. Your support, ideas, and encouragement throughout have been invaluable.

Thank you to my aunt Leslee Mayo, for sending me a copy of great aunt Eva's manuscript during my lineage research, helping me unpack the heritage of my given name. What a precious gift.

Thank you to my cousin Kristine Miller for staying in touch all these years, and for helping me find helpful bible passages referring to choosing a new name.

Thank you to the rest of my extended family — cousins, nephews, nieces, aunts, uncles, and in-laws. For those not mentioned in the book directly, you are 100 percent inside my adventures. Each of you are fundamental to my evolution and I love you with all my heart.

Thank you Sage Adderly for bringing your expertise and assembling a rock-star publishing team to help bring this book into the world. Without your creativity, support, guidance, and gifts of synthesis and organization, this book would still be on training wheels held hostage inside my hard drive.

A slide, twirl, and hip bump of joy to my soul brother Atasiea. Thank you for dancing into my life a decade ago to help me remember my star name and then years later, writing the forward to my book. Thank you for your bonus notes in the final days. Until I can dance on the sand next to you at the edge of the Pacific, a big cosmic sashay to you from the heartland to express my thanks to have found you after lifetimes.

Life unfolds while I write — in all its beauty and strife. Thank you brave, creative, and inspiring Daria Hlazatova for designing the exquisite cover art for this book which arrived during a dangerous time in your world. I am beyond grateful for the divine timing of you in my life, and now your art on my book. Continued blessings to you in the Ukraine.

Big gratitude to the Souljourn Soul Council I am privileged to collaborate with: Kristi Pederson, Frank Wolfe, Christina Pierce, and Jill Schrack — your willingness, bravery, love, energy, and support has buoyed me while completing this healing book. You remind me of the beauty that can happen when I say yes to the holistic collaborative magic sauce of the universe.

I am forever thankful to the ancestors whose stories I carry in my blood. I stand on your shoulders knowing I am living the wildest dream you never thought imaginable. You are the ones who made living into my dreams possible.

I bow to all the teachers, peer mentors, and clients who have crossed my path over the years, you have taught me so much. You have contributed vast knowledge, wisdom, and understanding to this book.

To my soul family across time and space that I have not named here, thank you for helping me become more me than I know how to be. Each of your names are written in the stars by the knowing in my heart.

I love you.

Notes

1. Raven, Astara. "Vernal Equinox." Illuminate Blog. Illuminating Hearts, 2022, astararaven.love/illuminate-blog/vernal-equinox.

The Future is Relational

2. Story is defined as "a true narrative, or one presumed to be true, relating to important events and famous people of the past; a historical account or anecdote…with discernible theme or meaning. The development or past existence of a person, thing, country, institution, etc., considered as narrated or as a subject for narration." (OED) I add to this definition: discernment. It is important to understand where a story originates — from either the "win-lose" or "either-or" or "lose-lose" of a fragmented ego to the "both-and" or "win-win" of a healthy ego.

3. Raven, Astara. "Vernal Equinox." Illuminate Blog. Illuminating Hearts, 2022, astararaven.love/illuminate-blog/vernal-equinox.

4. Selig, Paul. Beyond the Known: Realization. St. Martin's Publishing Group, 2019.

5. The New Shorter Oxford English Dictionary. Oxford University Press, 1993.

6. Selig, Paul. The Book of Love and Creation. Penguin Group, 2012.

7. The Matrix. Directed by Lana Wachowski and Lilly Wachowski, Warner Brothers, 1999.

8. The New Shorter Oxford English Dictionary. Oxford University Press, 1993.

9. Revelation 21:5. Holy Bible. King James Version, Zondervan, 2002, www.biblegateway.com.

10. Selig, Paul. The Book of Truth. Penguin Group, 2017.

11. Haramein, Nassim. Quantum Gravity and the Holographic Mass. Physical Review & Research International, 2012, ISSN: 2231-1815, Page 270-292.

12. "Shifting from Disconnected to Connected." World View Shift, Unified Science Course, Module 1.4.2, Resonance Science Foundation, 2021, www.resonancescience.org/products/unified-science-course.

13. Selig, Paul. Sourced from I Am the Word to The Kingdom book. Penguin Group and St. Martin's Publishing, 2010-2021.

14. Raven, Astara. "Wisdom Within." Illuminate Blog. Illuminating Hearts, 2021, astararaven.love/illuminate-blog/wisdom-within.

More Things

15. Shakespeare, William. Hamlet. Act 1, Scene 5, www.sparknotes. com/nofear/shakespeare/hamlet/act-1-scene-5.
16. "Shifting from Disconnected to Connected." Module 1.4.2, World View Shift, Unified Science Course, Resonance Science Foundation, 2021, www.resonancescience.org/products/unified-science-course.
17. Morter, Dr. Sue. The Energy Codes. Simon & Schuster, 2019.
18. Rollin McCraty, Ph.D. "The Science of the Heart: Exploring the Role of the Heart in Human Performance." Volume 2. HeartMath Institute, 2015, www.heartmath.org/resources/downloads/ science-of-the-heart.

Science is a Verb

19. www.sciencebuddies.org/science-fair-projects/science-fair/ steps-of-the-scientific-method.
20. Rovelli, Carlo. The Order of Time. Riverhead Books, 2018.
21. www.gutenberg.org/files/3485/3485-h/3485-h.htm.
22. www.sheldrake.org/reactions/tedx-whitechapel-the-banned-talk.
23. Heliocentric, or sun-centered, represents the sun as the center of the accepted astronomical model of the solar system. Astronomy measured from or considered in relation to the center of the sun.
24. Geocentric, or earth-centered, represents the Earth as the center in former astronomical systems. Former astronomy was measured from or considered in relation to the center of the Earth.
25. A unified field theory attempts to unite the big scale of Einstein's Field Equations relating to the curvature of space-time and the smaller scale of Yang-Mills and Dirac equations relating to particle interactions at the quantum level.
26. Because of these incredible discoveries, the word quantum has become a popular household word. Quantum science. Quantum healing. Quantum Touch. And so on. Some criticize the wide use of the term as un-scientific. Yet the frequency of use reflects its importance to humans in our world. Regardless of your personal opinion, the increased use of this word implies a stretch of reality beyond what we previously knew. The term quantum as a trend indicates a fundamental shift is in progress – from depending not only on what we see as "real" to being more curious about what we cannot see as a part of our reality too.
27. A fractal is an object or quantity that displays self-similarity at all scales; it is a pattern repeating at all scales.

28. Oestreicher, Christian. A History of Chaos Theory. PubMed.gov, 2007, www.ncbi.nlm.nih.gov/pmc/articles/PMC3202497.

29. Holograph means the image of the whole is present at every point; rooted in holo meaning whole, and graph meaning image. Hologram means the information of the whole is present at every point; rooted in the term gram, as in grammar.

30. Haramein, Nassim. Quantum Gravity and the Holographic Mass, Physical Review & Research International, 2012, ISSN: 2231-1815, Page 270-292.

31. geometricunity.org

32. Erdelyi, Karina Margit. "Can Trauma be Passed Down from One Generation to the Next?" Psycom.net, March 2020, www.psycom.net/epigenetics-trauma.

33. Wallace, David Foster. "Plain Old Untrendy Troubles and Emotions" theguardian.com, September 2009, www.theguardian.com/books/2008/sep/20/fiction.

34. Pollack, Gerald H. The Fourth Phase of Water: Beyond Solid Liquid Vapor. Ebner and Sons Publisher, 2013.

35. Benyus, Janine. Biomimicry: Innovation Inspired by Nature. Harper Perennial, 2002.

36. Rovelli, Carlo. The Order of Time. Riverhead Books, 2018.

37. Tamburo, Mike. Sounds Eternal, soundseternal.com.

Truth's Stretch Marks

38. I define alchemy in the introduction as seeing the divine within and around us. An alchemist knows there is nothing that is not God. (see introduction)

39. Shainberg, Catherine. Kabbalah and the Power of Dreaming: Awakening the Visionary Life. Inner Traditions, 2005.

40. Selig, Paul. The Book of Love and Creation. Penguin Group, 2012.

Ghosts

41. Soul loss is defined as when part of our soul, may flee, fracture, or hide in an effort to protect itself during an overwhelming event.

42. The word shaman is derived from the language of the Tungusic peoples of Siberia and literally means 'the one who sees in the dark' or 'one who knows' depending on the resource. There is no single agreed-upon definition for the word "shamanism" among anthropologists, www.sharedwisdom.com/shamanwisdom.

43. Since time is happening all at once, past lives are actually parallel lives or other lifetimes — other expressions of our soul in other dimensions. I use the term past lives here for accessibility.

44. "What is Change?" Rewired, created by Dr. Joe Disepnza, season 1, episode 2, Gaia, 2019.

The Heart of Things

45. "The Power of the Heart: Heartmath." YouTube, uploaded by Beyond Words Publishing, 2015, youtu.be/4MNHsNn19ug.

46. Akasha is a Sanskrit word that means primary substance or that out of which all things are formed.

47. "8th Dimension & the Akashic Records" Initiation, created by Matias de Stefano, Season 1, Episode 8, Gaia, 2019.

48. Awakening the Illuminating Heart Workshop (ATIH) teaches Drunvalo Melchizadek's method to activate the Merkaba. I attended trainings in San Francisco, 2012, led by Ron LaPlace and in Portland, 2016, led by Viola Rose, theschoolofremembering.com.

49. Illuminating Hearts, LLC, astararaven.love/illuminating-hearts.

50. Raven, Astara. "Healing and Alchemy" Illuminate Blog. Illuminating Hearts, 2019, astararaven.love/illuminate-blog/healing-and-alchemy.

A Song Singing You Into Being

51. Raven, Astara. "A Song Singing You Into Being." Illuminate Blog. Illuminating Hearts, 2022, astararaven.love/illuminate-blog/a-song-singing-you-into-being.

The Middle

52. Szymborska, Wislawa. "Love at First Sight" MAP: Collected and Last Poems. Houghton Mifflin Harcourt Publishing Company, 2015.

Los Angeles

53. Rovelli, Carlo. The Order of Time. Riverhead Books, 2018.

Time Portal

54. Church, Dawson. The Genie in Your Genes. Energy Psychology Press, 2014.

The Power of Words

55. Holy Bible. New Revised Standard Version, National Council of the Churches of Christ, 1989, www.biblegateway.com.

The Pool

56. van der Kolk, Bessel. The Body Keeps the Score. Penguin Publishing Group, 2015.

Judith and Hannah

57. Rovelli, Carlo. Helgoland. Riverhead Books, 2021.
58. Judd, Eva Torf. Stones for Bread. Unpublished Memoir Final Draft, 1939.

Astara

59. Holy Bible. King James Version, Zondervan, 2002, www.biblegateway.com.
60. Solara. The Star-Borne: A Remembrance for the Awakened Ones. Star Borne Unlimited, 1989.

Reunited

61. Raven, Astara. "A Thousand Poems Ask for You by Name." Illuminate Blog. Illuminating Hearts, 2022, astararaven.love/illuminate-blog/a-thousand-poems-ask.
62. Colvin, Shawn. "Orion in the Sky." Fat City, Columbia Records, 1992, Track 6.

Cliff Jumping

63. Washington-Alexandria Architecture Center (WAAC), archdesign.caus.vt.edu/waac.
64. Gongs Unlimited, gongs-unlimited.com.

Wedding Trail

65. Raven, Astara. "Risking Everything." Illuminate Blog. Illuminating Hearts, 2022, astararaven.love/illuminate-blog/risking-everything.
66. Kern Family Farm, www.kernfamilyfarm.com.

67. Worldwide Opportunities on Organic Farms (WWOOF), wwoof.
net.

68. Artemis Music, bandcamp.com/artemis.

69. James Groft Music, jamesgroft.com.

The Donut

70. Double Torus Dynamic: Nassim Haramein. YouTube. Thrive
Movement, October 13, 2011, youtu.be/JyqBnd3Xwck.

Willow Tree

71. Raven, Astara. "The Forest is Lit From Within." Illuminate Blog.
Illuminating Hearts, 2022, astararaven.love/illuminate-blog/
the-forest-is-lit-from-within.

72. Selig, Paul. The Book of Knowing and Worth. Penguin Group,
2013.

73. Arrien, Angeles. The Second Half of Life: Opening the Eight Gates
of Wisdom. Sounds True, Incorporated, 2007.

Flying at Night

74. As told to me by my psyche in a dream at age 35, rediscovered in a
journal at age 43, found and shared at age 47. I love time travel.

Out of the Blue

75. Tippett, Krista, host. "Junot Diaz – Radical Hope is Our
Best Weapon." On Being with Krista Tippett, The On
Being Project, 14 Sept 2017, onbeing.org/programs/
junot-diaz-radical-hope-is-our-best-weapon-sep2017.

The Secret to Life

76. Amos, Tori. "Upside Down – B-Side Version." A Piano: The
Collection. Rhino Atlantic, 2006.

San Diego

77. Bach, Richard. Bridge Across Forever: A True Love Story. Harper
Collins, 2006.

Architecture

78. Bach, Richard. Bridge Across Forever: A True Love Story. Harper Collins, 2006.

Black Whole

79. Gaugelin, Michael. The Cosmic Clocks: From Astrology to a Modern Science. ACS Publications, 1982.

80. HeartMath Institute, www.hearmath.org.

81. Jensen, Janice, director. Haramein, Nassim, actor. The Black Whole. Gaiam – Entertainment, 2011.

82. C. W. Misner, K. Thorne, J.A. Wheeler, D.I. Kaiser. "Present day quantum field theory gets rid by a renormalization process of an energy density in the vacuum that would formally be infinite if not removed by this renormalization." Gravitation. Princeton University Press, 2017.

83. The Fibonacci sequence is also known as Phi or the Golden Ratio.

84. Humans are at the exact midpoint of two scales: the Universe and Planck's distance. Microtubules make up the boundary condition of our biological cells, they fall exactly in half between the extremely large, the universe, and the extremely small, the Planck's distance, where relativity ceases to be valid, and quantum law takes over. Planck's length is not the smallest length, it's only a reference point. Thanks to the infinite nature of the universe, there is always something smaller than we can know. Just like Nassim removes 'renormalization' to discover the true density of the vacuum, he recalculates the density of the mass of a proton, which is different than traditionally accepted calculations. Nassim discovers a more accurate mass of a 'black hole proton'. This true proton mass creates a gravitational force that can overcome the strong Coulomb force that tends to push protons apart. (The Black Whole. Gaiam, 2011)

85. The mathematical pattern or structure of the vacuum is a 64-tetrahedral grid. It is comprised of 8-star tetrahedrons, each with their vector equilibrium pointing out. When they come together into the 64-tetrahedron grid the vector equilibrium points in. (The Black Whole. Gaiam, 2011)

86. Flower of Life image at back of book or astararaven.love/meet-astara/#startime.

87. Jensen, Janice, director. Haramein, Nassim, actor. The Black Whole. Gaiam – Entertainment, 2011.

Tiny Space

88. "If someone should say to you: | In the fortified City of the Imperishable, |Our body, there is a lotus, | And in this lotus a tiny space: | What does it contain that one | Should desire to know it? | You must reply: | As vast as this space without | Is the tiny space within your heart: | Heaven and earth are found in it, | Fire and air, sun and moon, | Lightning and the constellations, | Whatever belongs to you here below | And all that doesn't, | All this is gathered in that tiny space | Within your heart." (Chandogya Upanishad 8.1.2-3)

89. Agnew, Brooks. Remembering the Future: The Physics of the Soul and Time Travel. IUniverse, 2010.

90. "The Power of the Heart: Heartmath." YouTube, uploaded by Beyond Words Publishing, 2015, youtu.be/4MNHsNn19ug.

91. Martin, Steve. Monologue. SNL Transcripts Tonight, 10/23/76, snltranscripts.jt.org/76/76emono.phtml.

The Return

92. Ingerman, Sandra. "Soul Retrieval" Sandra Ingerman. 2013, www.sandraingerman.com/soulretrieval.html.

93. Ingerman, Sandra. Soul Retrieval: Mending the Fragmented Self. Harper, 1991.

The Claim

94. Raven, Astara. "Leap," Illuminate Blog. Illuminating Hearts, 2020, astararaven.love/illuminate-blog/leap.

95. Holy Bible. King James Version, Zondervan, 2002.

Change the Channel

96. www.therecoveryvillage.com/mental-health/ptsd/related/ptsd-vs-ptsi.

97. Beck, Martha. Diana, Herself. Cynosure Publishing, 2016.

98. Lamott, Anne. Bird by Bird. Anchor Books, 1995.

99. Tao, Lin. "DMT: You Cannot Imagine a Stranger Drug or a Stranger Experience" Vice.com, 2014, www.vice.com/en/article/5gkkpd/dmt-you-cannot-imagine-a-stranger-drug-or-a-stranger-experience-365.

100. Mirante, Daniel. "Introductions" Ayahuasca.com, 2018, www.
ayahuasca.com/introductions/an-introduction-to-ayahuasca.
101. "Entheogen", New World Encyclopedia, 2017, www.
newworldencyclopedia.org/entry/Entheogen.
102. Frindel, Jeremy, director. Dass, Ram, actor. One Track Heart: The
Story of Krishna Das, Zeitgeist Films, 2012.
103. Glennon, Doyle. Carry on Warrior. Scribner, 2014.

Other Lives, Genetics, Culture, and Me

104. Raven, Astara. "There is Always Movement No Matter How Small,"
Illuminate Blog. Illuminating Hearts, 2022, astararaven.love/
illuminate-blog/there-is-always-movement.
105. Rosen, Michael, author. Oxenbury, Helen, illustrator. Going on a
Bear Hunt. Alladin Paperback, Reprint Ed., 2003.

Cosmic Conference Call

106. COVID-19 is the disease caused by a new coronavirus called
SARS-CoV-2. WHO first learned of this new virus on 31 December
2019, following a report of a cluster of cases of 'viral pneumonia'
in Wuhan, People's Republic of China, www.who.int/emergencies/
diseases/novel-coronavirus-2019/question-and-answers-hub.
107. Stevens, Jose. "Perceiving COVID-19 as an Ally" Powerpath.
com, March 18 2020, thepowerpath.com/power-path-library/
articles-by-jose-stevens/perceiving-covid-19-as-an-ally.
108. Melchizadek, Drunvalo. Awakening The Illuminating Heart
Workshop, The School of Remembering, theschoolofremembering.
com.
109. Astara Raven is the first certified Energy Codes © Facilitator in
Nebraska. Read more: Morter, Dr. Sue. The Energy Codes. Simon &
Schuster, 2019.
110. Home Base of the Soul online course, Inner Space Academy,
Illuminating Hearts, innerspaceacademy.love/#homebaseofthesoul.
111. The Beatles. "Let it Be." Let it Be. Apple, 1970.
112. The upper room came into my field of reference when I read
Alchemy by Paul Selig. My guides use this phrase since it is
terminology I am familiar with. To learn more: Selig, Paul.
Alchemy. St. Martin's Publishing Group, 2020.

Planetary, Intergalactic

113. Raven, Astara. "Vernal Equinox." Illuminate Blog. Illuminating Hearts, 2022, astararaven.love/illuminate-blog/vernal-equinox.
114. I call my soul healing work Heartifact Archaeology and created my Heartifact Archaeology eco-system of offerings where I synthesize decades of spiritual experience into one multidisciplinary system. Heart-i-fact describes soul artifacts and facts of the heart — our immense timeless wisdom. Each session is customized for an individual's unique nature and soul instructions. To see our nose, we need a mirror. I utilize a myriad of soul mirrors to reflect, reveal and translate soul knowing: channeling, conscious tarot, sound healing, shamanism, Energy Codes, embodiment, quantum dowsing, akashic records, and more: astararaven.love/offerings.
115. www.nationalgeographic.org/encyclopedia/equinox.
116. Parton, Dolly [@DollyParton]. "Find what you love and do it on purpose." Twitter, 8 April, 2015, https://twitter.com/dollyparton/status/585890099583397888
117. Inspired from: Selig, Paul. The Kingdom. St. Martin's Publishing Group, 2021.
118. Beastie Boys. "Intergalactic – Remastered." Hello Nasty. Capitol Records, 2009.

How The Stars Tell Time

119. Raven, Astara. "How the Stars Tell Time" Illuminate Blog. Illuminating Hearts, 2022, astararaven.love/illuminate-blog/how-the-stars-tell-time.

Lily age 5

Lily age 12

Astara age 50

About the Author

Astara is a California transplant to the heartland. Inside of her life already she's contained a multitude of lifetimes. She is an author, dancer, and sustainable architect. She's also a songstress, coach to the stars, quantum time traveler, and alchemist. She's all these roles—and none of them—and so much more. After two decades as a sustainable leader, she now advocates for the Earth by building bridges of awareness. Years ago, she gave herself permission to *psychic prosperity* — expanding her senses to hear the cosmos whisper its wisdom to her. As a systems thinker, she formed the *Heartifact Archaeology Eco-System* as well as *Inner Space Academy* to create the healing she wished was in the world, and intimacy is one of the golden keys. *How the Stars Tell Time* is Astara's first book.